Tort Law in the European Union

Tort Law in the European Union

Second Edition

Gert Brüggemeier

This book was originally published as a monograph in the International Encyclopaedia of Laws/Tort Law.

Founding Editor: Roger Blanpain
General Editor: Frank Hendrickx
Volume Editor: Britt Weyts

Wolters Kluwer

Published by:
Kluwer Law International B.V.
PO Box 316
2400 AH Alphen aan den Rijn
The Netherlands
E-mail: international-sales@wolterskluwer.com
Website: lrus.wolterskluwer.com

Sold and distributed in North, Central and South America by:
Wolters Kluwer Legal & Regulatory U.S.
7201 McKinney Circle
Frederick, MD 21704
United States of America
Email: customer.service@wolterskluwer.com

Sold and distributed in all other countries by:
Air Business Subscriptions
Rockwood House
Haywards Heath
West Sussex
RH16 3DH
United Kingdom
Email: international-customerservice@wolterskluwer.com

ISBN 978-94-035-0070-6

e-Book: ISBN 978-94-035-0071-3
web-PDF: ISBN 978-94-035-0072-0

This title is available on www.kluwerlawonline.com

The Author

Gert Brüggemeier (1944) is Professor emeritus of Civil and Comparative Law at the Law Faculty, University of Bremen, Germany (1978–2009). He was a Managing Director of the Research Institute *Centre of European Law and Politics at the University of Bremen (ZERP)* 1991–2004 and Judge at the *Oberlandesgericht* (Superior Regional Court) *Bremen*, part-time.

He was a Visiting Professor at the Law Schools of UC Berkeley, Yale and Tulane (USA), at the Universities of Paris I – *Panthéon-Sorbonne* (France), *Fribourg* (Switzerland), Strathclyde (Glasgow, Scotland), and at the European University Institute (EUI), Florence, and the *Scuola Superiore Sant'Anna*, Pisa (Italy).

His main monographs are *Deliktsrecht* (Baden-Baden: Nomos 1986); *Prinzipien des Haftungsrechts* (Baden-Baden: Nomos: 1999); in English: Common Principles of Tort Law (London: BIICL 2004; reprint 2006); *Haftungsrecht. Struktur, Prinzipien, Schutzbereich* (Heidelberg: Springer 2006); Modernising Civil Liability Law in Europe, China, Brazil and Russia (Cambridge: CUP 2011).

In addition he is editor and co-editor of numerous books and author of more than 100 articles and book reviews.

The Author

Table of Contents

Preface to the Second Edition

This text is a thoroughly revised version of the first edition of 2015. It adheres to the original structure but elaborates it in a more detailed version. It stresses the bifurcated structure of the Union's liability under Article 340(2) TFEU: (a) vicarious liability for torts of EU servants and bodies (factual conduct) and (b) breach-of-law liability of EU institutions (legislative and administrative acts), and develops the multi-facetted liability of Member States for breach of EU law. The third pillar of this breach of EU law liability is the responsibility of private parties. Special sections are dedicated to compensation for lawful acts and to the principal's liability of the EU for impairments of EU servants (staff cases).

The part on EU civil liability in tort has its main focus, as in the previous edition, on products liability. Recent ECJ judgments in the field of medical devices, such as *Boston Medizintechnik, Sanofi Pasteur*, and *Schmitt v. TÜV Rheinland*, are critically commented.

From a geographical and political point of view, this text covers twenty-eight Member States. At the time of completing this manuscript, the UK was still a Member State of the EU.

For lectoring and linguistically checking the manuscript, I like to thank Monika Hobbie, Bremen (*ZERP*). Some slight errors of the first edition could be corrected. For remaining mistakes, misconceptions and misunderstandings I take the sole responsibility. Critical comments are welcome under gbruegge@uni-bremen.de

Gert Brüggemeier
Bremen, December 2017

Preface to the First Edition and Acknowledgements

When the editor of the Tort Law division of the International Encyclopaedia of Laws contacted me with the request to write a monograph on tort law of the EU, I hesitated. I was convinced that such a subject does not exist. One year later, after having written the monograph on this non-issue, I felt confirmed. There is a maze of public liability with an uncountable amount of judgments of the courts of the EU, and as genuine civil tort law – there is product liability. That is it. Hence, this monograph contributes two things: It approaches the public liability of the EU from a tort lawyer's perspective which leads to a reconstruction of this field of law. And it delivers a critical restatement of EU product liability. The focus is on restructuring. Additional fine-tuning is left to future editions. Critical comments and helpful information are very welcome (gertbrueggemeier@web.de). Torts' aspects of international procedural law (Brussels Ia) and conflict of laws (Rome II) have not been taken up in depth. They are of no relevance for public liability.

Due to the international character of the Encyclopaedia's monographs, the authors are asked by the publisher to cite and quote only sources in English. With some exceptions (including author's own works), I tried to comply with this demand. Therefore, I address my apologies to the numerous authors who delivered valuable contributions in French, German, Italian or other languages of the EU for non-citation.

No money of European or German taxpayers has been burnt through this project. But I benefitted a lot from the invitation by the Scuola Superiore Sant'Anna in Pisa to deliver the Lezioni Pisane di Diritto Civile in summer 2014. Thus, I spent three months in the inspiring atmosphere of the beautiful former monastery of Benedictines, in splendid isolation and full concentration on the EU tort law project. The basics of this monograph came there into existence. That is the reason why I dedicate this monograph to this institution (and to a lot of supportive individuals). If this book presents some new insights, they are due to the genius loci, the birthplace of Galileo Galilei. All errors remain mine.

For a linguistic check of the English manuscript, I like to thank Jason Dinse, American lawyer at the Centre of European Law & Politics at the University of Bremen (ZERP). Here, too, the poorness of the English falls in my responsibility. I also owe a debt of gratitude to Antje Kautz, ZERP, for the technical support in finishing this manuscript.

Gert Brüggemeier
Bremen, January 2015

Guide for Readers

The terminology is following the Treaty of Lisbon, entering into force on 1 December 2009. The Articles of all Treaties are thoroughly cited in the new numeration of the Lisbon Treaty (TEU, TFEU), unless it was indispensable in historical contexts.

The term 'Court of Justice of the European Union' (CJEU) is only used to define the judicial structure of the EU (Article 19(1) TEU). It comprises two operating courts: European Court of Justice (ECJ) and European General Court (EGC; former European Court of First Instance). The European Civil Service Tribunal (ECST), established in 2004, was dissolved again in 2016.

Cases are always cited with their case numbers. Till 2010, the European Courts Reports are used: (ECR): [2001]ECR I-(page no.) for judgments of the ECJ from 1989 onwards; ECR II-(page no.) for judgments of the EGC (former Court of First Instance). – From 2010 onwards, cases are cited using the European Case Law Identifier (ECLI) ECJ: EU:C:2010:(page no.)/EGC:EU:T:2010:(page no.).

Cases with Arabic numbers (No. 1 or 2) define different judgments in cases with identical case number and identical case parties. Cases with Roman numbers (I or II) define cases with identical claimants but different case numbers, different subject matter and often different defendants.

Claimants in procedures before EU courts are called 'applicants'; claimants in procedures before national courts are called 'plaintiffs'.

Until 1996, cases of the European Court of Human Rights (ECtHR) are cited by reference to the Series A of the official reports (X v. UK A 161 (1989)). From 1996 onwards, the European Human Rights Reports (EHRR) are used. Recent judgments are also cited using the HUDOC database (X v. UK hudoc (2009)).

List of Abbreviations

AC	Appeal Cases
ACP	African-Caribbean-Pacific States
AFNOR	Association française de la normalisation
AG	Advocate General
ALI	American Law Institute
All ER	All England Law Reports
BEF	Francs belges (former Belgian currency)
BGB	(German) Bürgerliches Gesetzbuch (Civil Code)
BGH	(German) Bundesgerichtshof (Federal Court of Justice)
BGHZ	Reports of cases before the Bundesgerichtshof in civil matters
BIICL	British Institute of International and Comparative Law
BSI	British Standards Institution
BVerfG	(German) Bundesverfassungsgericht (Federal Constitutional Court)
BVerfGE	Reports of cases before the Bundesverfassungsgericht
CA	Court of Appeal (England and Wales)
CAL	California Reporter
Cass	(French) Cour de Cassation
C. civ.	(French) Code civil
CEN	European Committee for Standardization
ChFR	(EU) Charter of Fundamental Rights
CJEU	Court of Justice of the European Union
CMLR	Common Market Law Reports
CML Rev	*Common Market Law Review*
Cod. civ.	(Italian) Codice civile
COM	Document of the European Commission

List of Abbreviations

CUP	Cambridge University Press
CYELS	Cambridge Yearbook of European Legal Studies
DIN	Deutsches Institut für Normung
EAEC	European Atomic Energy Community/Euratom
EC	European Community/Communities
ECB	European Central Bank
ECHR	European Convention for the Protection of Human Rights and Fundamental Freedoms
ECJ	European Court of Justice
ECLI	European Case Law Identifier
ECR	Reports of cases before the European Courts
ECSC	European Coal and Steel Community
ECST	European Civil Service Tribunal
ECtHR	European Court of Human Rights
ed./s	editor/s//edition
EEA	European Economic Area
EEC	European Economic Community (Common Market)
EFTA	European Free Trade Association
EFTA Court	Court of Justice of European Free Trade Association States
EGC	European General Court
EIB	European Investment Bank
EJCL	*European Journal of Comparative Law and Governance*
ELJ	*European Law Journal*
ELM	*Environmental Law and Management*
EL Rev	*European Law Review*
EMLR	Entertainment and Media Law Reports
EMU	Economic and Monetary Union
EP	European Parliament
EPL	*European Public Law*
EU	European Union
EuLR	European Law Reports
EuR	*Europarecht*
EURATOM	European Atomic Energy Community
EuZW	*Europäische Zeitschrift für Wirtschaftsrecht*
EWCA (Civ)	Court of Appeal of England and Wales (cases in civil matters)

EWHC	High Court of England and Wales
Foro it.	Il Foro Italiano
GLJ	*German Law Journal*
HR	(Dutch) Hoge Raad
IMF	International Monetary Fund
JETL	*Journal of European Tort Law*
KLI	Kluwer Law International
LG	(German) Landgericht (Regional Court)
L.G.D.J.	Librairie Générale de Droit et de Jurisprudence
MC	Montreal Convention on International Carriage by Air
MedR	*Medizinrecht*
MJ	*Maastricht Journal of European and Comparative Law*
MLR	*Modern Law Review*
MN	Minnesota
NE	North Eastern Reporter
NJ	Nederlandse Jurisprudentie
NJW	*Neue Juristische Wochenschrift*
NVwZ	*Neue Zeitschrift für Verwaltungsrecht*
nyr	not yet reported
OJ C/L	Official Journal of the European Communities/European Union (Communication/Law)
OLG	(German) Oberlandesgericht (Superior Regional Court)
OUP	Oxford University Press
p./pp.	page/s
P.	Pacific Reporter
para./s	paragraph/s
Rec.	Recueil
RG	(German) Reichsgericht (Imperial Court (1879–1945))
RGZ	Reports of cases before the Reichsgericht in civil matters
r.p.r.	Reference for preliminary ruling
s.	section
SDR	Special Drawing Rights of the IMF
TEAEC	Treaty establishing the European Atomic Energy Community
TECSC	Treaty establishing the European Coal and Steel Community
TEEC	Treaty establishing the European Economic Community

List of Abbreviations

TEU	Treaty on the European Union
TFEU	Treaty on the Functioning of the European Union
UKHL	House of Lords (former Judicial Dept.) of the United Kingdom
UKSC	Supreme Court of the United Kingdom
U.S.	Reports of cases before the US Supreme Court
USD	US American Dollars
Va L Rev	*Virginia Law Review*
VersR	*Versicherungsrecht*
vol./s	volume/s
WC	Warsaw Convention on International Carriage by Air
WLR	Weekly Law Reports
WPNR	*Weekblad voor privatrecht, notariat en registratie*
WTO	World Trade Organization
YEL	(Oxford) Yearbook of European Law
ZvglRWiss	*Zeitschrift für vergleichende Rechtswisenschaft*

List of Tables

List of Tables

General Introduction

§1. European Union: History and Structure

I. The European Communities

1.

> World peace cannot be safeguarded without the making of creative efforts proportionate to the dangers which threaten it.
> The contribution which an organised and living Europe can bring to civilisation is indispensable to the maintenance of peaceful relations. In taking upon herself for more than 20 years the role of champion of a united Europe, France has always had as her essential aim the service of peace. A united Europe was not achieved and we had war.
> Europe will not be made all at once, or according to a single plan. It will be built through concrete achievements which first create a de facto solidarity. The coming together of the nations of Europe requires the elimination of the age-old opposition of France and Germany. Any action taken must in the first place concern these two countries.
> With this aim in view, the French Government proposes that action be taken immediately on one limited but decisive point: It proposes that Franco-German production of coal and steel as a whole be placed under a common High Authority, within the framework of an organisation open to the participation of the other countries of Europe. … .

2. The declaration of 9 May 1950 of the French Foreign Minister *Robert Schuman* (born 1888 as a German citizen in Luxembourg) was the starting point of the European integration process finally leading to the establishment of the European Union. It enshrined the founding myth of this unique historical process: preventing future war in Europe by integrating the European States economically and politically. (A distinctly different process of Europeanization was launched with the Treaty of London of 5 May 1949, establishing the *Council of Europe*. Its European Convention on Human Rights came into force in 1953.[1] The ECtHR was set up in 1959, located in Strasbourg. Currently, the Council of Europe has forty-seven Signatory States, with Montenegro being the latest to join).

1. As a commentary in English compare W.A. Schabas, *The European Convention on Human Rights* (OUP 2017).

3. Schuman's proposal was taken up and in 1951 six European States – Belgium, France, Italy, Luxembourg, the Netherlands and West Germany – signed the *Treaty* of Paris *establishing the European Coal and Steel Community* (TECSC). The ECSC Treaty went into force in 1952. Its mission (Article 2) was 'to contribute to the expansion of the economy, the development of employment and the improvement of the standard of living'. The European Coal and Steel Community (ECSC) had legal personality of its own. Its institutional organs were composed of a *High Authority* as executive, assisted by a Consultative Committee, a *Common Assembly*, a *Special Council* composed of Ministers as representatives of the governments, and a *Court of Justice*. All institutions were located in the City of Luxembourg, with the exception of the Assembly being based in Strasbourg. The first president of the High Authority became *Jean Monnet* (1952–1955), who resigned from presidency in protest in 1955 when the project of a *European Defence Community* was rejected by the French Parliament. This failure also implied the end of the parallel project of a *European Political Community*.

4. Despite these political setbacks, shortly afterwards two other supranational European Communities were created: The Treaties of Rome (1957) established the European Economic Community – the future core of the integration process – and the European Atomic Energy Community (or Euratom). The Treaties of Rome entered into force in 1958 with six Contracting States identical to the founding Member States of the ECSC.

5. The *Treaty establishing the European Economic Community (TEEC)* was designed to create a common market among its Member States through the elimination of most trade barriers and the establishment of a common external trade policy (Customs Union[2]). The Treaty also provided for a 'common agricultural policy' (CAP). Created in 1962, CAP became one of the most important policies and a cornerstone of the European Integration.[3]

Three political institutions were introduced which held the executive and legislative power: the *Council* (representing the governments), the *Parliament,* and the *Commission.* Council, Parliament or a Member State could place a request for legislation to the Commission. The Commission would then draft a Bill and present it to the Council for approval and to the Parliament for an opinion. To exercise the Community's competences, the institutions adopt regulations, directives and decisions. The EEC Commission was located in Brussels and its first president was *Walter Hallstein.*

The EEC inherited two institutions of the ECSC: The Common Assembly in Strasbourg and the Court of Justice in Luxembourg extended their authority to the EEC in the same role.

6. The Treaty establishing the *European Atomic Energy Community* or Euratom (TEAEC) provided a similar structure.

---

2. Articles 12–29 TEEC.
3. Regulation (EEC) No. 25 on the financing of the common agricultural policy, OJ 1962 No. 30/1.

7. By the Merger (or Brussels) Treaty of 1967,[4] the executive and legislative organs of ECSC and Euratom were united with that of the EEC, creating a *Single Commission of the European Communities* running three separate and independent Communities with legal personality of their own – ECSC, EEC and Euratom – and a *Single Council of Ministers* for the Communities.

In 1987, the Single European Act (SEA),[5] amending the Rome Treaties, added new momentum to the integration process. It launched the project of an 'internal market', provided necessary adaptations for its completion, and expanded the Communities' powers.

8. The European Communities also grew in number of Member States. Three former members of the *European Free Trade Association (EFTA,* founded in 1960) – United Kingdom, Denmark and Ireland – joined in 1973, followed by Greece in 1981, and Portugal and Spain in 1986. East Germany was admitted as part of the reunified Germany in 1990.

II. Towards the European Union

A. Maastricht Treaty

9. With the Maastricht Treaty (Treaty on European Union – TEU) of 1992,[6] which went into force in 1993, a dramatic structural change occurred. The European Union (EU or Union) as a structurally sophisticated polity was created, but without having its own legal personality. The Maastricht Treaty represents an eminent shift to a more political process of Europeanization. It postulated for the first time the objective of an 'ever closer union among the peoples of Europe' (Article A(2)). This Union, established in 1993, consisted of three pillars. The European Communities (ECSC, EEC, EAEC) with its supranational institutions – Commission, Council, Parliament and Court of Justice – became the main pillar embedded into the artificial three-pillar structure of the new European Union. The EEC was renamed *European Community*.[7] The second pillar was the common foreign and security policy and the third was justice and home affairs. Unlike the European Communities, the other two pillars were essentially intergovernmental in nature with decisions being made by committees composed of Member States' politicians and officials. They remained outside of the jurisdiction of the Court of Justice.

Additionally the concept of a European citizenship was introduced (Article 8).[8]

---

4. Treaty establishing a Single Council and a Single Commission of the European Communities (Merger Treaty) of 1965, OJ 1967 No. 152/2.
5. OJ 1987 L 169/1.
6. OJ 1992 C 191/1.
7. Treaty on European Union, OJ 1992 C 191/1, at 5 et seq.
8. Compare the contributions in *The Court of Justice and the Construction of Europe* (Part III: The Area of Citizens, p. 425) (CJEU ed., Asser & Springer 2013).

10. The Maastricht Treaty also provided the foundation of an *Economic and Monetary Union (EMU),* which included the creation of a single currency, the euro. Article 121 defined the so-called Maastricht or convergence criteria a Member State must comply with if it wishes to enter the Economic and Monetary Union and adopt the euro as its currency.

11. The Maastricht Treaty (TEU) and the Rome Treaties (TEEC and TEAEC) were amended by the Amsterdam Treaty of 1997 (in force 1999),[9] introducing a High Representative for EU foreign policy and strengthening the role of Parliament. The Treaty of Nice of 2001 (in force 2003)[10] failed to introduce overdue institutional reforms. The process to modify EU institutions began after the turn of the twenty-first century, resulting in a '*Treaty establishing a Constitution for Europe*'[11] which would have repealed the various existing Treaties and replaced them with one legal document – a 'Constitution of the EU'. This project was abandoned after having been rejected in 2005 by 54.67% of French and 61.54% of Dutch voters in national referenda. As a part of it, a Charter of Fundamental Rights had already been drafted in 2000 by a European Convention[12] and had been solemnly proclaimed by the EU institutions.[13]

The ECSC Treaty of Paris expired formally in 2002.

12. In the meantime further enlargements of the EU continued. In 1995 Austria, Finland and Sweden acceded to the EU. In 2004, the then fifteen Member States of the EU were joined by ten new accession countries: Cyprus, Czech Republic, Estonia, Hungary, Latvia, Lithuania, Malta, Poland, Slovenia and Slovakia. Additionally Bulgaria and Romania acceded in 2007. As of now, the last State to join the EU as the twenty-eighth Member State was Croatia in 2013.

The EU has a combined population of over 500 million inhabitants or 7.3% of the world population.[14]

B. Treaty of Lisbon: 'Constitution Without Constitutional Treaty'

13. The actual structure of the EU is enshrined in the (Reform) Treaty of Lisbon (2007), effective in 2009.[15] The Treaty presented three documents as 'constitutional charter'[16] on which the Union is based:

---

9. OJ 1997 C 340/85.
10. OJ 2001 C 80/1.
11. OJ 2004 C 310/1.
12. Compare http://European-convention.eu.int.
13. OJ 2000 C 364/1.
14. As of 2010. Compare Intern'l Institute for Applied Systems Analysis. Download data sheet 2010.
15. Treaty amending the Treaty on European Union and the Treaty establishing the European Community, OJ 2007 C 306/202.
16. Formulation used by the ECJ for the Treaties. Compare Case 294/83, *Les Verts v. European Parliament* [1986] ECR 1339, para. 23.

(i) The structure of the European Union was thoroughly amended. The Lisbon Treaty (TEU) brought the end of the EC. The pillar system of the Maastricht Treaty was abolished. The three pillars were united under the roof of the European Union, which succeeded the legal personality of the European Community, alias European Economic Community: '*EU Inc.*'. After the expiry of the ECSC Treaty, only the Euratom Treaty remained in force. The EAEC did not merge with the EU and retained a separate legal personality, while sharing the same institutional organs.

The organs of the EU are the *Parliament* with an increase of powers, the *European Council* with a full-time president and now formally separated from the *Council of Ministers*, the *Commission*, the *Court of Justice* and the *Court of Auditors*.[17] Additionally, the *European Central Bank (ECB)* gained the status of being an EU institution.[18]

(ii) The classical EEC Treaty was adapted to the new structure and renamed 'Treaty on the Functioning of the European Union (TFEU)'.[19]

(iii) The EU Charter of Fundamental Rights (ChFR) was made legally binding.[20]

All three documents, TEU, TFEU and ChFR, have equal legal value and collectively constitute the European Union's legal basis – the EU constitution.

14. In 2017, the EU internal market comprised twenty-eight national economies, including the UK. In 1994, the (then) EC was enlarged to the *European Economic Area (EEA)* by an Agreement with three EFTA-States, Iceland, Liechtenstein and Norway.[21] Novel EC/EU legislation with relevance for the EEA is continuously adopted through decisions of the EEA Joint Commission. For dispute resolution under the EEA Agreement, a special judicial body has been established: the *EFTA Court*.[22] – The Economic and Monetary Union (EMU) consisted in 2017 of nineteen Member States with a common currency, the euro.[23]

17. Article 13 TEU, Arts 285–287 TFEU. Established in 1975 in Luxembourg, the Court of Auditors started operating in 1977 and was recognized as an institutional organ by the Maastricht Treaty.
18. Article 13 TEU, Arts 282–284 TFEU.
19. OJ 2007 C 326/47.
20. OJ 2007 C 303/1, annexed with Protocols on a Charter-opt-out by the United Kingdom and Poland (concerning 'social rights'). Compare S. Peers, T. Hervey, J. Kenner & A. Ward, *The EU Charter of Fundamental Rights – A Commentary* (Hart 2014).
21. Agreement between the Community, on the one hand, and the Countries of the European Free Trade Association (EFTA), on the other, relating to the Creation of the European Economic Area of 17 Mar. 1993, OJ 1994 L 1/3. The remaining fourth former EFTA State, Switzerland, rejected an accession to the EEA by a referendum in 1992. As a recent stock-taking, compare H.H. Fredriksen & C. Franklin, *Of Pragmatism and Principles: The EEA Agreement 20 Years on* (2015) 52 CML Rev 629.
22. The EFTA Court consists of three judges, one from each of the three States. The original plan for a joint EEA Court has been blocked by the ECJ (*see* ECJ, Opinion 1/91, *EEA (No 1)* [1991] ECR I-6079). Compare generally EFTA Court (ed), *The EEA and the EFTA Court – Decentred Integration* (Hart 2014).
23. In 2015, the last Member State to join the EMU was Lithuania.

15. The border-free *Schengen Area*, installed in 1985 under the Luxembourg presidency,[24] actually encompasses twenty-two EU States and four former EFTA States (Iceland, Liechtenstein, Norway and Switzerland). It guarantees free movement to more than 400 million persons, but fails to install a system of effective protection of its external frontier. During the refugee crisis of 2015/2016, the workability of the Schengen principles and the idea of free movement of persons in an 'area of freedom, security and justice without internal frontiers' (Article 3(2) TEU) suffered a serious crisis. The actual lack of the stipulated common EU policy on immigration and asylum, 'based on solidarity between Member States, which is fair towards third country nationals' (Article 67(2) TFEU), became virulent.

16. The EU somehow managed to survive the financial crisis of 2008, in the end due to the active interventions of the ECB.[25] In the aftermath of the crisis, a variety of intergovernmental agreements under public international law complemented classical EU law. An important example is the European Stability Mechanism (ESM).[26] However, a solution of both the structural problems of the EMU ('euro crisis') and the intricacies of an EU policy on immigration and asylum is yet to come. Additionally and surprisingly, on 23 June 2016, a majority of 51.9% of the voters in the UK decided in a national referendum to leave the EU ('Brexit'). When in January 2017 the UK Supreme Court ruled that Westminster Parliament's vote is needed for the UK government to trigger Article 50 TEU,[27] both houses of Parliament passed an approving Act in February 2017. On 29 March 2017, the British government delivered its exit notice to the EU. If not negotiated differently, the exit of the UK takes effect two years later, from 29 March 2019 (Article 50(3) TEU).[28]

17. In face of this multitude of setbacks and crises, a road map towards an 'ever closer Union of the peoples of Europe' (Article 1(2) TEU) is actually not in sight. *Schuman's* vision of a '*Fédération européenne*' is in 2018 farther from realization than it was in the 1950s, while the (future) Union of twenty-seven Member States finds itself in search of new constituting principles for the twenty-first century as fundamental as the peace formula of the 1950s which lost integrative vigour among the Member States and their citizens. The new principles may be democratic legitimacy, rule of law, social justice and solidarity.

---

24. Named after the small village on the river Mosel in Luxembourg where the Agreement was signed.
25. On the legality of the measures of the ECB compare ECJ, C-8/15 P to C-10/15 P, *Ledra Advertising Ltd and Others v. Commission and ECB* EU:C:2016:701 (European Stability Mechanism (ESM)); ECJ, Case C-62/14, *Gauweiler and Others v. Deutscher Bundestag* EU:C:2015:400 (Outright Monetary Transactions (OMT)). In the latter case the ECJ granted a wide margin of discretion to the ECB. It held that the OMT programme does not exceed the powers of the ECB under EU law and does not contravene the prohibition of monetary financing of Member States (Art. 123(1) TFEU). *See also* Bundesverfassungsgericht, 18.7.2017, 2 BvR 859/15, r.p.r. (Public Sector Purchase Programme (PSPP)).
26. The EU Commission and Some Member State governments intend to develop the ESM to a veritable European Monetary Fund.
27. *R v. Secretary of State for Exiting the European Union* [2017] UKSC 5, confirming [2016] EWHC 2768.
28. Compare, *inter alia, Secession from a Member State and Withdrawal from the European Union* (C. Closa ed., CUP 2017); *The Law & Politics of Brexit* (F. Fabbrini ed., OUP 2017).

Table 1 Table of Treaties

Signed	1951	1957	1965	1986	1992	1997	2001	2007
In Force	1952	1958	1967	1987	1993	1999	2003	2009
Document	Paris Treaty	Rome Treaties	Merger Treaty	Single European Act	Maastricht Treaty	Amsterdam Treaty	Nice Treaty	Lisbon Treaty
	ECSC	EEC EAEC	EEC EAEC ECSC		EU with three pillars structure: 'EC plus' EAEC ECSC Treaty expired in 2002			EU EAEC

§2. Judicial System of the European Union

I. Court of Justice

18. In 1951, the foundations for a revolutionary judicial development were laid with the inauguration of a 'Court of Justice' in Luxembourg on the basis of the Treaty of Paris.[29] Its function was 'to ensure the rule of law in the interpretation and application of the ECSC Treaty and of its implementing regulations'.[30] The Court, established in 1952,[31] was originally conceived as an international administrative court. It was composed of seven judges, one from each founding Member State plus an additional one. The uneven number should guarantee majority votes of the Court with the seventh seat rotating among the three large Member States France, Italy and West Germany. The judges were appointed for six years being eligible for reappointment. Following the French model of procedural law with its '*Commissaire du Gouvernement*', the judges were assisted in their task by two 'Advocates General' (AG) presenting reasoned submissions (opinions) to the Court on the cases assigned to them.[32] Unlike similar institutions in some Member States they are not entrusted with the defence of the general interest and do not form a hierarchy. The Court can decide without participation of an AG only in cases 'raising no new point of law'.[33]

19. After the establishment of EEC and EAEC by the Treaties of Rome, a new judicial body was constituted in 1958 – the '*Court of Justice of the European Communities*' (ECJ) – inheriting the former ECSC court, but facing a considerably enlarged field of application such as, e.g., the four fundamental economic freedoms and the rules of competition.[34] It exercised the competences referred to it in the three Treaties and operated in accordance with the separate Statutes of the Court annexed by a protocol to each Treaty.

20. With the successive enlargements of the European Communities, the number of judges and AG grew accordingly. Correspondingly, the workload of the Court rose steadily. Under the Single European Act of 1987, the Court was provided with an additional lower court to deal with supposedly less important cases. This *Court*

---

29. Compare Arts 7, 31–45 TECSC and the Protocol on the Statute of the Court of Justice annexed to the Treaty.
30. Article 31 TECSC.
31. For a publication on occasion of its 60th anniversary, compare *The Court of Justice and the Construction of Europe: Analyses and Perspectives on Sixty Years of Case Law/La Cour de justice et la construction de l'Europe: analyses et perspectives de soixante ans de jurisprudence* (CJEU ed., Asser & Springer 2013).
32. Compare Arts 10 and 11 Protocol on the Statute of the Court of Justice of the ECSC; Art. 166 TEEC. *See* generally K. Borgsmidt, *The Advocate General at the European Court of Justice* (1988) 13 EL Rev 106; T. Tridimas, *The Role of the Advocate General in the Development of Community Law* (1997) 34 CML Rev 1349.
33. Article 20(5) Statute of the Court of Justice. In the years 2004–2008, the percentage of judgments issued without an AG's opinion rose from 30% to 41%. *See* T. de la Mare & C. Donnelly, *Preliminary Rulings and EU Legal Integration*, in *The Evolution of EU Law* 363, at 405 (2nd ed. P. Craig & G. de Búrca eds, OUP 2011).
34. Compare Arts 164 et seq. TEEC and Arts 136 et seq. TEAEC.

of First Instance was established in 1989.[35] Originally restricted to administrative law, under the Nice Treaty of 2003 its competences were extended, leading to a veritable two-tier court system. The cases under its jurisdiction comprised, *inter alia*, non-contractual liability of Community institutions and staff matters. Appeals against its decisions on point of law could be made to the ECJ.

II. Court of Justice of the European Union

21. The Lisbon Treaty established the institution of a '*Court of Justice of the European Union*' (CJEU).[36] Until recently it was composed of three judicial bodies: the Court of Justice (ECJ), the General Court (former Court of First Instance – EGC) and additionally one specialized court – the Civil Service Tribunal (CST) with competence for staff cases (Article 19(1) TEU).

22. The Court of Justice (ECJ) is a 'judicial anomaly' (G.F. Mancini), unparalleled in the legal orders of the Member States. It is the Constitutional Court of the European Union, safeguarding the objectives and rules of law laid down in the Treaties and the Charter. It is the highest Administrative Court, and at the same time it is the Supreme Court in private, labour, commercial, competition law and other fields of law (like e.g., criminal law) covered by EU primary or secondary legislation. Its tasks and structure are defined in Articles 251–281 TFEU and detailed in the Statute of the CJEU.[37] Its procedure is regulated in the ECJ Rules of Procedure.[38] In 2017, the ECJ employed twenty-eight judges (one judge per Member State) and eleven AGs.[39] The Court sits in Chambers of five (or three) judges. It may also sit as a Grand Chamber (thirteen judges) or as a Full Court (at least fifteen judges) when the legal complexity or importance of the case justifies it.[40]

23. As mentioned above, a Court of First Instance was attached to the ECJ as an inferior court in 1989. The Treaty of Nice established it as an independent court. Renamed *EGC* by the Treaty of Lisbon, it consisted also of one judge per Member

35. Council Decision 88/591/ECSC, EEC, Euratom establishing a Court of First Instance of the European Communities, OJ 1988 L 319/1.
36. Article 19 TEU.
37. Protocol on the Statute of the Court of Justice of the European Union, OJ 2001 C 80/53.
38. Rules of Procedure of the Court of Justice of the European Communities, OJ 1991 L 176/7; last amended as Rules of Procedure of the Court of Justice of the EU of 29 Sep. 2012, OJ 2012 L 265. For a commentary on Statute and Rules of Procedure compare B. Wägenbaur, *Court of Justice of the EU* (C.H. Beck 2013).
39. From September 2015 onwards. One post of an advocate general is reserved for France, Germany, Italy, Spain and the UK. The six remaining ones alternate between the other Member States.
40. On this in greater detail, compare K. Laenerts, D. Arts & I. Maselis, *Procedural Law of the European Union* (2d ed. Sweet & Maxwell 2006).

State. After the judicial reform of 2015,[41] in its present composition as from 1 September 2016, the EGC has forty-eight judges. It sits in chambers of three or five judges, and no AGs are attached to the EGC. Its competences and structure are regulated in Article 256 TFEU and in Articles 47–62b Statute of the Court of Justice of the EU.[42] The EGC hears and determines cases as Court of First Instance in its field of competence and rules on appeals against decisions of Specialized Courts (not yet created).[43]

24. The Treaty of Nice empowered the Council to create judicial panels to be attached to the (then) Court of First Instance. One of those Specialized Courts was set up in 2004 – the EU *Civil Service Tribunal (ECST)*.[44] It was composed of seven judges, sitting regularly in chambers of three judges.[45] The ECST exercised the jurisdiction in staff matters: pay, promotion, pension, accidents, etc. of civil servants and public employees.[46] With the establishment of this first Specialized Court a decisive step towards a veritable three-tier system of the EU judiciary supposedly had been taken. But rather surprisingly after twelve years of existence, in 2016, the ECST was dissolved and its functions were conferred to the EGC which thus became again the general Court of First Instance in the EU judicial system.[47] – The *Unified Patent Court* (*UPC*) to be established by the Treaty will be a common patent court of the participating Member States outside the structure of the 'CJEU'.[48]

§3. European Courts and National Courts

I. Institutionalized Cooperation

25. The European courts are just one side of the coin. The European Union is an unprecedented supranational governance polity, which passes law addressed to the Member States and their residents. EU law has to be implemented and executed by the Member States. The relationship between EU law and national law of the Member States is characterized by the primacy of EU law and the direct effect of a whole series of provisions of EU law (*van Gend en Loos* and *Flaminio Costa*).[49]

---

41. Regulation (EU, Euratom) 2015/2422 of 16.12.2015 amending Protocol 3 on the Statute of the Court of the European Union, OJ 2015 L 341/14. As from 1.9.2019, the EGC will consist of two judges per Member State. On the current judicial reforms *see The New EU Judiciary* (E. Guinchard & M.P. Granger eds, Kluwer 2017).
42. Footnote 37; compare also Rules of Procedure of the General Court, OJ 2013 L 173/66.
43. Article 256(2) TFEU.
44. Council Decision 2004/752 EC, Euratom establishing the European Union Civil Service Tribunal, OJ 2004 L 333/7.
45. For details *see* Art. 62c Statute of the Court of Justice and Annex I to the Statute, OJ 2004 L 333/7.
46. On this in greater detail, *see infra* text (Part VI, Ch.2).
47. Regulation (EU, Euratom) 2016/1192 of 6.7.2016 on the transfer to the General Court of jurisdiction at first instance in disputes between the European Union and its servants, OJ 2016 L 200/137.
48. Compare Agreement on a Unified Patent Court, OJ 2013 C 175/56.
49. On this in greater detail, *see infra* text (Part II, Ch. 1, §1).

26. The EU Treaties do not provide for 'European courts' in the Member States. Instead, they introduce a decentralized system of judicial protection. The division of powers between the judicial bodies of the Union and the Member States does not fit neatly into traditional political or legal moulds. It implies that it is up to the national courts to review the application of EU law by the Member States' authorities in their jurisdiction. The national courts thus turned into a sort of regular European courts,[50] hearing and determining all cases related to EU law which do not fall within the exclusive jurisdiction of the 'CJEU'. In any case of breach of EU law by a Member State institution or a Member State resident, a private party whose rights are infringed can bring an action for damages to the national courts. The ECJ determines the EU law, the national court hears and determines the breach and decides on damages.

27. This co-application process of EU law by the ECJ and the national courts is institutionalized by the ingenious preliminary ruling procedure (Article 267 TFEU).[51] Each Member State court can and each court of last instance must – if there are uncertainties about the content of provisions of EU law or the validity of an act of an EU institution – refer a request for preliminary ruling to the ECJ. This obligation of national courts is limited where previous decisions of the Court have already dealt with the point of law in question (*acte éclairé*),[52] and where the correct application of EU law may be so obvious as to leave no scope for any reasonable doubt as to the manner in which the question raised is to be resolved (*acte clair*)[53] The system set up by Article 267 TFEU constitutes direct judicial cooperation between the ECJ and the national courts, as part of which the latter are closely involved in the correct application and uniform interpretation of EU law and also in the protection of individual rights conferred by that legal order.[54] The functioning of this inter-judicial cooperation depends to a great extent on the precision of the preliminary rulings ('*actes éclairants*') given by the ECJ.[55]

28. The national courts are under an obligation to ensure 'full effect' of EU law norms.[56] This full effect is achieved only if private parties can invoke before their national courts the rights which they derive from EU law. Article 19(1)(ii) TEU stipulates that 'Member States shall provide remedies sufficient to ensure effective legal protection in the fields covered by Union law.'[57] This provision of remedies

---

50. ECJ, Opinion 1/09 [2011] ECR I-1137, para. 80: calling the national courts '"ordinary courts" within the EU legal order'.
51. Articles 93–118 (Arts 107 et seq.: urgent procedure) Rules of Procedure. Compare M. Broberg & N. Fenger, *Preliminary References to the European Court of Justice* (2nd ed. OUP 2014); T. de la Mare & C. Donnelly, *Preliminary Rulings and EU Integration*, in *The Evolution of EU Law* 363 (2d ed. Craig & de Búrca eds, OUP 2011).
52. Case 283/81, *Srl C.I.L.F.I.T. and Others v. Ministero della Sanità* [1982] ECR 3415, para. 14.
53. *C.I.L.F.I.T.*, para. 16.
54. Compare, *inter alia*, ECJ, Opinion 1/09, para. 84.
55. For a taxonomy of preliminary rulings compare T. Tridimas, *Bifurcated Justice*, in *The Court of Justice and the Construction of Europe* 367, 369 et seq. (CJEU ed., Asser & Springer 2013).
56. Case 106/77, *Amministraztione delle Finanze dello Stato v. Simmenthal SpA (Simmenthal II)* [1978] ECR 629, para. 24.
57. The formula has been taken over from Art. I-29 Treaty Establishing a Constitution for Europe.

can be performed by legislative acts or by judge-made case law. Anyway, the autonomy of procedural and substantive law of the Member States is put under the important constraint that it has to meet the condition of *effective protection* of rights of private parties. For the subject matter of this monograph, this means that the principles of non-contractual liability under EU law developed by the ECJ over fifty years (and featured *infra* the text) must lead to corresponding procedures and remedies in the laws of the Member States as far as the liability of Member States or their residents for breach of EU law is concerned. These national rules should not be less favourable than those governing similar rights under domestic law (principle of equivalence) and not render the exercise of EU rights excessively difficult or virtually impossible (principle of effectiveness).[58] Nevertheless, remedial discrepancies between requirements of EU law and intricacies of domestic law often lead to pragmatic out-of-court settlements of these cases.

II. Jurisdiction in Liability Cases

A. Union Liability

29. The *non-contractual* liability of the Union is in principle determined by EU law, especially Article 340(2) TFEU. The 'CJEU' has exclusive jurisdiction for any claim grounded in Article 340(2) TFEU.[59] Within the CJEU, since its establishment in 1989, damages actions against the Union come under the jurisdiction of the EGC (Articles 256(1), 268 TFEU). As to the number of damages actions against the Union, between 1995 and 2010 some ten to twenty new damages cases were introduced each year before the EGC. This represents on average less than 4% of the cases before the EGC.[60] For matters of law, damages actions can get to the ECJ only on appeal.

30. The *contractual* liability of the Union is determined by the respective private law of the Member State applicable to the concrete contract (Article 340(1) TFEU). The claims have to be brought before the national courts, unless the jurisdiction of the European courts is provided for by the existence of an arbitration clause.[61] In the latter case, the EGC has to apply national law. This raises the

58. The principles of equivalence and effectiveness have been postulated by the ECJ in the 1970s and repeated relentlessly from then onwards. Compare Case 33/76, *Rewe v. Landwirtschaftskammer für das Saarland* [1976] ECR 1989; Case 45/76, *Comet BV v. Produktschap voor Siergewassen* [1976] ECR 2043; in the sequel, *inter alia*, Joined Cases C-46 and 48/93, *Brasserie du pêcheur and Factortame III* [1996] ECR I-1131, para. 67. For a critical account *see* M. Bobek, *Why There Is No Principle of 'Procedural Autonomy' of the Member States*, in *The European Court of Justice and the Autonomy of the Member States* 305 (H.W. Micklitz & B. de Witte eds, Intersentia 2011).
59. Article 268 TFEU.
60. Compare Annual Reports of the Court of Justice; *see also* P. Aalto, *Public Liability of the EU* 104 (Hart 2011).
61. Compare Arts 272, 273 TFEU. *See also* T. Heukels, *The Contractual Liability of the European Community Revisited*, in The Action for Damages in Community Law 89 (T. Heukels & A. McDonnell

intricate question of the ECJ's competence to review the application of national laws by the EGC.[62]

31. In the *Grifoni II* judgment of 1991,[63] the Court clarified that quasi-contractual claims for payment for performance of work, based on *unjust enrichment*, fall outside the scope of arbitration clauses in the sense of Article 272 TFEU. Actions for unjust enrichment against EU institutions must be pursued under the heading of non-contractual liability (Article 340(2) TFEU) though they are different in the conditions to be satisfied and not expressly provided for in the Treaties. Their exclusion would infringe the principle of effective judicial protection.[64]

B. Civil Liability[65]

32. The jurisdiction in trans-border claims between private parties based on non-contractual civil liability (tort, delict, quasi-delict) in cases, where at least the defendant is domiciled or has its statutory seat in a Member State of the EU, is determined by Regulation (EU) No. 1215/2012 – Brussels Ia (recast).[66] The Lugano Convention 2007 has made the Brussels I rules also applicable to Iceland, Norway and Switzerland.[67] Thus the Brussels I-Lugano provisions constitute a European judicial area which comprises thirty countries of the EEA[68] plus Switzerland. The Brussels Ia Regulation (recast 2012) provides for a general rule that 'persons domiciled in a Member State shall, whatever their nationality, be sued in the courts of that Member State' (Article 4(1)). Companies or other legal persons are domiciled at the place where they have: (a) a statutory seat, or (b) their central administration, or (c) their principal place of business.[69] Additionally, tort actions can be brought before the courts of the State, where the 'harmful event occurred or may occur' (Article 7 No. 2). The expression 'place where the harmful event occurs' has been interpreted by the Court as covering both the place where the injury/damage

---

eds., KLI 1997); M. Taschner, *Vertragliche Schuldverhältnisse der Europäischen Union – Zuständigkeit und anwendbares Recht*, in Festschrift U. Magnus 531 (Sellier 2014).

62. Compare Art. 58 Statute of the Court of Justice; *see also* AG Kokott, Opinion, C-531/12 P, *Commune de Millau and SEMEA*, EU:C:2014:1946, paras 71 et seq.
63. Case C-330/88, *Grifoni v. EAEC (Grifoni II)* [1991] ECR I-1045, para. 20; *see also* Case C-47/07 P, *Masdar (UK) Ltd v. Commission* [2008] ECR I-9761. For a comparative stock-taking, including EU law, compare R. Williams, *Unjust Enrichment and the Public Law* (Hart 2010).
64. Case C-47/07 P, *Masdar*, paras 49, 50 with further case law.
65. Compare Parts VII and VIII: Civil Non-contractual Liability.
66. Regulation (EU) No. 1215/2012 on jurisdiction and the recognition and enforcement of judgments in civil and commercial matters, OJ 2012 L 351/1. *See European Commentaries on Private International Law*, vol. I: *Brussels Regulation* (U. Magnus & P. Mankowski eds, O. Schmidt 2016). On the application of the former EC Brussels I Regulation in twenty-five Member States compare B. Hess, T. Pfeiffer & P.F. Schlosser, *The Brussels I Regulation (EC) No. 44/2001* (C.H. Beck/Hart/Nomos 2015).
67. (Lugano) Convention on jurisdiction and the enforcement of judgments in civil and commercial matters, OJ 2007 L 333/3.
68. With the exception of Liechtenstein. On the EEA *see supra* text.
69. Article 63(1) Brussels Ia.

occurred and the place of the event giving rise to it.[70] Article 7 No. 5 makes it clear that an enterprise can also be sued in another EEA State where a (dependent or independent) 'branch, agency or other establishment' is operating and causes damage.[71]

33. In product liability actions, the Court held that the place of the event giving rise to the injury/damage is the place where the activity which caused the product defect took place. In principle, this is the place where the product was manufactured. If the place where the damage occurred as a result of the defective product is different from the country of manufacture, the plaintiff may choose to bring proceedings in that country.[72]

34. Some case law of the European courts is dedicated to the conceptual distinction of *contractual* and *non-contractual* claims under the Brussels I Regulation. 'Matters relating to a contract' will be regularly dealt with by the Member States' courts of the place of the performance of the contractual obligation (Article 7 No. 1). Problems can arise in cases where the breach of contract constitutes at the same time a tort or delict. In this respect, the ECJ held that under contracting parties a claim is only contractual in nature where the conduct complained of may be considered a breach of contractual duties which are essential for the purpose of the contract (*Brogsitter* formula).[73]

35. Under the Brussels I-Lugano regime *extraterritorial* civil jurisdiction is permitted. The tortfeasor/defendant must be European, though the tort may be committed by a subsidiary and the place of the occurrence of harm may be outside the EEA (plus Switzerland). In the *Group Josi* case the ECJ confirmed once more that under the Brussels I Regulation the plaintiff need not be a European resident.[74] In the *Owusu* case the Court additionally held that the *forum non conveniens doctrine* does not bar a claim under the Brussels I-Lugano law.[75] On the basis of this established case law, one can state that the Brussels I-Lugano regime grants *locus standi* for non-European plaintiffs to sue in an EEA-State court or in a Swiss court, e.g., in cases where (dependent or independent) subsidiaries cause damage outside Europe by activities which can be attributed to Switzerland- or EEA-based parent companies. This jurisdictional aspect, however, does by no means determine the doctrinal question of accountability and liability of parent companies for operations of subsidiaries.[76] It is up to the national courts of the EEA-States to tackle this problem

70. Case C-51/97, *Réunion européenne SA and Others v. Spliethoff's Bevrachtingskantoor BV and Other* [1998] ECR I-6511, para. 28 with further case law.
71. Case C-218/86, *SAR Schotte GmbH v. Parfums Rothschild SARL* [1987] ECR 4905, para. 17: independent company with the same name and identical management.
72. Case C-45/13, *A. Kainz v. Pantherwerke AG* EU:C:2014:7 with further case law.
73. Case C-548/12, *M. Brogsitter v. Fabrication de Montres Normandes and Other* EU:C:2014:148.
74. Case C-412/98, *Société Group Josi Reinsurance Company SA v. Compagnie d'Assurances Universal General Insurance Comp. (UGIC)* [2000] ECR I-5925, paras 53–57.
75. Case C-281/02, *Andrew Owusu v. N.B. Jackson* [2005] ECR I-1383 (abolishing for EU law the *Re Harrods* doctrine of English common law: *Re Harrods (Buenos Aires) Ltd* [1991] 4 All ER 334 (CA)).
76. *See* European Parliament, Resolution on EU standards for European enterprises operating in developing countries: Towards a European Code of Conduct, OJ 1999 C 104/176. For an international

when applying the tort law to be determined under the EU Rome II Regulation or under the international private law of the *forum* State.

III. Applicable Law in Civil Liability Cases

36. The choice of law in cross-border torts is dominated by the *lex loci delicti* rule. This is a common principle in most conflict-of-laws regimes. It also holds true for the European codification – the Regulation (EC) No. 864/2007 (Rome II).[77] The *locus delicti* can be defined as being the place of conduct or the place of injury. Most recent codifications follow the *favor laesi* principle: namely, they authorize the application of the law of whichever of the two States (State of place of conduct or State of place of injury) is more favourable to the victim. Rome II also adheres to this principle (Article 4(1)). An acknowledged exception to the *lex loci delicti* rule is the 'closer connection principle'. This principle leads to the application of the law of the State to which both parties have a common affiliation through domicile, habitual residence, or nationality (Article 4(2)), or through a pre-existing relationship (Article 4(3)). The Rome II Regulation contains special rules for certain types of torts, such as products liability, environmental torts, unfair competition, intellectual property infringements, and industrial actions.[78]

---

legal contribution to this subject compare the 'Ruggie Framework' and the 'UN Guiding Principles': J. Ruggie, *Protect, Respect and Remedy: a Framework for Business and Human Rights*, UN doc. A/HRC/8/5 of 7.4.2008; *id.*, *Guiding Principles on Business and Human Rights: Implementing the United Nations 'Protect, Respect and Remedy Framework'*, UN doc. A/HRC/17/31 of 31.3.2011.

77. Regulation (EC) No. 864/2007 on the law applicable to non-contractual obligations, OJ 2007 L 199/40.

78. Articles 5–9 Rome II.

Book I. Non-contractual Liability of the European Union, Member States and Private Parties

Introduction: Various Types of Responsibility and Responsible Parties under EU Law

37. Non-contractual responsibility under EU law has long been, and to a certain extent still is, a juristic jungle. Orientation and structure are not easily accessible in this abundance of case law. At its core, one principal ground of liability can be identified, though its contours remain blurred: *breach of EU law*. But on the edge, in the shadow of this supposedly overarching topic, some other independent grounds of non-contractual responsibility of the Union exist.

38. The first and by far most important ground of liability entails the violation of a provision of EU law which confers rights to private parties, i.e., it must have a *protective* effect towards legitimate private interests. The legal interest may be one arising under the Treaties, secondary legislation or general principles of law recognized by the Court. The breach can be committed by EU institutions and bodies, by Member States' authorities, and by private parties.[79] Hence there are in principle three potential addressees of non-contractual liability: the *Union*, the *Member States* (and their institutions respectively), – and *private parties* (individuals as well as businesses).[80] For the Member States, liability for breach of EU law is achieved through the doctrines of vertical direct effect and supremacy.[81] For private parties to incur such liability, the condition of horizontal direct effect must be met.

39. With respect to the Union and its predecessors, the Court of Justice started to develop principles governing this breach-of-law liability in the 1960s and 1970s,

79. The term 'private party' is used throughout the monograph to name persons of private law, namely individuals and companies. Private bodies which are so-called emanations of the State are not covered. For the latter *see infra* text and fn. 400.
80. Compare W. van Gerven, *Non-contractual Liability of Member States, Community Institutions and Individuals for Breaches of Community Law with a View to a Common Law for Europe* (1994) 1 MJ 6; C. Sieburgh, *EU Law and Non-Contractual Liability of the Union, Member States and Individuals*, in *The Influence of EU Law on National Private Law* 465 (A.S. Hartkamp ed., et al. Kluwer 2014).
81. On this in greater detail, *see infra* text (Part II, Ch. 1, §1).

under ECSC law (*Vloeberghs*) and EEC law (*Lütticke II/Schöppenstedt*).[82] The injured private party has to sue the Union itself or its 'institutional organs',[83] especially Council as legislative and Commission as executive body, before the Luxembourg Courts. Uncertainties remained for a long time concerning the liability of Member States and of private parties for breach of EU law. With respect to *Member States*, the first ground of liability was breach of vertically directly effective EU law by Member States. These cases primarily cover unduly levied duties and discrimination committed by Member States' authorities (e.g., *Russo* and *Marshall*).[84] The actions for damages had to be brought before the national courts which apply their domestic law of governmental liability. To that extent, Member States in principle enjoyed procedural autonomy. For claims regarding breach of EU law, national courts, however, were under an obligation to adhere to a compensatory standard equivalent to that available under domestic law in similar cases, but also appropriate to secure the protective effectiveness of the remedies available.[85]

40. A special variant of the Member States' breach-of-EU-law liability became the *Francovich* type of responsibility.[86] The ECJ began to elaborate this concept in the 1990s. It reacts to the absence of horizontal direct effect of directives and covers failures of Member States to transpose EU directives properly. Next to the (above-mentioned) vertical direct effect cases[87] and the *Francovich* doctrine, two additional variants of Member States' liability for breach of EU law were developed: the breach of a State's affirmative duty to prevent harm to the internal market: *Schmidberger,*[88] and the liability of States' judicial bodies of last instance*: Köbler.*[89] The vicarious State liability for breach of EU law by national public servants has yet to be elaborated (*A.G.M.-COS.MET Srl v. Finland and Lehtinen*).[90]

41. Liability of *private parties* was theoretically recognized in EU antitrust law, but remained in an embryonic stage due to the underdeveloped status of the Member States' law of damages in this field. Only recently the question of horizontal direct effect of provisions of EU law has been pushed tremendously to the fore. To harmonize the national legal remedies which allow full compensation of the losses

82. *See infra* text (Part I, Ch. 2).
83. Under the Lisbon Treaty the European Union has legal personality of its own (Arts 47 TEU, 335 TFEU). Its institutional organs are listed in Art. 13 TEU. The EC ceased to exist. *See supra* text.
84. Case 60/75, *Russo v. AIMA* [1976] ECR 45; Case 152/84, *Marshall v. Southampton and South-West Hamshire Area Health Authority* [1986] ECR 723.
85. Laid down by the *Rewe* and *Comet* judgments of the ECJ. *See infra* text and fns 383–385. . Compare also *The European Court of Justice and the Autonomy of the Member States* (H.W. Micklitz & B. de Witte eds, Intersentia 2011).
86. Joined Cases C-6 and C-9/90, *Francovich and Others v. Italy* [1991] ECR I-5403; *see infra* text (Part II, Ch. 1, §2).
87. *See infra* text (Part II, Ch. 1, §1).
88. Case C-112/00, *Schmidberger v. Austria* [2003] ECR I-5659; *see infra* text (Part II, Ch. 1, §3).
89. Case C-224/01, *Köbler v. Austria* [2003] ECR I-10239; *see infra* text (Part II, Ch. 1, §4).
90. Case C-470/03, *A.G.M.-COS.MET v. Finland/Lehtinen* [2007] ECR I-2798. Compare Brüggemeier, *EU Product Safety Law, Whistleblowers, and Member State Liability for Acts of Officials* (2015) 2 EJCL 212.

incurred, the EU passed Directive 2014/104/EU on antitrust damages actions which, in principle, extends the right to sue also 'indirect purchasers', including consumers.[91]

42. Whilst developed at different times, on separate tracks and in a sometimes confusing way, these varied types of *liability of public bodies* – Union's breach-of-law liability under (now) Article 340(2) TFEU and evolving Member States' breach-of-EU law liability (from vertical direct effect (type I) and *Francovich* (type II) to States' protective duty (type III) and responsibility of State courts of last instance (type IV)) – have become more and more approximated and consolidated towards the end of the twentieth century. This has been implemented by landmark judgments of the Court of Justice such as *Brasserie du pȩcheur and Factortame III, Hedley Lomas,* and *Bergaderm.*[92]

43. The *liability of private parties* in horizontal direct effect cases has finally also gained contours, to mention for competition law simply the cases of *Courage Ltd* and *Manfredi*. In addition, a new phenomenon has emerged in EU liability law after the passing of the Charter of Fundamental Rights: the third party effect of fundamental rights. The European courts find themselves confronted with the challenging task of balancing horizontally competing fundamental economic freedoms and fundamental human rights: *Laval*, *Viking*, and *mutatis mutandis*, *A.G.M.-COS.MET Srl v. Finland and Lehtinen.*[93]

44. Additionally, there are two branches of Union liability law which are rather marginalized and neglected compared to the 'grand subjects' of constitutional and administrative EU law mentioned *supra*, but from their substance, however, they are closer to the conventional law of torts.[94]

One is the traditional *vicarious liability* of the Union for the *torts* committed by acts of its servants towards third parties 'in performance of their official duties'. These cases of personal fault were expressly regulated in ex-Article 40(2) TECSC. Today, this branch, included as an independent strand in Article 340(2) – 'by its servants', also encompasses the liability of EU bodies and institutions for regular torts: *Grifoni I.*[95] – The other is its inverse pendant: *injuries to persons of the EU staff.* This is the responsibility of the Union as public principal for harm incurred by its

---

91. Directive 2014/104/EU on certain rules governing actions for damages under national law for infringements of the competition law provisions of the Member States and of the European Union, OJ 2014 L 349/1. *See infra* text (Part IV, Ch. 1, §2).
92. On this process in greater detail, *see infra* text. Compare also P. Aalto, *Public Liability in EU Law* (Hart 2011).
93. Compare N. Reich, *General Principles of EU Civil Law*, 146 et seq. (Intersentia 2014): 'principle of balancing'; D. Leczykiewicz, *Private Party Liability in EU Law* (2009/10) 12 CYELS 257. *See infra* text (Part IV, Ch. 2).
94. The relevance of private law in this context of non-contractual liability has, not surprisingly, been stressed by British authors. Compare D. Edward & W. Robinson, *Is there a Place for Private Law Principles in Community Law?* in *The Action for Damages* 339 (Heukels & McDonnell eds, KLI 1997).
95. Case 308/87, *Grifoni v. EAEC (Grifoni I* No 1*)* [1990] ECR I-1203.

own officials and caused by administrative failure of its own institutions. Responsibility is here grounded on the close principal-servant relationship and a *faute de service*, i.e., a breach of the principal's duty to have reasonable regard to the interests of the public servants. – The personal liability of the servants *towards the Union* is governed by the provisions laid down in the Staff Regulations or in the Conditions of Employment applicable to them (Article 340(4)).[96]

45. Lastly, some attention must be paid to a still embryonic phenomenon: the responsibility of the Union for damage caused to private parties by *lawful measures* of its institutions.[97] This concept should be clearly separated from the context of public or private parties' liability for breach of law and wrongful acts or omissions. Whilst not explicitly excluded by the wording of Article 340(2), it is nevertheless an original head of public responsibility to pay 'fair compensation', *not damages*, with its own genuine rationales: distributive justice and equal treatment. (A comparable differentiation of remedies could already be found in the ECSC Treaty of 1951: Article 34(1) provided primarily for 'equitable redress' determined by the High Authority, whereas Article 40(1) awarded 'pecuniary reparation' (= damages) assessed by the Court.)

96. This provision has been originally introduced with Art. 26 of the Merger Treaty 1965.
97. *See infra* text (Part VI, Ch. 1).

Part I. Non-contractual Liability of the European Union (Article 340(2) TFEU)

Chapter 1. Introduction: Two Types of Liability of the European Union: Vicarious Liability for Torts and Liability for Breach of Law

§1. History of Article 340(2) TFEU

46. Article 340(2) TFEU can be traced back to Article 215(2) of the EEC Treaty of Rome 1957.[98] Its wording has remained unchanged throughout the decades, though the Treaty itself underwent dramatic changes. It still reads:

> In the case of non-contractual liability, the [now] Union shall, in accordance with the general principles common to the laws of the Member States, make good any damage caused by its institutions or by its servants in the performance of their official duties.

47. The drafters of the Treaties of Rome would not spend too much thought and time on formulating this liability provision. Article 215(2) TEEC (and the homonymous Article 188(2) EAEC) did not belong to the regulatory core of the Treaties of 1957. The EEC Treaty's target was to abolish tariffs and trade restrictions between the six Member States and to help a customs union and common market to come into existence. Nevertheless, the Member States conferred sovereign powers on the EEC institutions and in recognition of this, those institutions were to be responsible for damage however wrongfully arising. Confronted with this subject of liability, the provision on non-contractual liability in the ECSC Treaty of Paris (1951) served as a point of orientation.[99]

---

98. It corresponded to Art. 188(2) Euratom Treaty.
99. G. Bebr, *The Non-Contractual Liability of the European Coal and Steel Community*, in *The Action for Damages* 71 (T. Heukels & A. McDonnell eds, KLI 1997); M. Lagrange, *The Non-Contractual Liability of the Community in the ECSC and in the EEC* (1965/1966) 3 CML Rev 10; W. Much, *Die Amtshaftung im Recht der Europäischen Gemeinschaft für Kohle und Stahl* (Klostermann 1952).

48. Article 40 TECSC adhered very closely to the French model of State liability and recognized two distinct causes of actions for damages: wrongful acts/maladministration (*faute de service*) of the Community (Article 40(1)[100])[101] as main, and personal fault/torts (*faute personnelle*) of public servants in the performance of their duties (Article 40(2)) as secondary head of liability.[102] The latter concerned the ordinary everyday operations of the public service: regular torts committed by the servants 'on the official job'. These cases were in French law governed by private law, and jurisdiction was in the civil courts.[103] The first cause of action (*faute de service*), however, was rooted deeply in public law. It required a wrongful act of the State, and jurisdiction lay with the administrative courts, with the *Conseil d'Etat* as last instance, developing their case law autonomously and independently from the civil code's law of delict and its categories.[104]

49. Article 40 TECSC kept both causes of actions separately in its two paragraphs, but both were, different from French law, conferred to the sole comprehensive jurisdiction of the Court of Justice. An institutional separation of administrative and civil courts remains still today alien to the European courts system.[105] Wrongful acts of the ECSC institutions led to administrative liability of the Community. Originally redress was only admissible subsequent to an annulment of the wrongful measure as far as decisions and recommendations are at issue (Article 34 TECSC).[106] With no annulment procedures available, the Court recognized that

100. A special head of Community liability was Art. 34 TECSC which provided for an equitable redress after annulment of a decision or recommendation of the High Authority.
101. Article 40(1) ECSC Treaty 1951 read: ' … , the Court shall have jurisdiction to assess damages against the Community, at the request of the injured party, in cases where injury results from a fault involved in an official act of the Community in execution of the present Treaty'.
102. Article 40(2) read: 'It shall also have jurisdiction to assess damages against any official or employee of the Community, in cases where injury results from a personal fault of such official or employee in the performance of his duties. If the injured party is unable to recover such damages from such official or employee, the Court may assess an equitable indemnity against the Community.'
103. The same holds true for English common law and most of the continental civil law regimes. The German law of delict differentiates additionally between regular public servants (workers, employees – §§823 et seq. BGB) and servants with the status of civil servants ('Beamte' – §§839 BGB) with the latter being privileged.
104. Since the arrêt *Blanco*, 8 Feb. 1873, Rec. 1873, 61. Compare Lagrange, (1965/66) 3 CML Rev 10; M. Fromont, *France*, in *Haftung des Staates für rechtswidriges Verhalten seiner Organe/Liability of the State for Illegal Conduct of its Organs/La responsabilité de l'Etat pour le comportement illégal de ses organs*) 135 (H. Mosler ed., Heymanns 1967).
105. Even among the chambers of the ECJ, no specialized chamber for civil law or (public and private) liability law has been established. This is one of the reasons why the vicarious liability of the Union for torts by its officials gradually vanished from the Court's agenda.
106. On the relationship between liability under Arts 34 and 40(1) TECSC and Art. 215(2) TEEC, compare Case T-120/89, *Stahlwerke Peine-Salzgitter AG v. Commission* [1991] ECR II-279, paras 71 et seq. (78) and Case C-220/91 P, *Commission v. Stahlwerke Peine-Salzgitter AG* [1993] ECR I-2393. *See also* J. Wakefield, *Judicial Protection through the Use of Article 288(2) EC* (KLI 2002).

damages actions are independently admissible (Article 40(1)).[107] Torts of public servants triggered their personal liability; the Community could be addressed only subsidiarily to pay an (equitable) 'redress' (Article 40(2)(ii) TECSC).[108]

50. In the Rome Treaties, the authors wanted to avoid the strong adherence to French law in the new article on non-contractual liability. At the same time the drafters were reticent about getting too deeply involved in the complex issues of *faute* and 'wrongfulness' of personal or institutional conduct and into disputes over the private or public law character of this liability in tort. So, they first decided to settle the odd problem of formulating a principle of non-contractual liability diplomatically, by plain reference to the 'general principles common to the law of the Member States'.[109] Well aware that a 'common' corpus of 'general principles' governing State liability for officials and public authorities did not exist in the law of the six founding Member States,[110] they secondly left it to the Court, through its case law, to fill in these principles in greater detail. Thus, they merged the two distinct causes of action of Article 40 TECSC into one head of Community liability (Article 215(2) TEEC), but nevertheless kept up the two variants of State liability: vicarious liability of the Union for *personal torts* of public servants 'in the performance of their official duties' and public liability for *wrongful acts of the State*, which then developed into the breach-of-law liability of the Union. Addressee of the actions for damages under Article 215(2) TEEC is, in any case of tort liability, exclusively the [then] Community (or its institutional organs).

51. These two regimes of non-contractual Community liability, Article 40(1)(2) TECSC and Article 215(2) TEEC, coexisted till 1967 when the Merger Treaty of 1965 came into force.[111] This Merger Treaty replaced Article 40(2)(i) TECSC by the following provision, realigning it to EEC law: 'The Court shall also have jurisdiction to order the Community to make good any injury caused by a *personal wrong* by a servant of the Community in the performance of his duties.'[112] This is an unambiguous declaratory statement, with the legislative authority of the European Council, that torts of servants also remain a separate and independent strand of Union liability under Article 215(2) TEEC/Article 288(2) TEC/Article 340(2) TFEU.

107. Joined Cases 9 and 12/60, *Société commerciale A. Vloeberghs SA v. High Authority* [1961] ECR 197 (inaction of High Authority).
108. On personal liability of servants under EU law *see infra* text (paras 68–72).
109. Classified as a purely 'diplomatic formula' by the former AG Lagrange. Lagrange, *The Non-Contractual Liability* (1965/66) 3 CML Rev 10, at 32.
110. Compare as comprehensive comparative stock-akings The Liability of Public Authorities in Comparative Perspective (K. Oliphant ed., Intersentia 2016), and *Staatshaftung in Europa. Nationales und Unionsrecht* (O. Dörr ed., de Gruyter 2014); for an earlier comparative account *see Haftung des Staates für rechtswidriges Verhalten seiner Organe/Liability of the State for Illegal Conduct of its Organs/La responsabilité de l'Etat pour le comportement illégal de ses organs* (H. Mosler ed., Heymanns 1967).
111. Merger Treaty (or Brussels Treaty) of 1965, OJ 1967 No. 152/1: merging the legislative and administrative bodies of the three European Communities. *See supra* text.
112. Article 26(2)(i) Merger Treaty 1965. On the other hand it abolished both, the requirement to sue at first the servant himself/herself, and the discretion of the Court to assess an equitable redress (Art. 40(2)(ii) TECSC).

52. Thus the fundamental ambivalence of state liability which characterizes most Member States' legal systems survives also in EU tort law: *regular torts* of officials and public bodies (fault) committed 'on the public job', which are in English common law and in continental European civil law covered mostly by private law of delict/torts – and *wrongs of the State* fulfilling sovereign tasks (maladministration/*fonctionnement défectueux du service public*). In the latter case, liability developed in many Member States exclusively in public law:[113] from original immunity of the State ('The king can do no wrong.') to diverse causes of liability with specific conditions. Article 215(2) TEEC/340(2) TFEU comprises the two types of private/public non-contractual liability under the exclusive jurisdiction of the European courts. These two variants of Union liability under Article 340(2) TFEU must therefore be the starting point of any restatement of EU tort law.

§2. Two Variants of Union Liability

53. Having legal personality of its own (*'EU Inc.'* – Articles 47 TEU, 335 TFEU), the Union shall be sued in tort, described in the language of the Treaty as non-contractual liability. As the law actually stands, non-contractual liability under Article 340(2) TFEU encompasses two distinct variants of liability:

> *The first entails the classical vicarious liability* (respondeat superior). *That is responsibility for regular torts by any public servant employed by the EU and committed in the course of his/her public employment. This variant corresponds to Article 40(2) ECSC Treaty of Paris and has parallels to the legal systems of the Member States. However, this variant today covers not only personal torts of individual officials, employees and workers, but also encompasses the torts of EU bodies and institutions. Insofar this monograph speaks of quasi-vicarious liability. Traditional (private and public) vicarious liability and its rules are restricted to the relationship of employer/principal and (dependent) employee/public servant.*[114]

54. The second variant comprises the *breach-of-law liability* of EU institutions and bodies. It embraces the 'relevant breaches' of rules of EU law for the protection of private parties by legislative or administrative acts. The principal ground of liability is not a tort (fault) committed by a public servant or an institution, but the unlawfulness of a legislative or administrative act or omission. Main defendants in

113. German law is characterized by the particularity that it provides at least three different legal regimes: one private law approach for regular torts of individual officials and emanations of the State (§§823 et seq./§839 (Beamte) BGB); one private-public law concept for wrongful acts of officials or public authorities fulfilling sovereign tasks (Art. 34 Federal Constitution (Grundgesetz)/ §839 BGB) – and a public law regime of compensation for unlawful acts of the State (*enteignungsgleicher und aufopferungsgleicher Eingriff*). In all three cases the amount of damages has to be determined by civil courts. Compare U. Magnus, *Germany*, in *The Liability of Public Authorities in Comparative Perspective* 177 (K. Oliphant ed., Intersentia 2016).

114. *See, inter alia*, P. Giliker, *Vicarious Liability in Tort. A Comparative Perspective* (CUP 2010). On this in greater detail, *see infra* text.

this field of law are the Council (of the EU) and the Commission. This second variant of Union liability had roots in the State responsibility for 'wrongful acts'/*faute de service* in French law and was addressed in Article 40(1) TECSC.[115] It cannot be traced back to the 'general principles common to the law of the Member States'. It is a genuine achievement of the ECJ case law developed out of the multi-layered supranational governance system of the EU, as originally intended by the drafters of Article 215(2) TEEC.

55. This twofold structure has been adopted by Article 41(3) ChFR. It stipulates a constitutional right of any private party to claim compensation for damage caused by *institutions* and *public servants* of the Union.

56. 'Institutions' means primarily the 'institutional organs' of the Union, i.e., European Parliament, European Council, Council of the EU, European Commission, Court of Justice, Court of Auditors.[116] Their concrete legislative or administrative measures[117] must infringe protective EU law. Concerning the ECB, a special homonymous paragraph has been additionally introduced by the Maastricht Treaty. It provides for a standard of liability equal to that of the other institutional organs, but different insofar as the ECB is the sole addressee of liability.[118] From the point of view of corporate law, torts and unlawful acts of the organs are imputed to the superior corporate entity as 'wrongs' of its own. Therefore, the corporate body, i.e., the Union, and institutional organs are necessarily and per se jointly and severally liable. In contrast to the literal wording of Article 340(2), the liability of the 'institutional organ' is not absorbed by the Union as '*superior qui respondeat*'. In practice, it is rather the institutions which are sued and less so the Union,[119] though the latter is by Article 340(2) exclusively named as *the* addressee of non-contractual liability. Sometimes the institution is sued, but the Court's judgment orders the Union to pay the compensation.[120]

In addition and secondarily, this liability of the Union encompasses breach of EU law by its 'bodies'. A body is any organization (of private or public law) which is authorized to act 'in the name and on behalf' of the EU or which is an 'emanation'

115. In its early decisions, the ECJ referred to its case law under Art. 40(1) TECSC. Compare Case 25/62, *Plaumann & Co v. Commission* [1963] ECR 95; Joined Cases 5, 7 and 13–24/66, *E. Kampffmeyer and Others v. Commission* [1967] ECR 245; Case 30/66, *Becher v. Commission* [1967] ECR 285.
116. As a rare example of an action for damages compare ECJ, Case 220/13 P, *K. Nikolaou v. Court of Auditors of the EU* EU:C:2014:2057.
117. In principle, also judgments of EGC and ECJ can constitute a relevant breach of EU law leading to liability of the EU. On this intricate problem, *see infra* text (Part I, Ch. 3, §4, I).
118. Article 340(3) TFEU. On liability of the ECB (though not mentioning Art. 340(3) TFEU) *see* Joined Cases C-8/15 P to C-10/15 P, *Ledra Advertising Ltd and Others v. Commission and ECB* EU:C:2016:701 (ESM). Instead, many Member States recognize immunities for their central banks.
119. Different, *inter alia*, the *Grifoni* cases (EAEC) and the cases of *K. Kampffmeyer KG* [1976] and *Bayerische HNL* (EEC). *See infra* text.
120. *See*, e.g., Joined Cases 64 and 113/76, 167 and 239/78, 27, 28 and 45/79, *Dumortier Frères and Others v. Council* [1979] ECR 3091.

of the EU. Here again, de facto a joint and several liability of the EU and the respective body exists. – Private law activities of these bodies, however, will regularly fall under the vicarious liability variant.[121]

57. As indicated *supra*, this second variant of non-contractual responsibility under Article 340(2), liability for unlawful 'official acts', will be called *breach-of-EU law liability*, to distinguish it clearly from vicarious liability for individual torts of public servants and quasi-vicarious liability for torts of bodies and institutions of the EU.

With respect to the diverse independent Agencies which are deployed in Member States to fulfil certain EU regulatory functions,[122] their statutes provide for an equivalent liability rule such as Article 340(2) TFEU.[123]

58. This breach-of-law liability for institutional maladministration, to stress it for the last time, is clearly opposed to classic vicarious liability. The latter had its ground in the general rules common to the Member States' laws of governmental responsibility, which mostly refer to the respective private law of delict/torts. The institutional liability for breach of protective EU law, however, had to be developed autonomously by the Court of Justice, greatly aided (and sometimes pushed) by its AG,[124] with less support by supposedly common principles of the governmental liability laws of the Member States. The Court focused instead on emergent 'general principles' of (primary) EU law. This type of breach-of-law liability clearly dominates the discussion on EU tort law throughout the Union.

59. That being said, Book I of the monograph starts with a section on vicarious liability in tort of the Union.[125] The various types of liability for breach of EU law, by Union *and* Member States' public institutions and bodies, and their partial merger will be featured extensively afterwards (Part I, Chapter 3 and Parts II & III), followed by a section on liability of private parties for breach of EU law (Part IV). The Union's liability for injuries to its own staff, and EU responsibility for lawful acts will be treated as separate issues in Part VI.[126]

---

121. On EU liability for legal persons under private law compare Case 18/60, *L. Worms v. High Authority* [1962] ECR 195; Case C-370/89, *SGEEM and Etroy v. EIB* [1992] ECR I-6211. *See also* A.Z. Steiner, *Die außervertragliche Haftung der Europäischen Union* 79–86 (Mohr Siebeck 2015) and *infra* text (Part I, Ch. 2, §2, II).
122. On the process of agencification in the EU compare M. Chamon, *EU Agencies: Legal and Political Limits to the Transformation of the EU Administration* (OUP 2016); M. Shapiro, *Independent Agencies*, in *The Evolution of EU Law* Ch. 5 (P. Craig & G. de Búrca eds, OUP 2011); *Agencies in European and Comparative Perspective* (T. Swart & L.F.M. Verhey eds, Intersentia 2003).
123. Compare M. Busuioc, *European Agencies. Law and Practices of Accountability* (OUP 2010).
124. On the role of Advocates General compare fn. 24 and N. Burrows & R. Greaves, *The Advocate General and EC Law* (OUP 2007).
125. W. van Gerven & J. Lever & P. Larouche, *Common Law of Europe Casebooks: Tort Law,* Ch. 9, 889 (Hart 2000), proceed in the same way.
126. *Locus classicus* for the non-contractual liability under EU law still is *The Action for Damages in Community Law* (T. Heukels & A. McDonnell eds, KLI 1997), as a successor volume of *The Non-Contractual Liability of the European Communities* (H.G. Schermers, T. Heukels & P. Mead eds, Nijhoff 1988).

Table 2 Non-contractual Liability of the European Union(I)

Non-contractual Liability of the European Union (I)

ECSC Treaty of Paris (1951)

Article 40(2)
Injury resulting from personal fault of official 'in performance of his duties'

Article 40(1)
'fault' involved in an official act of the Community

Article 215(2) Treaty of Rome
Article 288(2) TEC
Article 340(2) TFEU

'In the case of non-contractual liability, the Union shall, in *accordance with the general principles common to the laws of the Member States*, make good any damage caused *by its institutions* or *by its personnel* in the performance of their official duties.'

[A] vicarious liability for torts

- factual conduct

by EU officials: *Sayag/Adams*

quasi-vicarious liability for torts

by EU executives: -
by EU bodies: *Grifoni I*
by EU institutional organs: *Leussink*

[B] liability for breach of EU law by EU institutions

- legislative acts
- administrative acts

cumulative conditions of liability:

- protective rule/ conferral of rights
- unlawfulness/relevant breach,
- damage,
- causation.

Chapter 2. EU Vicarious Liability: Torts of Staff, Bodies and Institutions (Article 340(2) TFEU)

§1. Vicarious Liability: EU Staff

60. Vicarious liability of the Union as 'superior' for torts of its officials is subject to three conditions: (1) employment, (2) tort of the public servant, (3) commission in the performance of official duties. When these conditions are fulfilled, the public employer is exclusively or jointly and severally liable for the tort of its servant. This traditional 'strict' concept of *respondeat superior* complies in substance with the general principles common to the Member States' laws of governmental and employers' liability.[127] Only the Germanic laws of Austria, Germany and Switzerland still formally recognize fault of the employer as an additional requirement for liability of the 'superior'. In the two latter countries, this black letter law of 'superior's fault' has tremendously lost importance due to the case law developed through the courts.[128]

I. Employment

61. Public servant or employee is every person, man or woman, who by appointment or by an employment contract is obliged to supply services for EU institutions. In this regard, reference is to be made to the so-called Staff Regulations[129] as the official document describing the rules, principles and working conditions of the European civil service.

II. Delict/Tort

62. The employee must have committed a delict or tort. In this context, 'to commit a tort' means: *to cause an injury or damage to a private party by wrongful behaviour*. Such a tort of an official or private EU body can encompass:

> *all criminal acts that are committed by a public servant in the performance of his/her office. Crimes regularly also meet the conditions of private law torts and of grave personal misconduct. Then, each ordinary everyday tort, committed 'on the official job', constitutes a wrongful act in office. This can imply*

---

127. *See* for comparative accounts *Unification of Tort Law: Liability for Damage Caused by Others* (J. Spier ed., KLI 2003), and P. Giliker, *Vicarious Liability in Tort* (CUP 2010).
128. Compare S. Galand-Carval, *Comparative Report on Liability for Damage Caused by Others, Part I: General Questions*, in *Liability for Damage Caused by Others* 289, at 302 (J. Spier ed., KLI 2003).
129. Regulation (EEC) No. 31/1962 laying down the Staff Regulations of Officials and the Conditions of Employment of Other Servants of the EU, OJ 1962 L 45/1385; lastly amended 2014.

*intentional acts such as sexual harassment, or a mishap like negligently pouring hot coffee on a visitor, or a traffic accident caused by a car owned or leased by EU institutions and used for an official trip (*Sayag*),*[130] *or the non-procurement of safety on EU run premises which are open to the public (*Grifoni*). It can comprise the supply of incorrect information,*[131] *or the utterance of an opinion or statement which is detrimental to another's reputation or marketing of products (*A.G.M.-COS.MET*). – Generally it can be stated that this EU tort law covers the whole range of activities of EU bodies, agencies and officials which is usually described in scholarly writing as 'factual conduct'.*[132]

63. A tort can also be constituted by the breach of an *official protective duty*, which the respective employee has to comply with. A wrongful breach of an official duty by a public servant has been determined in an exemplary manner by the ECJ in the case of a 'delegate' in charge of the enforcement of a development aid project in Somalia, financed from resources by the European Development Fund.[133]

64. A relevant example of a *personal* official duty is the duty to keep secret (Article 339 TFEU).[134] A case of breach of the duty of confidentiality can be found in the bizarre *Adams* affair.[135] Mr *Adams*, then a Maltese national and an employee of *Hoffmann-La Roche & Co*, Basel, secretly supplied the EC Commissioner for Competition with confidential evidence concerning antitrust practices of the Swiss pharmaceutical company in the common market. That information led the Commission finally to impose a penalty on *La Roche*. Subsequently, on request of *La Roche*, criminal procedures against Mr *Adams* were initiated in Switzerland and he was sentenced (*in absentia*) to one year's imprisonment for breach of business confidentiality.[136] Mr *Adams* claimed that the Commission's officials did not keep his identity secret as they were bound to by law and additionally by an order of their head of division. He sued the Commission for compensation of the damage he sustained resulting from the discovery of his identity. The Court indeed held that the

---

130. On car driving as an 'official act' *see* H.G. Schermers & C.R.A. Swaak, *Official Acts of Community Servants and Art. 215(4) EC*, in *The Action for Damages* 167 (Heukels & McDonnell eds, KLI 1997).
131. Compare the 'staff cases' 19/69, 20/69 and 30/69, *D. Richez-Parise and Others v. Commission* [1970] ECR 325, para. 38.
132. *See*, *inter alia*, M.H. van der Woude, *Liability for Administrative Acts*, in *The Action for Damages* 109, at 117 (Heukels & McDonnell eds, KLI 1997); P. Machnikowski, *The Liability of Public Authorities in the European Union*, 559, at 574, in *The Liability of Public Authorities in Comparative Perspective* (K. Oliphant ed., Intersentia 2016).
133. Case T-491/93, *San Marco Impex Italiana Srl v. Commission* [1994] ECR II-1061.
134. Article 339 TFEU is unambiguous. It is addressed to individual servants and members of institutions, but not to the EU institutions themselves. Misconduct leads to liability for torts, not to breach-of-law liability of EU institutions.
135. Case 145/83, *S.G. Adams v. Commission* [1985] ECR 3556. *See also* M. Hunnings, *The Stanley Adams Affair or the Bitter Bit* (1987) 24 CML Rev 65.
136. Mr Adams' application to the (then) European Commission of Human Rights in Strasbourg was not admitted because barred by time. On the recent 'whistleblower' judgment of the ECtHR in the *Heinisch* case *see infra* text and fn 597.

Commission's officials[137] failed to make all reasonable efforts to impede the discovery of Mr *Adams*' identity by *Hoffmann-La Roche* and ordered compensation.

65. A tort can be an act or an omission. For the latter to trigger liability, an affirmative duty of the servant is required, e.g., the duty to provide for safe premises or to keep confidentiality. With regard to injury/damage and causation, the general rules apply.[138] Wrongful behaviour of an individual employee implies personal fault; that is (unlawful) intent or negligence.[139] Unequivocal in this regard was Article 40(2) TECSC, which stipulated that the injury must result from 'personal fault' of the public servant or employee.[140]

III. Scope of Employment

66. The wrong must have been committed 'in the performance' of the official duties. There must be a relationship to the service performed. The ECJ has construed this criterion of relationship narrowly. One of the first cases on liability for physical conduct of a public servant was *Sayag II.*[141] Mr *Sayag*, an engineer employed by Euratom, was instructed to take two representatives of a private enterprise on an inspection tour to a nuclear power plant at Mol in Belgium. He drove them there in his own car. For this, he had obtained a travel order enabling him to claim expenses for the trip from Euratom. Mr *Sayag* caused an accident by which one of his passengers was injured. The passenger sued *Sayag* and the latter's liability insurer for damages before the Belgian courts.[142] Mr *Sayag* argued that he drove the car 'in the performance of his official duties' and that therefore Euratom would be the right defendant. On preliminary ruling before the ECJ, the Court held that the Euratom would be 'only liable for those acts of its employees which, *by virtue of an internal and direct relationship*, were the necessary extension of the tasks entrusted to the European institutions'.[143] An official's use of his private car during the course of his duties could only satisfy this condition in the case of force majeure

137. As usual the Court did not distinguish between wrongful acts (torts) of public servants and breach-of-law by the institution (Commission) itself.
138. *See also infra* text (Part I, Ch. 4).
139. This aspect of *personal* fault should not be mixed up with the highly controversial question whether the Union's breach-of-law liability for its institutions comprises, next to unlawfulness, elements of fault as a precondition of responsibility. On this in greater detail, *see infra* text.
140. Article 40(2) ECSC Treaty: An action could be brought against the official 'in cases where injury results from personal fault of such official or employee in the performance of his duties'.
141. Case 9/69, *Sayag and S.A. Zürich v. Leduc and Others* (*Sayag II*) [1969] ECR 329.
142. *Sayag I* was about the question whether criminal proceedings could be pursued against Sayag as the person responsible for the accident and the resulting injuries of the passengers: Case 5/68, *Sayag v. Leduc* [1968] ECR 575. The Court held there that immunity under Art. 11(a) Protocol (acts performed in official capacity) does not prejudge any liability on the part of the Community, 'this being governed by special rules designed for a purpose separate from that of the provisions of the Protocol'. More on this *see infra* text.
143. *Sayag II* [1969] ECR 329, paras 7–8, and *Sayag I* [1968] ECR 575, at 600. *See also* Schermers & Swaak, *Official Acts of Community Servants and Art. 215(4)*, in *The Action for Damages* 167, at 174 et seq. (Heukels & McDonnell eds, KLI 1997).

or exceptional circumstances of such overriding importance that without the official's using private means of transport the Union would have been unable to carry out the tasks entrusted to it.

67. Thus, the case went back to the national Belgian courts applying Belgian law. Already in this case without success, the AG pleaded to take into account the respective laws of the Member States when determining the standards for the concrete case.[144] A comparison with the laws of the Member States would have shown that there, the range of acts triggering state liability is significantly wider.[145] The ECJ gave no justification for this limited nature of vicarious liability under Article 340(2) TFEU. It seems to be in contradiction with the broad concept of Union liability for torts of public servants presented here, as well as with the wide approach adopted by the European courts when they decide on 'emanations of the State' in vertical direct effect cases.[146] It remains to be seen whether the European courts nowadays will still adhere to this narrow concept of relationship.[147]

IV. Public Servants' Responsibility in Their Own Personal Capacity?

68. Many Member States' laws of governmental liability do not recognize a responsibility of the public servant in *his or her personal capacity* to the third party damaged by wrongful performance of official duties,[148] or, if so, restricts it to cases of serious misconduct.[149] The laws of the Member States predominantly channel the liability exclusively onto the State.[150] In other words: There is in principle *no joint and several liability* of the State and its servant. This is different from the private law of the Member States governing the responsibility of employers for torts of their employees.[151] Whether this exclusivity doctrine of governmental liability also applies in EU law is not free from doubt. Exclusivity is supported by the fact that Article 26(2)(ii) of the Merger Treaty of 1965, which replaced Article 40(2) TECSC with its principle of personal liability of public servants, mentions only the 'personal liability of servants *towards the Community*'. This corresponds from 1993

144. AG Gand, Opinion, Case 9/69, *Sayag II* [1969] ECR 337, 340 et seq.
145. Compare S. Galand-Carval, *Comparative Report on Liability for Damage Caused by Others, Part I: General Questions*, in *Liability for Damage Caused by Others* 289, at 294 (J. Spier ed., KLI 2003).
146. Compare C-188/89, *Foster v. British Gas Plc* [1990] ECR I-3313; Case 177/88, *Dekker v. Stichting Vormingscentrum* [1990] ECR I-3941; *see* in greater detail *infra* text.
147. The *Sayag* formula has, however, recently been affirmed by the EGC in Case T-124/04, *Jamal Ouariachi v. Commission* [2005] ECR II-4653, para. 18.
148. For example Austria, France, Germany, Poland, Portugal, Switzerland.
149. For example, Italy: personal liability of officials was excluded till 1948. Afterwards, it was restricted to serious misconduct of the public servant. The same holds true for the Scandinavian laws.
150. This is opposed to the law of the ECSC Treaty 1951. According to Art. 40(2) the injured private party had first to sue the responsible official or employee. Only if the injured party could not recover, the Community could be addressed subsidiarily.
151. *See* for comparative accounts *Liability for Damage Caused by Others* (J. Spier ed., KLI 2003) and P. Giliker, *Vicarious Liability in Tort* (CUP 2010).

onwards to the Treaty law (now Article 340(4) TFEU).[152] The (internal) personal liability is governed by the provisions laid down in the Staff Regulations[153] applicable to the servant at issue. It comprises internal offences such as embezzlement or breach of trust and recourse claims by the Union acting as principal.

69. Another argument in favour of exclusivity can be found in Article 11 lit. a of the Protocol (No. 7) on the Privileges and Immunities of the European Union.[154] It provides for immunity of officials and other servants of the Union from legal proceedings through Member State courts in respect of acts performed 'in their official capacity'. As benchmark serve the rules on servants' liability towards the Union.[155]

70. The personal liability subject can be summarized as follows:

– no external liability of servants, in addition to the Union, for acts performed in 'official capacity';
– recourse by the Union only in cases of serious misconduct;
– regular liability of EU servants under national law for tortuous acts committed outside 'official capacity'.

71. However, in the *A.G.M.-COS.MET* case, the ECJ held with regard to Member State liability:

> Union law does not preclude an individual other than a Member State from being held liable, in addition to the Member State itself, for damage caused to individuals by measures which that individual has taken in breach of Union law.[156]

Closer examination shows, however, that the Court did not differentiate between public-law bodies[157] and individual public servants. What may make sense in the former case, makes less sense in the latter. Therefore, it is still not completely free from doubt what the EU law in this respect is actually about. The question may be of less relevance because the damaged private party will mostly sue the deep pocket, i.e., the public fund. Nevertheless, as the *A.G.M.-COS.MET* case proves, State *and* official are often sued jointly and severally.

72. Be that as it may, if the Union is *not* held liable, because the servant's act was not performed 'in his/her official duties', then an action can be brought against

152. Compare Art. 215(4) (Maastricht Treaty), Art. 288(4) (Amsterdam Treaty).
153. The Staff Regulations of officials and the conditions of employment of other servants of the European Communities, OJ 1968 L 56, as amended.
154. OJ 2012 C 326/266.
155. Compare Art. 22 Staff Regulations: 'An official may be required to make good, in whole or in part, any damage suffered by the Union as a result of serious misconduct on his part in the course of or in connection with the performance of his duties.'
156. Case C-470/03, *A.G.M.-COS.MET*[2007] ECR I-2798, para. 98. *See infra* text.
157. Public-law bodies are concerned in the case quoted in *A.G.M.-COS.MET*: Case C-424/97, *S. Haim v. Kassenzahnärztliche Vereinigung Nordrhein (Haim II)* [2000] ECR I-5123.

the official in his or her personal capacity before a national court and governed by the national law of delict/torts.[158] The general rules of international private law and international procedural law apply.

If the Union or its institution is held vicariously liable, it has in cases of 'serious misconduct' of the official – arguably criminal offences and intentional injuries or gross negligence – a right to internal recourse against the public servant.[159] This recourse claim has to be brought before the EGC.

V. Immunities

73. A puzzling point needs finally to be addressed. Pursuant to Article 343 TFEU, the Union enjoys certain privileges and immunities in the Member States.[160] The same holds true for its officials and employees.[161] Article 11(a) of the Protocol (No. 7) on the Privileges and Immunities grants immunity from suits in national courts in relation to 'acts performed by them in their official capacity', whereas under Article 340(2) liability is conditional on the 'performance of their official duties'. Does it make a relevant difference? The ECJ oracled that Article 340(2) and Article 11(a) deal with separate issues.[162] That may mean that servants' acts 'in the performance of official duties', which lead to EU liability, may include but are not limited to acts 'performed by them in their official capacity', which lead to the employees' immunity from suit in national courts.[163] 'Official capacity' is said to be in its meaning narrower than 'official duties'.[164] Whether this makes sense may here be left undecided. If the Union *is* vicariously liable, then the servant's personal liability *should* be absorbed, regardless of whether his/her act in performance of his/her duty falls outside his/her 'official capacity'. That is the corollary of State vicarious liability, and it results from the obvious fact that the applicant cannot collect twice. There seemed to be only one case scenario imaginable where this discrepancy may work out: incidents of serious misconduct by the servant leading to criminal proceedings by the national authorities. Here, the liable Union might address its official for redress, and the criminal proceedings under national law are not exempted by Article 11(a).

158. Compare Case 9/69, *Sayag II* (fn. 141).
159. The personal liability of the EU officials towards the Union is taken up in Art. 340(4) TFEU. It refers to the conditions of the respective employment. The recourse is covered by Art. 22 of the Staff Regulations of Officials of 1962, OJ 1962 L 45/1385; now Regulation amending the Staff Regulations of Officials and the Employment of the Other Servants of the EU, OJ 2013 L 287/15. On this compare Schermers & Swaak, *Official Acts of Community Servants and Art. 215(4) EC*, in *The Action for Damages* 167 (Heukels & McDonnell eds, KLI 1997).
160. Compare Protocol (No. 7) on the Privileges and Immunities of the European Union, consolidated version, OJ 2012 C 326/266.
161. Compare Chap. V of the Protocol (No. 7).
162. Case 5/68, *Sayag v. Leduc* (*Sayag I*) [1968] ECJ 395, at 402.
163. That is the interpretation of the ECJ's oracle by Schermers & Swaak, *supra* fn. 130, at 167, 177.
164. Schermers & Swaak, *supra* fn. 130.

§2. Special Case: EU Ombudsman

74. A new field of liability in tort had come up before the European courts: liability of the European Ombudsman.[165] The Treaty of Maastricht introduced the European Ombudsman into the framework of the Union. Article 228(1) TFEU provides:

> The European Parliament shall appoint an Ombudsman empowered to receive complaints from any citizen of the Union or any natural or legal person residing or having its registered office in a Member State concerning instances of maladministration in the activities of the Union institutions or bodies, with the exception of the Court of Justice of the European Union acting in their judicial role. The Ombudsman shall inquire the complaints and shall then forward a report.

The EU intended to improve with this body the non-judicial settlement of cases of maladministration within its institutions. The body was finally established in 1994, with seat in Luxembourg.[166] The first European Ombudsman was elected and took office in 1995.

75. In *European Ombudsman v. Lamberts*, the ECJ had to tackle the problem of whether and under which conditions the EU could be made liable for an alleged malperformance by the Ombudsman.[167] Mr *Lamberts* sought compensation for economic and non-economic damage purportedly suffered as a result of the manner in which the Ombudsman had dealt with his complaint concerning an administrative decision of the Commission in a recruitment procedure. The Court, in plenary session, found that the Ombudsman is required solely to cooperate with the institution concerned in order to seek a friendly solution such as to eliminate the instance of maladministration and satisfy the complainant. In that regard, he enjoys a very wide discretion.[168] It finally upheld the judgment of the General Court which had held that the Ombudsman acted without being 'guilty of wrongful conduct'.[169]

76. In *M v. European Ombudsman*, a damages action was brought by a Commission official. The applicant sued the Ombudsman for infringement of his right to respect for private life. The latter had in a decision concerning a suspected instance of maladministration mentioned the applicant by name. The EGC found a plain breach of the applicant's right to respect for private life and of the principle of proportionality sufficient to lead to liability without further requirements, although the European Ombudsman enjoys in principle a wide margin of discretion. The EGC awarded compensation for non-pecuniary damage of EUR 10,000.[170]

---

165. On history and powers of the European Ombudsman, *see* Craig, *EU Administrative Law* 739 (OUP 2010) with further references.
166. Resolution 94/262/ECSC, EC, Euratom, European Parliament, OJ 1994 C 113/15.
167. Case C-234/02 P, *European Ombudsman v. Lamberts* [2004] ECR I-2838.
168. Case C-234/02 P, para. 82.
169. Case T-209/00, *Lamberts v. European Ombudsman* [2002] ECR II-2203, para. 85.
170. Case T-412-/05, *M v. European Ombudsman* [2008] ECR II-197, paras 140, 143.

§3. QUASI-VICARIOUS LIABILITY

I. EU Executive Officers

77. Unlike the regular public servants/employees, executive officers – the 'organ persons' – are indispensable for incorporated institutions to operate. Their will is regarded as the corporation's own will: their acts are deemed to be the corporation's own acts. In other words: these persons are 'the mouth and the hands' of the incorporated entity. That is why their torts are often regarded as torts of the corporation itself. Hence in German civil law for example, executives' liability is clearly not a case of vicarious liability (§831 *BGB*) but a special matter of corporate law. The tort of the 'organ person' is automatically attributed to the corporation, always leading to joint and several liability of both,[171] though each party can be sued separately (*'in solidum'*).

78. With regard to the European Union, its 'organ persons' are no longer individuals, but institutions (which in their turn may have 'organ persons'). These institutions are separately liable next to the Union. With respect to them, the focus is mostly on depersonalized processes and outcomes – malfunctioning instead of malfeasance. What the law vis-à-vis executive officers' liability looks like under Article 340(2) TFEU remains uncertain. As far as can be seen, there is no specific case law at hand. – A rare example of an EU institution's liability for injurious behaviour of its organ persons seems to be the case *K. Nikolaou v. Court of Auditors of the EU*. The applicant claims injuries and damage through faulty omissions of the president of the defendant institution. The Court, however, did not recognize this type of EU liability in tort.[172]

II. EU Bodies: *Grifoni I*

79. EU bodies of public or private law can also commit torts in their field of competence. In the private law of delict/torts, this type of liability corresponds to enterprise liability, where the enterprise is directly responsible for its malfunctioning or its defective outcome, without having prior recourse to any individual failure of employees or executives.[173] An excellent example of this organizational liability in tort is given in the case of *Grifoni I*.

80. For reconstruction works to be undertaken in the European joint research institute at Ispra, Italy, Mr *Grifoni*,[174] a tenderer for the performance of these works,

171. Compare §31 BGB. This principle is recognized by the law of most EU Member States. *See* S. Galand-Carval, *Comparative Report,* in *Liability for Damage Caused by Others* 289, at 293 (Spier ed., KLI 2003) with further references.
172. ECJ, C-220/13 P, *K. Nikolaou v. Court of Auditors of the EU* EU:C:2014:2057.
173. On this in greater detail, *see* Brüggemeier, *Modernising Civil Liability Law* (CUP 2011); Brüggemeier, *Haftungsrecht* 117–184 (Springer 2006); *see also infra* text.
174. Case 308/87, *Grifoni v. EAEC* (*Grifoni I No. 1*) [1990] ECR I-1203 (interlocutory judgment). *Grifoni I No. 2* was dedicated to the final assessment of the extent of damages: Case 308/87, *Grifoni*

inspected the flat roof of the institute. Due to insufficient safety devices, he fell from the roof and was seriously injured. At that time, the Ispra centre was run by the European Atomic Energy Community (EAEC/Euratom). Mr *Grifoni* sued the EAEC for compensation of the damage allegedly resulting from that accident.[175] Was there a tort? Committed by whom?

81. The Court, when deciding the case, was completely misled. Trained in the practice of breach-of-law liability, it applied the standard rules on responsibility for legislative wrongs.[176] Thereby it found it necessary to consider whether an act of the Commission (*sic*!) was unlawful (i.e., breach of EU law) and whether there was a causal link between the act and the damage suffered (here by Mr *Grifoni*).[177] But there were no acts of the Commission, neither of legislative nor of administrative nature. It was just an accident in Italy, occurring on the premises of an EU research institute. Accident law is private law of delict/torts.

82. The joined research centres are independent bodies of the EU and participate as parties in the regular private law world. They conclude employment contracts, they purchase technical devices and other things, and they hire enterprises for reconstruction works. As such, they are in charge of the safety of their premises, be they owners or tenants of the building. In Ispra, too, it was the centre which controlled and supervised the premises as a whole. The correct question to be answered by the Court therefore would have been: Did the centre commit a tort?[178] To be able to give an answer, one needed an applicable law. Neither did the EAEC have nor does the Union nowadays dispose of a private law of delict or torts. In this situation, the original wisdom of the drafters of the Rome Treaty held good: The ECJ had to have recourse to the general principles of tort law governing the concrete case and which are common to the Member States. Starting point could be the law of the place of the accident, i.e., Italian law. AG *Tesauro* formulated a sort of *equivalence principle*: The compensation awarded in accident cases under EU law shall not be less than under the domestic law of the place of the accident:

> It would be 'strange for the victim of an accident to receive [under EU law] protection' … , which was inferior to that provided for by the Member State in which the accident occurred.[179]

---

v. EAEC [1994] ECR I-341. – The case *Grifoni II* (C-330/88, *Grifoni v. EAEC* [1991] ECR I-1045) deals with claims for unpaid performance of work. *See supra* text (para. 31).

175. Article 188(2) EAEC Treaty is identical with Art. 340(2) TFEU.
176. *See* the reference made by the Court in *Grifoni I No. 1* to Case 49/79, *Pool v. Council* [1980] ECR 569 (sic!).
177. Case 308/87, *Grifoni I No. 1*, para. 7.
178. This is precisely the question posed by the learned Advocate General Tesauro in his opinion. He delivered his answer focusing on Italian civil law (Arts 2043, 2051 Cod. civ.). Compare AG Tesauro, Opinion, *Grifoni I No. 1* [1989] ECR I-1212.
179. AG Tesauro, Opinion (fn. 178), para. 17.

83. The answer provided by Italian law[180] and by the general principles would be: the centre was under a general private law duty to ensure safe premises. The content of this duty as a normative matter was to be determined by the Court. Thereby, it may take into account respective Italian regulations on the prevention of accidents in the construction industry, if available.

Under the concrete circumstances, the outcome of the case was beyond doubt. As a matter of fact, in this case the centre had not taken any precautions at all. It was an organizational fault/*colpa d'apparato*. A causal link between this negligent omission and the injury was beyond dispute. In other words: A tort of the centre was given. This led to quasi-vicarious liability of its public 'superior', the European Atomic Energy Community.

84. The correct way to decide the case was straightforwardly offered to the Court by the excellent opinion of AG *Tesauro*. However, the ECJ ignored it completely. It treated the Commission as a tortfeasor.[181] Neither *the* Commission nor *any* Commissioner was related to the site of the accident, and there is no administrative measure of the Commission that infringes a protective provision of EU law conferring a right to Mr *Grifoni* (free movement of persons?). The Commission's involvement in the case was reduced to the formal procedural aspect that, as the 'institutional organ' of the (then) three European Communities, it had to represent the defendant European Atomic Energy Community before the Court.

III. EU Institutions: *Leussink and Others*

85. Though not in the *Grifoni* case, there are other case scenarios imaginable where also the Commission can take the role of a tortfeasor in the sense of quasi-vicarious liability. Such an incident is delivered in the *Leussink* case.[182] Originally, it was primarily a so-called staff case, i.e., a claim of an official against the Union as his principal,[183] but it was also a third party liability scenario, inasmuch as relatives of Mr *Leussink* were applying for damages, too.[184]

86. A road accident occurred in an EU Member State and an individual suffered bodily injuries and property damage by a car belonging to the Commission, used in official mission and driven by a Commission public servant. If the individual sues the Union for damages, it is again a case of enterprise or institutional liability in tort. The (now) competent EGC would have to refer to the general principles of law of delict/torts of the Member States as stipulated by Article 340(2). In the original

180. Articles 2043, 2051 Cod. civ.

181. Mistaken by its own arguments, the Court in *Grifoni I No. 2* erroneously named the Commission as defendant in *Grifoni I No. 1*. *See* Case 308/87, *Grifoni I No. 2* [1994] ECR I-341, para. 1.

182. Joined Cases 169/83 and 136/84, *G. Leussink and Others v. Commission* [1986] ECR 2822. On the *Leussink* case, *see also* W. van Gerven, J. Lever & P. Larouche, *Common Law of Europe Casebooks: Tort Law* 895 (Hart 2000).

183. On the staff cases, *see* in greater detail *infra* text (Part VI, Ch. 2).

184. *See infra* text and fn. 754.

Leussink case, it remained uncertain whether the driver was to blame for the accident. According to the expert's report presented in *Leussink*, the accident occurred because the tread came away from one of the tyres. The report listed as possible causes: poor maintenance or inadequate inspection of the vehicle or negligent use. The Commission did not furnish any evidence enabling the Court to determine the factual cause of the detachment of the tread. As the Commission was best placed to provide evidence in that respect, the *Leussink* Court based its order for payment of damages correctly on a presumption of organizational fault of the Commission.[185]

87. There is another possible path of EU institutions' liability in tort. It happens that private undertakings are intrusted with tasks which form part of the framework of the Union. They fulfil these tasks by activities under private law. The EU institutions have the public duty to supervise these activities. According to an early judgment of the Court under Article 40(1) TECSC, these private parties do not fall under the jurisdiction of the Court.[186] Wrongfulness of their private law activities is governed by national law and to be determined by domestic courts. However, as far as an alleged failure of the Commission or another body of the EU to supervise these private parties properly is concerned, an action for damages can be brought under Article 340(2).[187] – The question remains and has not yet been answered by the Court whether these 'intrusted private parties' should be considered as 'emanations' of the EU and treated like other regular bodies of the EU.[188] The Treaties want to reserve for the Court's jurisdiction all cases involving non-contractual liability of the *Union as a whole* towards third parties.

185. *Leussink*, para. 17.
186. C 18/60, *Worms v. High Authority* [1962] ECR 195.
187. C 18/60, *Worms*, at 205.
188. On the case law on 'emanations' of Member States *see infra* text.

Chapter 3. 'Breach-of-Law Liability' of the European Union (Article 340(2) TFEU)

88. Although covered by one and the same paragraph of Article 340 TFEU, the two types of EU liability have little in common. The EU vicarious and quasi-vicarious liability, featured *supra*, is traditional State liability for torts in public office/*schuldhafte Amtspflichtverletzung* committed by EU public servants or bodies. *Faute personelle* or organizational fault/*colpa d'apparato* is a regular precondition for these two variants of vicarious liability. In that regard, well-established legal rules exist in most of the twenty-eight Member States of the EU and principles of private law of delict/torts apply.

89. The type of public liability to be discussed in this section, however, developed without common principles in the law of the Member States. It is a merger of the French *faute de service* State liability and of the particularities of the EU legal system. The focus is on '*public subjective rights*' conferred by (superior) protective provisions of EU law to private parties, businesses or individuals, – and on *breach* of these protective provisions by EU institutions and bodies which are under a duty to secure these rights or legally protected interests and to prevent their impairment. The breach can be committed by legislative or administrative acts.[189] Individually acting persons disappear behind the veil of the public institution. Under scrutiny are depersonalized processes of public maladministration that produce a defective outcome – a breach of law.[190] Decisive is the *'relevant breach'*[191] of the protective law by the respective legislative or administrative measure. Breach of EU law or unlawfulness/illegality is the principal ground of this institutional liability.[192] To bring an action for damages, the relevant breach additionally must have caused damage. The aggrieved private party then can seek compensation from the Union (or its institutions) before the European courts (Article 268 TFEU).

---

189. With regard to the judicature (EU and Member States courts), *see infra* text.
190. *See* already the definition of faute de service by G. Teissier, *La responsabilité de puissance publique*, 49 (1906): 'Ce n'est pas, en effet, seulement l'erreur, l'acte illégal, la négligence, la faute en un mot d'un fonctionnaire de tel ou tel service qui peut causer un dommage; ce peut être la mauvaise organisation de ce service, son fonctionnement défectueux, sans qu'on allègue même la moindre faute à l'encontre d'un agent. *C'est le service public, c'est la machine gouvernementale ou administrative elle-même qui, dans ces divers cas, est la cause du dommage.*' (Emphasis added – G.B; quoted from Much, *Die Amtshaftung* 33 (1952)).
191. *Relevant breach* is chosen as a comprehensive category covering both 'plain breach' and 'manifest and grave breach', that is, cases with and without discretion of the public authority. W. van Gerven once proposed as a general standard the test of 'a reasonable authority acting under similar circumstances'. This, however, missed the point. It is the reformulation of the negligence principle for a new type of liability for unlawfulness under Art. 340(2), where the question of fault is a distinct non-issue. W. van Gerven, *A Common European Law in the Area of Tort Law,* in *Tort Liability of Public Authorities in Comparative Perspective* 125, at 136 (Fairgrieve, Andenas & Bell eds., BIICL 2002).
192. On the hidden fault elements which are nevertheless contained, *see infra* text.

90. The Court developed this type of liability by focusing on fundamental principles of EU law and only 'where necessary',[193] on general principles common to the legal systems of the Member States. Thus, the Court of Justice invented straightforwardly an EU law Aquilian action of *damnum iniuria datum*: that is, *compensation for damage caused by breach of European law.* This damages action was a necessary corollary of the command of full effectiveness of EU law.

§1. Union Rights

91. The 'CJEU' (Article 19 TEU) is the guardian of EU law. This is an obvious proposition, but nonetheless important. Therefore, its main interest is the full and complete implementation of EU law throughout the Union's twenty-eight Member States. The completion of the single market must be promoted; breaches of EU law must be prevented. The TFEU provides a variety of possibilities to sue before the European courts parties that have breached EU law, especially Member States,[194] but a monograph on tort law is not the place to address that in greater detail. The subject in this section is the breach of protective rules by the EU institutions. Effective prevention of infringements demands remedies; attributable causation of damage requires compensation. The two principal remedies against breach of EU law provided for by the Treaties are annulment of the illegal act and compensation of damage. The end of annulment is the abolition of a particular unlawful measure of an EU institution by the Courts (Articles 263, 264 TFEU). It is a subject matter of general EU law. In this section, the concern is exclusively on compensation or, to be more precise, on actions by private parties against the Union for recovery of damage caused by breach-of-law by an EU institution, based on Article 340(2). The aim of full effectiveness of EU law – which is the mantra constantly repeated by the Court – would be impaired if private parties were unable to obtain redress when their rights and legitimate interests were infringed by unlawful public acts or omissions.

92. From the 1960s onwards, the ECJ developed instruments to monitor breach of EU law by EU institutions. In the *Plaumann* case, the Court initially held that an annulment of the respective measure, incompatible with EU law, was a necessary condition before the Union could be sued under [now] Article 340(2).[195] In this regard, it adopted for EEC law the well-settled practice under Articles 34, 40 TECSC. Shortly later, this approach was generally discarded, and the action for

193. Formula used in ECJ, Joined Cases C-46 and 48/93, *Brasserie du ppêcheur and Factortame III* [1996] ECR I-1131, para. 27. This happens mostly as far as the consequences of liability are concerned: damages, limitations, etc.

194. On Treaty infringement procedures against Member States (Arts 258, 259 TFEU), *see* C. Harlow & R. Rawlings, *Accountability and Law Enforcement: The Centralised EU Infringement Procedure* (2006) 31 EL Rev 447.

195. Case 25/62, *Plaumann & Co v. Commission* [1963] ECR 95, at 108: 'An administrative measure which has not been annulled cannot itself constitute a wrongful act on the part of the administration.'

compensation became recognized as an independent and autonomous instrument across the (then) three Communities:

> The action for damages ... was established by the Treaty as an independent form of action with a particular purpose to fulfil within the system of actions and subject to conditions for its use, conceived with a view to its specific purpose.[196]

The action for annulment (Article 263 TFEU) and the action for damages (Article 340(2) TFEU) are two distinct procedural forms pursuing different purposes, the former aiming at the repeal of a legislative act or an administrative measure, the latter at the payment of compensation.

93. Today, two *normative questions* determine the non-contractual breach-of-law liability of the Union: (1) Is there a protective provision of law?[197] And (2) is there a relevant breach of this EU law?

Beforehand, one aspect deserves note here. Also, with regard to EU institutions and bodies a preliminary question must be answered in the affirmative: Did the institution in question act 'in the name and on behalf' of the European Union? This goes obviously without saying in cases of legislative or administrative measures by 'institutional organs' (Council, Commission, etc.). However, this aspect can be in dispute when EU bodies are engaged in private law activities. For example: In an action brought against the European Investment Bank (EIB), an interlocutory judgment of the ECJ, sitting as full court, was needed to decide this question in the affirmative.[198]

94. An example from another context is the *J.M. Le Pen* case.[199] In this scenario, the 'Socialist Group' of the EU Parliament distributed an allegedly defamatory pamphlet dealing with the rise of fascism in Europe. *Le Pen* and the *Front National* sued for damages under Article 340(2) TFEU. The Court held that there is no rule of EU law from which it may be inferred that the acts of a political group would be imputed to the EU Parliament as an institution of the Union.

§2. Protective Rule (*Schutznorm*)

95. To serve as a cause of action for damages, the infringed rule of law must fulfil one major condition: It must intend the protection of a conferred right or a

196. Case 4/69, *A. Lütticke GmbH v. Commission (Lütticke II)* [1971] ECR 325, para. 6 (for EEC law); compare for ECSC law: Joined Cases 9 and 12/60, *Société commerciale A. Vloeberghs v. High Authority* [1961] ECR 197, pp. 213/214; for EAEC law: Case 59/65, *H. Schreckenberg v. Commission of the EAEC* [1966] ECR 543, at 550.
197. *See supra* text.
198. Case C-370/89, *Société Générale d'Entreprises Electro-Mécaniques (SGEEM) and Etroy v. European Investment Bank (SGEEM No 1)* [1992] ECR I-6244 (interlocutory judgment on jurisdiction); Case C-370/89, *SGEEM No 2* [1993] ECR I-2583.
199. C-281/89, *J.M. Le Pen and the Front National v. D. Puhl and Others* [1990] ECR I-1183.

legitimate interest of a private party. This has been postulated for the first time in the *Vloeberghs* case (for ECSC law).[200] Like in the law of some Member States, the European courts use the formula that it is sufficient if the rule does not only concern the public at large but is also, maybe only implicitly, directed towards any particular private party or class of private parties.[201] Generally, the question of whether a provision of EU law is intended to confer individual rights or to protect private interests is determined through interpretation in accordance with the recognized interpretative methods. The crucial factors in that regard are the wording, spirit and purpose of the provisions at issue and the concerns of the EU legislature evidenced in the preamble to the respective legal instrument.

96. In *Kind*, e.g., the Court stated that alleged mistakes in the delivered reasons for the passing of a regulation do not violate private legal interests.[202] The European courts held constantly that the rules on the division of powers and competences between the various institutions of the EU, whose aim is to ensure the balance between the institutions provided by the Treaties, and between the Union and the Member States, as enshrined in Article 5 TEU, cannot be regarded as rules which are intended to confer rights on private parties. The position would be different if a measure of an EU institution was adopted which not only disregarded the division of powers between the institutions but also, in its substantive provisions, disregarded a superior rule of law protecting private parties.[203] In *Dillenkofer*, the ECJ insisted, against the opinion of some Member States Governments, that the directive on package travelling is not restricted to promoting the freedom of services and competition. The Court made once more clear[204] that the fact that a directive pursues other targets or is adopted in the general interest does not exclude that it also intends to protect individual interests, here consumer interests.[205]

The four economic freedoms of the TFEU[206] prominently confer rights on the enterprises and individuals acting in the respective sectors of the internal market.

97. The original criterion that an act must affect a limited *and* defined number of protected parties has later been modified. Iinstead, the sole criterion of the definability of the class of protected parties, be that class great or small, became the decisive element.[207]

---

200. Joined Cases 9 and 12/60, *Société commerciale A. Vloeberghs v. High Authority* [1961] 197, at 217.
201. Case C-282/90, *Industrie- en Handelsonderneming Vreugdenhil BV v. Commission (Vreugdenhil II)* [1992] ECR I-1937. *See also* P. Aalto, *Public Liability in EU Law* 158 (Oxford, Hart 2011).
202. Case 106/81, *J. Kind KG v. EEC* [1982] ECR 2887, paras 13 et seq.
203. *See* especially C-282/90, *Vreugdenhil II* [1992] ECR I-1937, paras 20–22; *see also* Case C-221/10 P, *Artegodan GmbH v. Commission* EU:C:2012:216.
204. *See* already Joined Cases 5, 7 and 13-24/66 *E. Kampffmeyer and Others v. Commission* [1967] ECR 245, at 262.
205. Joined Cases C-178, 179 and 188-190/94 *Dillenkofer and Others v. Germany* [1996] ECR I-4845.
206. Free movement of goods (Arts 28 et seq.), employees (Art. 45), services (Art. 56) and capital (Art. 63). Compare C. Barnard, *The Substantive Law of the EU – The Four Freedoms* (4th ed., OUP 2013).
207. Joined Cases C-104/89 and C-37/90, *J.M. Mulder and Others v. Council and Commission* (*Mulder II No. 1*) [1992] ECR I-3126, para. 16. *See also infra* text.

§3. RELEVANT BREACH OF LAW

I. Legislative Acts

98. Unlike in the private law world of torts, it is not the wrongfully caused personal injury or property damage that raises questions of liability. Here, it is a '*normative incident*', the defective outcome of the legislative machinery of the EU that leads to liability for normative injustice. As regards liability arising from legislative measures, the wrongful act with which an EU institution is charged must be the relevant breach of a *superior rule of law* for the protection of private parties.[208] Higher-ranking rules of law are regularly provisions of the Treaties and other primary EU law, and the general principles of law.[209] A Commission regulation implementing improperly a parent Council regulation would also be in breach of superior law.

99. A legislative act is any measure of general application. It is the substance, not the form of the measure which counts. Both regulations and directives will normally satisfy this test.[210] The legislative act is defective when it does not comply with a superior protective rule or general principle of EU law. Supposedly, hundreds of academic conferences held and innumerable law review articles and law books published in the last decades have been dedicated to this subject of a relevant breach (sufficiently serious breach). The following attempts to reconstruct the basic legal structure.

A. Schöppenstedt

100. In the beginning was the *Schöppenstedt* formula. In the case of *Zuckerfabrik Schöppenstedt*,[211] a German sugar producer felt unlawfully aggrieved by a Council regulation dealing with methods to calculate sugar prices. It alleged an infringement of its right from Article 40(2)(ii) TFEU. Addressing the question of a relevant breach, the Court held in 1971:

> In the present case the non-contractual liability of the Community [Union] presupposes at the very least the unlawful nature of the act alleged to be the cause

208. Case 5/71, *Aktien-Zuckerfabrik Schöppenstedt v. Council* [1971] ECR 975, para. 11; Joined Cases 83 and 94/76 and 40/77, *Bayerische HNL* [1978] ECR 1209, para. 4. *See also* A. Arnull, *Liability for Legislative Acts under Art. 215(2) EC*, in *The Action for Damages* 129 (Heukels & McDonnell eds, KLI 1997) – The thesis, put forward by P. Aalto, that the *Bergaderm* judgment of 2000 (fn. 259) generally did away with the superiority condition is incorrect. *Union* liability for *legislative* acts (!) structurally requires a breach of a superior rule of EU law. Compare Aalto, *Public Liability in the EU*, passim (Hart 2011).
209. *See* Tridimas, 2006, and Groussot, 2006 (fn. 332).
210. On this in greater detail, *see* A. Arnull, *Liability for Legislative Acts under Art. 215(2) EC*, in *The Action for Damages* 129 (Heukels & McDonnell eds, KLI 1997).
211. Case 5/71, *Aktien-Zuckerfabrik Schöppenstedt v. Council* [1971] ECR 975.

> of the damage. Where legislative action involving measures of economic policy is concerned the Community does not incur non-contractual liability for damage suffered by individuals as a consequence of that action, ... , unless a sufficiently flagrant violation of a superior rule of law for the protection of the individual has occurred.[212]

From the outset the ECJ distinguished clearly two cases of breach-of-law liability: a *plain* infringement of the protective superior rule of law (unlawful nature of the act) – so-called *Lütticke* test,[213] and, where the legislative implementation of economic policy was concerned, a '*sufficiently flagrant*' violation – so-called *Schöppenstedt* test.

101. In phase I after *Schöppenstedt*, the Union's breach-of-law liability was governed by these rigorous conditions, because it concerned exclusively legislative acts or at least acts of a general nature, such as decisions authorizing a certain Member State to adopt safeguard measures, which kept the Court of Justice busy. The Court's case law thus simply reflected the regulatory character of the activities of the Union whose institutions then were mainly legislative machineries. The *implementation and application* of EU legislation was the responsibility of the Member States. Concrete problems relating to the application of this legislation, e.g., proceedings seeking annulment of administrative acts, had to be raised before national courts.[214] Actions were exceptionally admitted before the European courts if the national authorities acted according to mandatory instructions of the Commission[215] or if the Commission failed to perform its supervisory function on the implementation by the Member States.[216]

As will be seen in the following, the regulatory activities leading to disputes on compensation relate mostly to the field of the Common Agricultural Policy, such as price support regulations and general rules on monetary compensatory amounts. Many actions for damages concerned the common organization of the market in cereals, especially durum wheat.[217]

---

212. *Schöppenstedt*, para. 11.
213. Case 4/69, *A. Lütticke GmbH v. Commission* (*Lütticke II*) [1971] 325, para. 10: ' ... liability of the Community presupposes ... actual damage, a causal link between the damage claimed and the conduct alleged, and the illegality of such conduct.' Compare before, Joined Cases 5, 7 and 13-24/66, *E. Kampffmeyer and Others v. Commission* (*E. Kampffmeyer*) [1967] ECR 245, at 262 and *see infra* text.
214. *See, inter alia*, Case 96/71, *R. & V. Haegeman v. Commission* [1972] ECR 1005, paras 8–16.
215. For example, Case 175/84, *Krohn v. Commission* [1986] ECR 753.
216. For example, Joined Cases 5, 7 and 13-24/66, *E. Kampffmeyer* [1967] ECR 245; Case 30/66, *K.A. Becher v. Commission* [1967] ECR 285; Case 4/69, *A. Lütticke GmbH v. Commission (Lütticke II)* [1971] ECR 325.
217. *See* Joined Cases 63–69/72, *W. Werhahn Hansamühle and Others v. Council* [1973] ECR 1229; Joined Cases 56–60/74, *K. Kampffmeyer KG and Others v. EEC (Kampffmeyer KG)* [1976] ECR 712. *See* on this A. Arnull, *Liability for Legislative Acts under Art. 215(2) EC*, in *The Action for Damages* 129 (Henkels & McDonnell eds, KLI 1997).

B. Bayerische HNL

102. In phase II after *Schöppenstedt*, things changed in so far as the Courts increasingly put the focus on the *margin of discretion* exercised by the legislative institution.[218] The new test was first enunciated in the case of *Bayerische HNL and Others v. European Economic Community*.[219] This case belonged to a complex of cases deeply rooted in the technicalities of the common market in milk and milk products. Despite its system of intervention prices, the Commission was facing a surplus of milk production giving considerable rise to the intervention stocks of skimmed milk powder. To reduce these stocks the Community adopted a regulation on compulsory purchase of skimmed milk for use in feeding-stuffs. This regulation has been declared null and void by the ECJ. Aggrieved were in particular firms engaged in the production and sale of chickens. Applicants in *HNL* were German producers of poultry. They claimed to have suffered losses due to the increased compulsory prices for skimmed milk. They sued the Union for compensation of the alleged financial consequences of the void regulation. The Court held:

> Although the principles [in the legal systems of the Member States governing the liability of public authorities for damage caused to private parties by legislative acts] vary considerably from one Member State to another, it is however possible to state that the public authorities can only exceptionally and in special circumstances incur liability for legislative measures which are the result of choices of economic policy.
> [Therefore] individuals may be required, in the sectors coming within the economic policy of the Community, to accept within reasonable limits certain harmful effects on their economic interests as a result of a legislative measure without being able to obtain compensation from public funds even if that measure has been declared null and void. In a legislative field such as the one in question, in which one of the chief features is the exercise of a wide discretion essential for the implementation of the Common Agricultural Policy, the Community does not therefore incur liability unless the institution concerned has manifestly and gravely disregarded the limits on the exercise of its powers.[220]

103. It was particularly for two reasons that the Court did not find such a 'manifest and grave' disregard. First, the annulled regulation affected a very broad class of traders, basically all buyers of compound feed-stuff containing protein. Second, the price increase of feed-stuff as a factor in the production costs was only limited. Thus, the negative effects of the regulation on the profit-earning capacity of the undertakings arguably did not exceed the bounds of the economic risks inherent in

218. Compare C. Hilson, *The Role of Discretion in EC Non-Contractual Liability* (2005) 42 CML Rev 677.
219. Joined Cases 83 and 94/76, 4, 15 and 40/77 [1978] ECR 1209.
220. Paragraphs 5 and 6.

the activities of the agricultural sectors concerned.[221] The latter became subsequently an often used formula in this context,[222] where legislative measures were at stake which involve choices of economic policies. Hence, *HNL*'s claim was dismissed as unfounded.

104. These criteria of liability for legislative acts were confirmed in the famous *swell flour*[223] and *maize grits*[224] cases, dealing again with matters of Common Agricultural Policy. In these cases, the Council had introduced production refunds for the maize used for the manufacture of groats and meal *(Gritz)* intended for the brewing industry and for *Quellmehl* used in the bakery industry. A main feature of these measures was equal treatment between the processing of swell flour, maize and starch. In a Council regulation deviating from the proposal of the Commission, the subsidies were removed from *Quellmehl* and *Gritz*. Thus, starch could undercut the two other products. This regulation was abolished by the ECJ.[225] The applicants, manufacturers of maize grits and swell flour from various countries, brought proceedings against Union/Council/Commission to recover the loss they allegedly suffered during the period when they were unlawfully without refund payments. The Court stated a grave and manifest disregard of the limits on the exercise of their discretionary powers by the EU institutions for the following reasons:

> In the first place it is necessary to take into consideration that the principle of equality, … ,[226] which prohibits any discrimination in the common organization of the agricultural markets, occupy a particularly important place among the rules of Union law intended to protect the interests of the individual. Secondly, the disregard of that principle in this case affected a limited and clearly defined group of commercial operators.[227] … Further, the damage alleged by the applicants goes beyond the bounds of the economic risks inherent in the activities in the sector concerned.[228]

---

221. Paragraph 7.
222. Another context is the responsibility for *lawful actions* where the damage arguably must be 'unusual and special'. *See* in greater detail *infra* text (Part VI, Ch. 1).
223. Case 90/78, *Granaria BV v. Council and Commission* [1979] ECR 1081; Case 238/78, *Ireks-Arkady v. Council and Commission* [1979] ECR 2955; Joined Cases 261 and 262/78, *Interquell Stärke-Chemie and Diamalt v. Council and Commission* [1979] ECR 3045 (interlocutory judgment).
224. Joined Cases 64 and 113/76, 167 and 239/78, 27, 28 and 45/79, *P. Dumortier Frères, S.A. and Others v. Council* [1979] ECR 3091; *see also* Joined Cases 241, 242 and 245–250/78, *DGV and Others v. Council and Commission* [1979] ECR 3017.
225. Joined Cases 124/76 and 20/77, *SA. Moulins et Huileries de Pont-à-Mousson and Société cooperative Providence agricole de la Champagne v. Office National Interprofessionnel des Céréales* [1977] ECR 1795 (*Gritz* cases); Joined Cases C 117/76 and 16/77, *A. Ruckdeschel & Co v. Hauptzollamt Hamburg-St. Annen* and *Diamalt AG v. Hauptzollamt Itzehoe* [1977] ECR 1753.
226. Reference made to Art. 40(2) TFEU.
227. As a matter of fact it comprised the entire maize grits and swell flour industry in the Community!
228. Paragraph 11. –*See* as a recent example of discriminatory distribution of fishing quotas by a Commission regulation: Case C-611/12 P, *J.F. Giordano v. Commission* EU:C:2014:2282. Less convincingly, the ECJ denied compensation. As a critique, compare Brüggemeier, *Revocation of Fishing Quotas* (2015) 6 JETL 304.

105. The criterion of a 'limited and clearly defined group' of protected parties has then been clandestinely buried in the *Mulder* case complex. It raised questions about deficits in a system of premiums for non-marketing of milk and milk products. Some provisions of the Council regulation in question have been declared invalid by the ECJ.[229] *Inter alia*, Mr *Mulder*, together with other Dutch and German producers of milk, sued for damages. In its interlocutory judgment *Mulder II* on the ground of liability, the Court adhered to the principles developed in *HNL*. With regard to the number of protected parties, it focuses now on the definability of the group of businesses, be that group great[230] or small. What matters is the 'specific situation of a clearly defined group of economic agents'.[231]

Because the applicants in *Mulder II* and the Commission could not agree on an out-of-court settlement, the case finally came twice back to the ECJ to assess the amount of damages.[232]

C. *Post-HNL Phase*

106. After the *Bayerische HNL*, the *Quellmehl* and *Gritz* cases and the milk quota case complex,[233] the rules of breach-of-law liability under Article 340(2) could be reformulated as follows: Next to the requirement of an infringement of a superior protective provision of EU law, the rigorous conditions of the *Schöppenstedt* test to trigger liability apply only if two cumulative conditions are met:

> First, the breach must be committed by a legislative act or a measure general in nature.
> Second, in adopting this general measure the EU institution concerned must have exercised broad discretionary power.

107. This means that, for determining breach-of-law liability of the Union, *two types of general measures* must be distinguished: those which involve a wide margin of discretionary powers, and those which do not. Only the first type of legislative measures is subject to the conditions set out in *Schöppenstedt*, that is that only

229. Case 120/86, *Mulder v. Minister van Landbouw en Visserij (Mulder I)* [1988] ECR 2321, and Case 170/86, *von Deetzen v. Hauptzollamt Hamburg-Jonas* [1988] ECR 2355.

230. According to W. Wurmnest, the Commission was confronted with more than 16,000 aggrieved agriculturists. Cf. U. Magnus & W. Wurmnest, *Casebook Europäisches Haftungs- und Schadensrecht* 162 (Nomos 2002).

231. Joined Cases C-104/89 and C-37/90, *J.M. Mulder and Others v. Council and Commission (Mulder II No. 1)* [1992] ECR I-3126, para. 16. For an annotation compare T. Heukels (1993) 30 CML Rev 368.

232. Joined Cases C-104/89 and C-37/90, *J.M. Mulder and Others v. Council and Commission (Mulder II No. 2)* [2000] ECR I-203, with an additional follow-up Case C-104/89 DEP, *J.M. Mulder v. Council and Commission (Mulder II No. 3)* [2004] ECR I-5.

233. Compare E. Sharpston, *Milk Lakes, SLOMs and Legitimate Expectations*, in vol. 1, *Judicial Review in European Law. Liber Amicorum Lord Slynn of Hadley* 557 (D. O'Keeffe & A. Bavasso eds, KLI 2000).

gross malfunctioning of the institution – *gross maladministration*[234] – will lead to liability. For the second type the plain unlawfulness of the measure, its illegality, constitutes a relevant breach and suffices as ground of liability. A damages action can be brought when the other requirements of damage and causation are additionally fulfilled.

Examples of the second type of general measures are regulations that merely implement other regulations. In the case of *de Boer Buizen*, a Dutch steel trading undertaking applied for declaration of liability for losses it arguably suffered as a result of a Trade Arrangement between the EU and the USA concerning steel pipes and tubes.[235] The Arrangement was implemented by a Council regulation, and the Court confined its analysis to the question of the illegality of the Council regulation.

108. Until the early 1990s most cases in which the Union's liability in damages had arisen as a result of legislative acts concerned *regulations* under the Common Agricultural Policy involving choices of economic policy.[236] However, what about the other type of legislative act – the *directive*? In other words: Are individual actions for damages against the Union based on illegal directives admissible? For a long time, the prevailing answer has been in the negative.[237] Not the directive, only addressed to the Member States, was considered as measure giving rise to damage, but the implementing provisions of the Member State. Therefore a directive could be challenged only indirectly by suing against the implementing measures before the national courts. By reference for preliminary ruling to the ECJ, the illegality of the directive had to be determined. In this case scenario the supposedly liable Member State then may have a right of reimbursement against the Union.[238] With its *Assurances du crédit* judgment in 1991[239] the Court took the opposite position, though very implicitly and completely ignoring the unequivocally disapproving opinion of the AG. It ruled that where a private party has suffered damage as a result of an illegal directive, it is appropriate to challenge the measure with a compensation action under Article 340(2) if direct and individual concern could be shown. The general principles of liability for legislative acts also apply in cases of illegal

234. Conduct 'verging on the arbitrary'. *See* Joined Cases 103 and 145/77, *Royal Scholten Honig and Tunnel Refineries Ltd v. Intervention Board for Agricultural Produce* [1978] ECR 2037, para. 19; compare also the *Peine-Salzgitter* case: T-120/89 [1991] ECR II-279 and C-220/91 P [1993] ECR I-2393.

235. Case 81/86, *de Boer Buizen BV v. Council and Commission* [1987] ECR 3689.

236. Compare *supra* paras 103 and 104.

237. Compare AG Tesauro, Opinion, Case C-63/89, *Assurances du crédit and Other v. Council and Commission* [1991] ECR 1813 (pleading for inadmissibility of damages actions) with further references.

238. On joint and several liability of Union and Member States *see infra* text (Part V, Ch. 1).

239. Case C-63/89, *Assurances du crédit and Other v. Council and Commission* [1991] ECR I-1799; annotated by D. Curtin, *The Non-contractual Liability of the Community Legislature for Illegal Directives* (1992) 17 EL Rev 46.

directives.[240] The most prominent example, the applicants brought a damages action based on a directive, became the *Bergaderm* case.[241]

109. In part, the same holds true for a third category of legal acts – the *decisions*. Decisions are binding in their entirety. A decision which specifies those to whom it is addressed is binding only on these parties (Article 288(4) TFEU). Therefore decisions were generally understood to be of direct and individual concern, i.e., non-legislative. However, in the *Antillean Rice Mills* case the Court held:

> The fact that the contested measure is in the form of a decision, ... , is not sufficient to preclude its being legislative in character. In the context of an action for damages the character depends on the nature of the measure in question, not its form.[242]

How unsatisfactory the explanation of the 'normativity' of decisions by the European Courts may ever be,[243] having characterized the decision at issue as legislative, the *Schöppenstedt* conditions of liability were to be imposed.

II. Administrative Acts

110. For thirty years the EEC and its organs were mainly engaged with regulatory activities, especially under the Common Agricultural Policy involving choices of economic policy. This EEC was a political body without administrative substructure. The Member States were charged with the implementation and administration of the EEC legislation. That is why the ECJ was primarily kept busy with liability for defective legislative acts. Only when a failure of the Commission to properly supervise the implementation through the Member States came up, the Court was confronted with the problem of the Union's liability for administrative acts and omissions.[244]

111. The leading case became *Lütticke GmbH.*[245] The dispute was on taxation. The applicant, a German importer of milk powder, contended a failure of the Commission to correct the calculation of turnover tax imposed on milk powder in Germany which allegedly was not in accordance with the principles contained in the Council directive in question. The applicant brought an action for damages and

240. *Assurances du crédit* [1991] ECR I-1799, para. 13; Case C-298/89, *Gibraltar v. Council* [1993] ECR I-3605, para. 16. Compare also Case T-135/96, *UEAPME v. Council* [1998] ECR II-2335 and Cases T-172, 175 and 177/98, *Salamander AG and Others v. European Parliament and Council* [2000] ECR II-2487.
241. Case C-352/98, *Bergaderm SA and Groupil v. Commission* [2000] ECR I-5291.
242. Case C-390/95 P, *Antillean Rice Mills and Others v. Commission* [1999] ECR I-769, para. 60.
243. Compare, *inter alia*, Arnull, *Liability for Legislative Acts*, in *Action for Damages* 129, 131 et seq. (Heukels & McDonnell eds, KLI 1997).
244. Compare the cereals and milk product Cases 5, 7 and 13-24/66, *E. Kampffmeyer and Others v. Commission* [1967] ECR 245; Case 30/66, *K.A. Becher v. Commission* [1967] ECR 285; Case 4/69, *A. Lütticke GmbH v. Commission (Lütticke II)* [1971] ECR 325.
245. Case 4/69, *A. Lütticke GmbH v. Commission (Lütticke II)* [1971] ECR 325.

interest. Though not focusing on the distinction between legislative and administrative measures explicitly, in 1971, the Court formulated unequivocal conditions of liability for non-legislative measures:

> By virtue of the second paragraph of Article 215 and the general principles to which this provision refers, the liability of the Commission presupposes the existence of a set of circumstances comprising actual damage, a causal link between the damage claimed and the conduct alleged against the Commission, and the illegality of such conduct.[246]

These are the three-part *Lütticke* conditions of liability for administrative acts.

112. From 1990 onwards, the Union's liability for administrative acts became a more common subject matter for the jurisdiction of the Luxembourg courts under Article 340(2).[247] The EU institutions and the Commission in particular got more occupied with the application of general rules. Hence, the question of the conditions for liability of the Union for unlawful administrative acts got on the agenda again: applicability of the *Schöppenstedt* formula – or back to a plain breach-of-law approach (*Lütticke* conditions)?

113. First, a definition of 'administrative acts' has to be given. The answer does not depend on the external form of the action. A measure is legislative in character and corresponds to the legislative function if its regulatory content is sufficiently abstract and it is of general application.[248] Conversely, a measure is *administrative* in nature if it is not of general application but intends to regulate an individual case. This issue was, *inter alia*, in dispute in the case of *Bergaderm*, where a directive was said to be an 'administrative measure in disguise' because in substance it arguably regulated just one individual case.[249]

114. H.M. van der Woude listed four categories of administrative acts by EU institutions which are of relevance for the jurisdiction of the European courts:

- failure to exercise supervisory powers;
- factual conduct;
- public procurement measures;
- funding operations.[250]

The first category has its basis in Article 17(1) TEU. It provides that the Commission shall ensure that the provisions of the Treaty and the measures taken by the institutions pursuant thereto (secondary legislation) are applied. The Commission

---

246. *Lütticke II* [1971] ECR 325, para. 10.
247. On this in greater detail, *see* M.H. van der Woude, *Liability for Administrative Acts*, in *The Action for Damages* 109 (Heukels & McDonnell eds, KLI 1997).
248. Joined Cases 16/62 and 17/62, *Confédération Nationale des Producteurs des Fruits et Légumes and Others v. Council* [1962] ECR 471.
249. C-352/98 P, *Bergaderm and Goupil v. Commission* [2000] ECR I-5291. *See infra* text.
250. On this in greater detail, *see* van der Woude (fn.), pp. 116–126.

has to supervise the application and implementation through the Member States. The instruments to exercise this supervision are partly foreseen by the TFEU itself, e.g., the possibility to forbid state subsidies which are incompatible with the single market,[251] and partly conferred by implementing legislation. Founding judgments of the ECJ on liability for administrative acts deal with failure of the Commission to exercise its supervisory powers.[252]

115. Public procurement covers the purchase of goods and services and the ordering of works *via* public tenders by EU institutions. It also comprises finance contracts granted by Non-member States in the context of specific aid programmes of the EU.

Funding operations mainly concern activities within the Union, such as, e.g., the modernization of the fishing fleet.[253]

116. By contrast, the category of *factual conduct* concerns the malfeasance of individual public servants or the misconduct of public bodies, and not measures of EU institutions. It belongs therefore to the division of vicarious liability for torts[254] and should not be intermingled with breach-of-law liability.

117. An additional important field for administrative measures taken by the Commission is EU competition law. According to Council Regulation (EEC) No. 4064/89 on the control of concentrations between undertakings,[255] the Commission must appraise merger projects of enterprises in the EEA. Here, a prior annulment of the administrative measure is normally conditional for a damages action. In the spectacular *Schneider-Legrand* affair, the EGC annulled a decision of the Commission declaring a merger incompatible with EU law.[256] The applicant *Schneider Electric* brought a damages claim of unprecedented EUR 1.6 billion (!) against the Commission, which was largely accepted at first instance.[257] On appeal, the ECJ with two judgments reduced the amount of damages considerably.[258]

III. Consolidated Approach: The Margin-of-Discretion Test – Bergaderm

118. As the law stood until recently with respect to administrative decisions, it could be restated as follows: Normally the plain infringement of a rule intended to

251. Articles 185, 186 TFEU.
252. Compare Joined Cases 5, 7 and 13-24/66, *E. Kampffmeyer and Others v. Commission* [1967] ECR 245; Case 30/66, *K.A. Becher v. Commission* [1967] ECR 285; Case 4/69, *A. Lütticke GmbH v. Commission (Lütticke II)* [1971] ECR 325.
253. *See* as an exemplary case T-514/93, *Cobrecaf v. Commission* [1995] ECR II-624.
254. *See supra* text. Also the cases of *Adams* and *Grifoni I* are featured in this section. Compare fns 135 and 174.
255. [1989] OJ L 395/1, as amended.
256. Case T-310/01, *Schneider Electric SA v. Commission (EGC No 1)* [2002] ECR II-4071, and Case T-77/02, *Schneider Electric SA v. Commission (EGC No. 2)* [2002] ECR II-4201.
257. Case T-351/03, *Schneider Electric SA v. Commission (EGC No. 3)* [2007] ECR II-2237.
258. Case C-440/07 P, *Commission v. Schneider Electric SA (EGC No. 1)* [2009] ECR I-6413 and (*EGC No. 2*) [2010] ECR I-73.

protect the interests of private undertakings, i.e., the unlawful nature of the measure as such, sufficed to constitute a relevant breach. That is, the *Lütticke* conditions – illegality, damage, causation – suffice to trigger liability. If, however, the implementing institution exercised a wide margin of discretion when taking the administrative measure, then the rigorous *Schöppenstedt* test applies here, too. – Therefore, both areas – legislative and administrative measures, which were in the early decades clearly separated – can no longer be treated per se differently. It was in the case of *Bergaderm* where the Court, after making explicit reference to *Brasserie* and *Hedley Lomas*, took this step ahead:

> *The individual nature of a measure taken by an institution (of the Union or the Member States) is not a decisive criterion for identifying the limits of the discretion enjoyed by the institution in question.*[259]

To determine the relevant breach, plain infringement or manifest and grave disregard, the margin of discretion of the acting institution has to be established under the circumstances of the concrete case. The general or individual nature of a measure taken, that is, whether it is a legislative or administrative act, is of less relevance.

IV. The High Complexity Test: Decisions Under Uncertainty

119. In the recent case law, however, a *new third* category – *between* no discretion/plain breach and wide discretion/serious breach – seems to have been introduced by the EGC: *institutional fault.*[260] This is connected with a paradigm change in the review politics of the European Courts.[261] From the 1970s to the 1990s, in conflicts with safety requirements and free movement of products in the context of Articles 34–36 TFEU, the ECJ constantly refrained from going into detail. It confirmed the Member States' powers to decide the level of protection, especially in situations of uncertainty where international scientific evidence had to be taken into account. This case law in turn provoked a host of regulatory activities in relation to health and safety protection at EU level. Regulatory agencies were established and scientific advisory committees attached to them. The so-called comitology system came into existence.[262] This process of scientification of the administrative practice finally reached the Court itself.

---

259. Case C-352/98, *Laboratoires Pharmaceutiques Bergaderm SA and Goupil v. Commission* (*Bergaderm*) [2000] ECR I-5310, para. 46; Case C-312/00 P, *Commission v. Camar and Tico* [2002] ECR I-11355, para. 55; Case C-472/00 P, *Commission v. Fresh Marine* [2003] ECR I-7541, para. 27; Case C-282/05 P, *Holcim (Deutschland) AG v. Commission* [2007] ECR I-2941, para. 48.

260. On this in greater detail *infra* text.

261. Compare E. Vos, *The European Court of Justice in the Face of Uncertainty and Complexity*, in *Judicial Activism at the European Court of Justice* 142 (M. Dawson, B. de Witte & E. Muir Cheltenham eds, Elgar 2011).

262. Compare C.F. Bergstrom, *Comitology: Delegation of Powers in the EU and the Committee System* (OUP 2005); *EU Committees: Social Regulation, Law and Politics* (C. Joerges & E. Vos eds, Hart 1999).

120. The turning point in this sense was the landmark case of *Technische Universität München.*[263] In a customs dispute, the question was raised whether electronic microscopes manufactured in the EU were scientifically equivalent with the scientific apparatus imported by the University from Japan. On preliminary ruling before the Court, it examined the composition of the group of experts the Commission had consulted before determining its decision. The Court ruled that such a group of experts must be composed of persons possessing the necessary technical knowledge in the relevant field. It found the composition of the group of experts insufficient. Consequently, the Court held that the Commission had infringed 'its obligation to examine carefully and impartially all the relevant aspects of the case in point'.[264]

121. This principle of due diligence or sound administration in cases of scientific uncertainty and complexity did not remain restricted to administrative law.[265] Supported by the General Court, this 'proceduralist' standard of review gained entrance at the law of liability. This reception began in some respect with the *Brasserie* and *Bergaderm* cases. The 'complexity of the situation to be regulated' is listed there for the first time as a decisive factor the Court has to take into account,[266] but it had no further impact on the reasoning of the Court. More telling is the *Artegodan* case complex. Both cases, *Bergaderm* and *Artegodan*, are centred on scientific uncertainties about the adverse health effects of a chemical active agent. In the latter case, the Commission ordered the Member States to withdraw the marketing authority for a pharmaceutical manufactured by *Artegodan GmbH.* Due to lack of competence of the Commission, its order was subsequently annulled by the General Court,[267] and as a result the Member States on their part cancelled the withdrawal of the national marketing authority. *Artegodan* sued the Commission for compensation of the losses purportedly incurred by the interim prohibition to sell its product. Neither courts, EGC or ECJ, could concede the Commission a wide discretion when it made its order to withdraw. Thus, reference to the *Schöppenstedt* criteria was barred. As unlawfulness/breach of a protective rule of law was free from doubt,[268] liability of the Union would have been the regular consequence. Instead, the General Court focused on the *legal complexity and factual uncertainties*, having regard as well to the precedence to be given to public health, and ruled:

---

263. Case C-269/90, *Technische Universität München v. Hauptzollamt München-Mitte* [1991] ECR I-5469; as an important follow-up case, compare Case T-13/99, *Pfizer Animal Health SA v. Council* [2002] ECR II-3305.
264. Case C-269/90, *Technische Universität*, para. 22.
265. *See* Craig, *EU Administrative Law* 333 (OUP 2010); H.P. Nehl, *Principles of Administrative Procedure in EC Law* (Hart 1999).
266. Joined Cases C-46 and C-48/93, *Brasserie du pêcheur and Factortame III* [1996] ECR I-1131, para. 43; Case C-352/98, *Bergaderm* [2000] ECR I-5310, para. 40.
267. Joined Cases T-74, 76, 83–85, 132, 137 and 142/00, *Artegodan GmbH and Others v. Commission* [2002] ECR II-4945.
268. Article 11 Directive 65/65/EEC on the approximation of provisions laid down by law, regulation or administrative action relating to medicinal products, OJ 1965–66, p. 24 (as amended).

It follows that only the finding that an irregularity would not have been committed in similar circumstances by an administrative authority exercising ordinary care and diligence enables the liability of the Union.[269]

122. On appeal, the Court of Justice did not take up this wording. Instead, it adhered to its system of rules worked out since *Bergaderm* and *Holcim (Deutschland) AG* where it incorporated the 'complexity of the situation' into the *Brasserie* factors.[270] According to these rules to determine breach-of-law liability, the courts must also take into account 'the complexity of the situations to be regulated [and] the difficulties in the application or interpretation of the legislation'.[271] Not surprisingly, these situations of factual and legal complexity are then again mingled up with the category of broad discretion and both, separately or jointly, constitute a 'sufficiently serious breach';[272] that means, judicial business as usual. Thus, the complexity formula, for the first time introduced in *Brasserie*,[273] covers all three scenarios: plain breach, complicated breach (*alias* institutional fault) and manifest breach (gross maladministration). The result is the opposite of clarity and precision of EU law. The formula 'sufficiently serious breach' finally means everything and nothing.

V. Summary

123. To put the record straight: After *Bergaderm* and *Holcim*, to determine the breach-of-law liability of the Union under Article 340(2) TFEU for legislative and administrative acts (or omissions) of its institutions, the well-elaborated focus on the character of the public measure at issue lost its distinguishing force. Instead, one has to face three case scenarios:

(1) Plain breach of a (superior) protective provision of law in situations without discretion and with less factual and legal complexity (*no-fault*).
(2) Breach of law in a situation without discretion but of factual (scientific) and legal complexity. Here additionally a 'sound administration' must have acted in a similar way (i.e., breach plus *institutional fault*). Unresolved is the question whether this has to be qualified as a defence of the EU institutions where the institutions have the burden to adduce evidence for the required conditions of complexity and for lack of fault.
(3) Manifest breach of law in situations with a wide margin of discretion (*gross maladministration*).

269. Case T-429/05, *Artegodan GmbH v. Commission* [2010] ECR II-491, para. 51.
270. Case C-352/98 P, *Bergaderm v. Commission* [2000] ECR I-5310, para. 40; Case C-282/05 P, *Holcim (Deutschland) AG v. Commission* [2007] ECR I-2941, paras 50 et seq.
271. *Bergaderm*, para. 40; *Holcim*, para. 50.
272. *Bergaderm*, para. 40; *Holcim (Deutschland) AG*, para. 51; Case C-221/10 P, *Artegodan GmbH v. Commission* EU:C:2012:216.
273. *Brasserie*, para. 51. *See infra* text .

§4. Special Institutions: EU Courts

124. For self-evident reasons, the institution of the 'CJEU' with its two operating judicial bodies has so far not been considered as a candidate whose potential breach of EU law would lead to liability of the Union. *Brasserie du pêcheur* in 1996, however, has made clear that, in principle, no institutional organ of the Union is excluded from liability.[274] For the time being no such damages actions against the European courts have been brought. This may have changed fundamentally after the accession of the EU to the ECHR. The Lisbon Treaty provided the legal basis for the Union's accession to the ECHR.[275] The accession process was on its way, an accession agreement had been drafted, and the formalities had been clarified.[276] After accession, the ECJ would have the same status as the Supreme Courts of the Member States. In cases of alleged infringements of fundamental rights through judgments of the EGC or the ECJ,[277] the aggrieved private parties could sue the Union before the ECtHR in Strasbourg. Cause of action would be: breach of ECHR by the ECJ, and the remedy: damages and/or payment of 'just satisfaction' by the Union according to Article 41 ECHR.[278]

125. However, by its Opinion 2/13, delivered on 18 December 2014,[279] the ECJ surprisingly has blocked this path for the accession to the ECHR. The Court seems here to be driven by an attitude to defend its own powers *vis-à-vis* the ECtHR. The implications of the obligation to accede to the ECHR as set forth in Article 6(2) TEU have not been discussed at all. – Anyway, after the entry into force of the EU Charter in 2009, Article 52(3) ChFR may already serve as a sufficient ground for such an action for compensation. It stipulates that the level of protection provided by EU Charter rights must be at least as high as that of the European Convention rights.

---

274. *Brasserie*, [1996] ECR I-1131, para. 32.

275. Article 6(2) TEU.

276. Compare P. Gragl, *The Accession of the European Union to the European Convention of Human Rights* (Hart 2013); J.P. Jacqué, *The Accession of the European Union to the European Convention on Human Rights and Fundamental Freedoms* (2011) 48 CML Rev 995, and see the contributions in 16 GLJ no. 1 (2015).

277. Compare the famous *Caroline von Hanover* case, where the ECtHR held that the German Federal Court of Justice *and* the Federal Constitutional Court (sic!) infringed with their judgments the applicant's right to privacy under Art. 8 ECHR. Germany was sentenced to pay a just satisfaction to the applicant: ECtHR, 24 Jun. 2004, *Caroline von Hanover v. Germany I* 40 EHRR 1. *See also* ECtHR, 21 Jul. 2011, *Heinisch v. Germany* hoduc (2011) (infringement of Art. 10 ECHR by German Labour Courts and by the Federal Constitutional Court for not admitting constitutional review); 21 Mar. 2000, *Dulaurans v. France* 33 EHRR 1093 (violation of Art. 6(1) ECHR by the *Cour de Cassation*).

278. For greater detail, compare the contributions of E. Steiner, W. Berka & W. Karl, *Tort Law in the Jurisprudence of the European Court of Human Rights* 3/237/345 (A. Fenyves, E. Karner, H. Koziol & E. Steiner eds, de Gruyter 2011).

279. ECJ, Opinion 2/13, *ECHR*, EU:C:2014:2454; *see also* the contrasting view of AG Kokott relating to Opinion 2/13, EU:C:2014:2475.

126. Already currently, a claim for unreasonable length of judicial proceedings can be brought.[280] This is a constituent of the right to a fair legal process, which is enshrined in Article 6(1) ECHR and Article 47(2) ChFR. Beforehand, it was safeguarded in EU law as a general principle of law. In *Baustahlgewerbe*, the ECJ awarded a fine for the excessive length of proceedings before the Commission, including the procedure before the General Court.[281] In the case of '*Der Grüne Punkt*', the Court noted expressly that 'failure on the part of the (then) Court of First Instance to adjudicate within a reasonable time can give rise to a claim for damages brought against the Union'.[282] Finally, the general rules of Member States' liability for decisions of State courts of last instance are also applicable on the ECJ.[283]

280. As a rare example of national legislation of this cause of action compare §97(a) German Act on the Federal Constitutional Court (Bundesverfassungsgerichtsgesetz). It reads: A party who suffers a detriment due to unreasonable length of procedures before the BVerfG can claim compensation.
281. Compare Case C-185/95 P, *Baustahlgewerbe v. Commission* [1998] ECR I-8417 (reasonable satisfaction for excessive duration: EUR 50,000). *See also* Joined Cases C-120 and 121/06, *FIAMM and others v. Council and Commission* [2008] ECR I-6513 (compensation for lawful acts denied; *see infra* text).
282. Case C-385/07 P, *Der Grüne Punkt – Duales System Deutschland v. Commission* [2009] ECR I-6155, para. 193.
283. *See infra* text. On Union liability for 'manifest errors' of the ECJ, compare. P.J. Wattel, *Staatsaansprakelijkheid voor EC-rechtelijk onrechtmatige hoogste rechtspraak* WPNR 6553 (2003), p. 840.

Chapter 4. Additional Conditions of Liability

127. The new EU *lex Aquilia* of 'breach-of-law liability' requires three cumulative conditions for compensation: relevant breach of law, damage and causation. The European courts, like national courts, handle liability cases as issues which are disposed of in the most rapid and expedient manner. Instead of examining whether all three cumulative liability conditions are met, the Courts focus on that condition which is not proven or not fulfilled, without paying any further attention to the remaining conditions.

§1. DAMAGE/INJURY

128. The criterion of damage was not at the centre of the early case law of the ECJ. It was a category too familiar to the judges and AG from the Member States' private law to consider it worthwhile to devote much time and thought to it. That eventually changed later. In this monograph, it suffices to state that there must be a *provable negative effect on a material or immaterial, legally protected interest* resulting from an EU institution's act or omission. That can be a bodily injury, property damage, an infringement of a conferred right or protected legal interest, a violation of a personality right without any loss, or just pure economic loss, past and future, without any injury. The latter was the case in most of the liability proceedings before the Court when the implementation of economic policies was at stake. The aforesaid suffices to satisfy the condition of 'damage' in this context. Article 41(3) ChFR recognizes in a comparable way a right to compensation for 'any damage' caused by EU institutions and their servants.

The section on 'Consequences of Liability' will deal in greater detail with the nature (e.g., economic and non-economic damage), extent (e.g., primary and secondary injury; primary and consequential damage) and amounts of damages under EU tort law.

129. On the basis of the foregoing, one additional clarification has to be made. From the early days of jurisdiction under both the ECSC Treaty of 1951 and the EEC Treaty of 1957, legislative measures – and later on administrative acts – which implemented the various economic policies were at the fore. These could have adverse financial effects on the enterprises operating in the respective economic sector, and actions were brought by businesses claiming loss of profit. For this class of actions, the ECJ developed a special criterion: the damage must be '*direct, certain and specific*'.[284] This criterion served to exclude the normal and foreseeable risks inherent in the market conditions from the reach of compensable damage. Those risks form part of the economic hazards connected with the activities of an industrial and commercial undertaking.[285]

284. Case 4/69, *A. Lütticke GmbH v. Commission (Lütticke II)* [1971] ECR 325, para. 10; Joined Cases 67–85/75, *Lesieur and Others v. Commission* [1976] ECR 797, at 804–806.

285. Joined Cases, 14, 16, 17, 20, 24, 26, 27/60 and 1/61, *Meroni and Others v. High Authority* [1961] ECR 161, at 166–167. *See also* the *Quellmehl* and *Gritz* cases, *supra* fns 224–226.

The criterion of directness and certainty of damage is also prominently applied in the case complex of compensation for damage arguably caused by lawful actions of the EU institutions.[286]

§2. Causation

130. For the Union to become an addressee of breach-of-law liability under Article 340(2), causation is additionally required.[287] The relevant breach of law must be the cause in fact of the concrete damage. Here, a field of law is addressed where again the general principles common to the law of the Member States come into play.[288] The common approach in both private and public law of the Member States is the 'but for test'. The breach must be a *conditio sine qua non* of the occurrence of the damage or injury. In the practice before the European courts, the negative version of the c.s.q.n test seemed to be preferred. Evidence for causation is lacking if the damage sought to be compensated would have also occurred, and in an identical manner, in the absence of the breach of law. In this regard, the Opinions of the AG are more explicit than the judgments of the Courts.[289] In cases of omissions, the *conditio cum qua non* test is applied. That is, to assess that in a hypothetical scenario the damage would not have occurred if the omitted act would have been performed.

For the 'vicarious liability' of the Union, a tort of the public servant or body is required. Here, with respect to causation of the injury or damage, the same general principles apply.

131. The onus to prove the causal link rests normally on the applicant. This will be taken up in the section on proof.

132. More does not need to be said here. Aspects of directness, certainty, etc. of the damage[290] do not belong to the complex of causation. These are deliberations

---

286. Compare, *inter alia*, Case 59/83, *Biovilac v. EEC* [1984] ECR 4057 and Case T-184/95, *Dorsch Consult v. Council and Commission* [1998] ECR II-667, confirmed on appeal: C-237/98 P, [2000] ECR I-4549. *See* in greater detail *infra* text (Part VI, Ch. 1).

287. Compare I.C. Durant, *Causation, in Tort Law in the European Community* 47, 56 et seq. (Koziol & Schulze eds, Springer 2008); K. Bitterich, *Elements of an Autonomous Concept of Causation in European Community Law Concerning Liability*, ZvglRWiss 12 (2007); A.G. Toth, *The Concepts of Damage and Causality as Elements of Non-Contractual Liability*, in *The Action for Damages* 179 (Heukels & McDonnell eds, KLI 1997). *See* generally, *Digest of European Tort Law, vol 1: Essential Cases on Natural Causation* (B. Winiger, H. Koziol et al. eds, Springer 2007).

288. For private law, compare the comparative accounts of A. Steel, *Proof of Causation in Law* (CUP 2015); *Perspectives on Causation* (R. Goldberg ed., Hart 2011); *Unification of Tort Law: Causation* (J. Spier ed., KLI 2000), and as locus classicus H.L.A. Hart & T. Honoré, *Causation in Law* (2d ed., OUP 1985): covering both cause in fact/natural causation and legal cause.

289. Compare AG Roemer, Opinion, Joined Cases 29, 31, 36, 39–47, 50 and 51/63, *Laminoirs de la Providence and Others v. High Authority* [1965] ECR 948, at p. 954; AG Gand, Opinion, Joined Cases 5, 7 and 13–24/66, *E. Kampffmeyer and Others v. Commission (E. Kampffmeyer)* [1967] ECR 245, at p. 278; AG van Gerven, Opinion, Case 201/86, *Société Spie-Batignolles v. Commission* [1990] ECR I-218, para. 17.

290. *See* infra text and paras 304 and 305

on whether a *caused* damage (sic!) will fulfil additional normative criteria to trigger liability in specific case scenarios. The same holds true when the courts decide on the liability for primary *and* secondary injuries or tackle the problem of attribution of consequential damages of an injury. The factual causation of a secondary injury or of arguably consequential damages is determined according to the rules presented above. The problem arising in cases of secondary injury and of consequential damages is a *normative* and not a factual one: Courts have to determine the protective or normative purpose of the legal rule. The House of Lords aptly coined the formula that it has to be assessed whether or not it is *fair, just and reasonable* to impute the remote incident.[291] In other words: The point here is not to determine causation but *attribution* of damage, i.e., the *scope of liability*. As incorrect as it may be, in judgments and law books the normative aspect is mostly intertwined with the issue of cause in fact. Examples of this mingling up are juristic terms like 'legal cause', 'proximate cause' or 'adequate causation'.

133. The causal relationship between breach and damage can be interrupted by *intervening causes.*

Such a cause may exist in an independent act or omission of a Member State or by an EU institution. The Court has held that where the damage arises from an autonomous decision of the national authorities taken in implementing EU law or from a legislative position in a Member State, the necessary relationship of cause and effect between EU measure and the damage will be missing.[292] Where, however, the decision of the Member State has been made possible by an illegal omission of the EU institution to exercise the supervisory powers conferred upon it by the Treaty, it is this failure that will be regarded as the cause of the damage. This has been correctly expressed by AG *Roemer* in his opinion in the case of *Vloebergh*s:

> The fact that conduct contrary to the Treaty on the part of a Member State is at the commencement of a chain of cause and effect does not prevent the subsequent omission of the High Authority[293] from being regarded as the direct cause of the damage. If the High Authority has failed to exercise its functions of supervision with regard to a Member State it is liable for the damage which follows from the original behaviour of a Member State contrary to the Treaty.[294]

291. Compare House of Lords, *Caparo Industries plc v. Dickman* [1990] 2 AC 605, 617–618, per Lord Bridge.
292. *See*, e.g., Case 132/77, *Exportation des sucres v. Commission* [1978] ECR 1061, paras 22–27; Joined Cases 197–200, 243, 245 and 247/80, *Ludwigshafener Walzmühle Erling KG and Others v. Council and Commission* [1981] ECR 3211 (market in cereals/durum wheat prices).
293. Under the ECSC Treaty 1951.
294. AG Roemer, Opinion, Joined Cases 9 and 12/60, *Société commerciale A. Vloebergh*s *SA v. High Authority* [1961] ECR 219, at 240.

If a national authority merely implements a given EU measure without being responsible for its unlawfulness, the Member State cannot be held liable on grounds connected with the illegality of the measure.[295]

§3. Fault

134. Does EU law require fault to make the Union liable for breach-of-law by its institutions and bodies? The answer given to this question was until recently mostly in the negative.[296] With respect to the recent case law, that has to be reconsidered.

I. General Concept of Fault

135. The term fault in the continental civil law systems has a strong personal and subjective connotation. This is due to the Roman law's influence and the legacy of natural law, completed by enlightenment philosophy and economic liberalism. Anglo-American common law of torts assimilated these ideas in the nineteenth century. The law of delict of the civil law codifications of the nineteenth century – from the French *Code civil* of 1804 to the German *Bürgerliches Gesetzbuch* (*BGB*) of 1896 – was dominated by the fault category. '*No liability without fault.*'[297] Fault meant individual misuse of freedom to act or personal failure of behaviour. It comprised intent and negligence (as a kind of fault[298]). Intent is the knowing and wilful causation of injury, and intentional wrongs require unlawfulness of the injurious conduct to trigger liability.[299] Most of the traditional delicts of the pre-industrial world were intentional wrongs like murder/manslaughter, treason, battery, rape, arson, theft, counterfeiting, etc. Negligence, though already recognized in Roman law, had its breakthrough with the industrial revolution. Conventionally, it is defined as the foreseeable and avoidable causation of injury or damage. Intent is by its very nature personal and subjective. Negligence attracted in private law, as opposed to

295. Joined Cases 106–120/87, *Asteris and Others v. Greece (Asteris II)* [1988] ECR 5515, para. 18.
296. *See* prominently Joined Cases C-46 and 48/93, *Brasserie du pêcheur and Factortame III* [1996] ECR I-1131, para. 79. Compare also, *inter alia*, M. Lukas, *Fault Liability*, in *Tort Law of the European Community* 81 (Koziol & Schulze eds, Springer 2008) with further references.
297. 'It is not damage, but fault which obliges to compensation.' R. von Jhering, *Das Schuldmoment im Römischen Privatrecht* (Roth 1867), at 40.
298. If not expressly introduced differently, *negligence* is used in this monograph exclusively as a kind of fault and not as the *common law tort of negligence*. On the latter and its emergence compare *Negligence. The Comparative Legal History of the Law of Torts* (E.J.H. Schrage ed., Duncker & Humblot 2001).
299. Plus knowledge of unlawfulness. On this in greater detail, *see*, *inter alia*, Brüggemeier, *Haftungsrecht*, pp. 20–41; Brüggemeier, *Common Principles of Tort Law*, pp. 59–65; J. Finnis, *Intention in Tort Law*, in *Philosophical Foundations of Tort Law* 226 (D.G. Owen ed., Clarendon Press 1995); compare also ALI (ed.), *Restatement (Third) of Torts: Intentional Torts to Persons* (2014 – Discussion Draft).

criminal law, mostly an objective interpretation.[300] That is, reference point to assess negligence became the conduct of the '(average) reasonable person under like circumstances'.[301] This holds true for the two private law regimes – civil law and common law. The Archimedean point for this concept of fault, however, remained the comportment of human beings, blessed with freedom and reason. Fault addresses individual wrongdoing.[302]

136. The societal conditions for this fault model of liability changed dramatically with the ongoing industrialization of the Western world.[303] The new paradigms of the industrial society became technical risks, enterprises and insurance. An ethically neutral mechanism of distribution of risks and losses was increasingly replacing the honourable culture of individual responsibility. The first civil code, enforcing this straightforwardly, was the Soviet Union's code of 1922.[304] This new risk pooling and liability channelling on enterprises were made possible through loss spreading by insurance – especially State social insurance and private third party (liability) insurance. Against this backdrop, 'stricter' forms of liability came to the fore, by legislation and through case law: quasi-strict enterprise liability and no-fault (strict) liability.[305]

II. No-Fault, Institutional Fault, Gross Maladministration

137. On the basis of the foregoing, the consequences for the Union's non-contractual liability have to be elaborated.

First, fault is still indispensable inasmuch as malfeasance is an issue. This is the case in the fields of *vicarious liability* of the Union.[306] Here, conventional torts committed by public servants 'in the performance of official duties' lead to liability. An individual tort of a public servant, as featured *supra* in the text, regularly comprises personal fault. Torts by EU bodies and institutions require organizational fault/ *colpa d'apparato*.

Second, and more importantly, fault and torts are in principle *not* an issue in the large field of *breach-of-law liability* of the Union (and the Member States). It is

---

300. Still not out of strife in some Germanic laws, *see* H. Koziol, *Liability Based on Fault: Subjective or Objective Yardstick?* (1998) 5 Maastricht J. Eur. & Comp. L. 111; as a comparative stock-taking compare *Unification of Tort Law: Fault* (P. Widmer ed., KLI 2005).
301. The classic model is Roman law's *bonus paterfamilias*. Dig. 16.3.32.
302. Tellingly the language of the European courts in the field of law, under scrutiny here, up to recently employed only the categories of *persons* and *individuals* though mostly dealing with incorporated enterprises. – As opposed to that, Art. 34 ECSC Treaty 1951 already spoke of 'injury to an enterprise or a group of enterprises'.
303. For a broad comparative historical analysis of the last 150 years *see* J. Bell & D. Ibbetson, *European Legal Development. The Case of Torts* (CUP 2012), passim, with references to other eight volumes of their research project.
304. C. Osakwe, *Russian Civil Code. Parts 1–3* (Wolters Kluwer 2008).
305. On this in greater detail compare Brüggemeier, *Haftungsrecht*, p. 117; Brüggemeier, *Risk and Strict Liability: The Distinct Examples of Germany, the United States, and Russia* (2013) 21 ERPL 923. On the development of tort law in Europe from 1850 to 2000, *see European Legal Development. The Case of Torts,* 9 vols. (J. Bell & D. Ibbetson gen. eds, CUP 2010–2012).
306. *See supra* text.

neither tort liability nor strict liability. It is liability for unlawfulness by processes of maladministration (public acts of unlawful nature). Having said this, at second regard things must be differentiated. Breach-of-law liability is by no means completely free of fault elements.

In the classic cases of liability for breach by legislative or administrative acts where the acting EU institution enjoys no or only limited discretion, no-fault is required to bring an action for damages. Unlawfulness or plain breach of law leads to liability (illegality/maladministration per se: *Lütticke II* 1971[307]).

138. In the novel type of cases, without discretion but characterized by *factual (scientific) and legal complexity*, liability seems to be conditional on a sort of institutional fault or qualified maladministration. What is institutional fault about? It corresponds to enterprise liability in general private law. Unfamiliar to the codifications of the nineteenth century, it is but until recently that concepts of enterprise liability show up in the proposals for a reform of civil liability law.[308] Enterprise liability means direct responsibility of the enterprise – incorporated or not – for defective processes and outcomes. It is then, *re vera*, only a question of whether the concrete damage could have been avoided by reasonable cost. If the burden for this exoneration is on the enterprise, then it is justified to speak of quasi-strict liability.[309] Be that as it may, of relevance here is the detail that the responsibility of organizations is not strict liability, but in last resort still liability for *malfunction*. It keeps the negligence structure. That is, enterprise negligence has to be determined. This determination operates as a comparison. One *factual* situation is paralleled with another *normative* one. If the normative standard of proper processing under the concrete circumstances, as a matter of law to be determined by the court, is (economically) reasonable for the enterprise to comply with, then in case of non-compliance the conditions of organizational fault or *colpa d'apparato*[310] are met. Enterprise liability is thus founded.

139. This can be transferred to the *supra* mentioned incidents of high complexity. The concrete processing of an applicant's case by the EU institution has to be compared with the normative standard of processing by an *administrative authority exercising ordinary care and diligence under similar circumstances* (principle of sound administration).[311] If the concrete procedural manner of operating the case falls out of the reach marked by the normative standard, then institutional fault or

307. Case 4/69, *A. Lütticke GmbH v. Commission (Lütticke II)* [1971] ECR 325.

308. European Group on Tort Law (ed), Principles of European Tort Law (Springer 2005): Art. 4:202; Avant-projet. de réforme du droit des obligations et de la prescription (Catala), 2005: Art. 1353. For a general overview on reform projects and recent legislation compare Brüggemeier, *Modernising Civil Liability Law* (CUP 2011).

309. The author introduced for this also the term 'reverse Learned Hand test'. Brüggemeier, *Modernising Civil Liability Law*, p. 70.

310. Corte di Cassazione, Sez. Un., 22 Jul. 1999, n. 500, in Foro it., 1999, I, 2487, with comments by A. Palmieri and R. Pardolsi, in Giur. Cost., 1999, 4045.

311. This corresponds to W. van Gerven's formula (fn.), intended by him as a 'comprehensive common principle, to be applied regardless of discretion'. W. van Gerven, *A Common European Law*, in *Tort Liability of Public Authorities* 125, at 136 (Fairgrieve, Andenas & Bell eds, BIICL 2002).

qualified maladministration is present. Institutional conduct of this kind involves Union liability.[312]

Still unanswered is the question of whether the contended high complexity and ordinary administration is a defence to be proven by the institution, or whether it is a regular condition for which evidence has to be adduced by the applicant.

140. In the third category of cases, where EU institutions enjoy a *wide margin of discretion*, only a 'manifest' breach shall lead to liability. Here, a reverse negligence structure is applied. Courts do not define a normative standard of *good* processing or *sound* administration which an institution or body has to match to be exempt from liability. They define a normative standard of *bad* processing, i.e., gross maladministration or grave mal-legislation, which an institution or body has to meet to trigger Union liability, as thoroughly deviant from the good standard of acting by an 'ordinary' administration or legislation under similar circumstances. Technically and structurally, this is comparable to the practice of general private law when it occasionally makes civil liability conditional on gross negligence.

141. In the cases of *Dekker* and *Brasserie*, on meticulous requests by the Dutch *Hoge Raad* and the German *Bundesgerichtshof*, on the question of whether the EU type of breach-of-law liability requires fault (a principle common to most of the Member States' laws of governmental liability[313]), the Court gave its well-known answer: '*breach of law, not fault obliges to damages*';[314] an answer, one author called 'genuinely overarchingly European'.[315]

On second regard, the answer must be more differentiated (being not necessarily less European though). 'Relevant breach', triggering Union liability for breach of law encompasses three case scenarios with different conditions of responsibility: (i) no-fault in cases without discretion, (ii) institutional fault in cases of high complexity, and (iii) gross maladministration in cases with wide discretion.

Be that as it may, the centre of this breach-of-law liability remains the unlawful nature of the respective legislative or administrative act or omission.

---

312. *See also* Case T-212/03, *MyTravel v. Commission* [2008] ECR II-1967.
313. In *Brasserie du pêcheur* the starting point of the Court's reasoning was incorrectly just the opposite: The EU breach-of-law liability is said to be 'simply an expression of the general principle familiar to the legal systems of the Member States that *an unlawful act or omission* [sic!] gives rise to an obligation to make good the damage caused'. Compare Joined Cases C-46 and 48/93, *Brasserie du pêcheur and Factortame III* [1996] ECR I-1131, para. 29. This 'general principle' simply does not exist outside the ECJ case law. It is genuinely Court made.
314. Case 177/88, *Dekker* [1990] ECR I-3968, para. 26: 'Any infringement of the prohibition of discrimination suffices in itself to make the person guilty [?] of it liable and no regard may be had to the grounds of exemption envisaged by national law.' On *Dekker see infra* text and para. 173. – *Brasserie* was a case of a legislative wrong in the context of wide discretion. The precise answer of the Court was restricted to this concrete case scenario: *any concept of fault going beyond that of a serious breach is* (in this case) *unacceptable*. Compare Joined Cases C-46 and 48/93, *Brasserie du pêcheur* [1996] ECR I-1131, paras 79 and 80.
315. C. van Dam, *European Tort Law* 566 (2d ed. OUP 2013).

Chapter 5. Burden and Standard of Proof

142. Any judicial trial contains in principle three steps: (i) stating the facts of the case, (ii) finding the relevant law, and (iii) applying the law to the assessed facts (subsumption). The new European Aquilian liability encompasses three preconditions – *iniuria*/breach of law, damage and causation.

§1. Burden of Proof

143. Generally, the onus of proof for the conditions of liability falls on the applicant. This approach is in broad accordance with the basic rules of the law of the Member States. The ECJ, on appeal, has no jurisdiction to examine and re-assess the evidence adduced before the EGC.

Evidence is concerned with the clarification of the factual scenario –'what happened?' Concerning the crucial first element of liability, however, breach of law or unlawfulness is a *question of law* and inasmuch not accessible to proof. In cases of qualified breach (institutional fault/gross maladministration), the factual circumstances have to be presented and, if contested, have to be proven. In so far, a procedural cooperation maxim is valid. The defendant institution is required to collaborate with the applicant by delivering relevant documents and information which it alone possesses.[316]

144. With respect to the damage, the suing party must provide evidence as to the actual occurrence and exact amount of the damage suffered. The same holds true in the case of causation.

Regular or exceptional shifts of the burden of proof to the defendant institution are not excluded. In cases where personal or institutional fault still matters, a presumption of negligence has occasionally been applied.[317] Generally, under the principle of effectiveness, facilitations of proof (from prima facie to reversal of proof) have been recognized by the Court when this is considered necessary to avoid depriving a party of any effective means of enforcing his/her rights.[318]

As far as the *rules of evidence* are concerned, the Court holds that, in the absence of EU legislation in this field, any type of evidence admissible under the procedural law of the Member States in similar proceedings is in principle applicable in EU

---

316. AG Lagrange, Opinion, Joined Cases 29, 31, 36, 39–47, 50, 51/63, *Laminoirs de la Providence and Others v. High Authority* [1965] ECR 911, 943–944; Lenaerts, Arts & Maselis, *Procedural Law of the European Union* 401 (Sweet & Maxwall 2006).
317. *See* Joined Cases 169/83 and 136/84, *Leussink and Brummelhuis v. Commission* [1986] ECR 2822. On further staff cases *see infra* text (Part VI, Ch. 2).
318. *See*, e.g., in cases of repayment of national charges levied in breach of EU law: Case 199/82, *Amministrazione delle Finanze dello Stato v. SpA San Giorgio* [1983] 3595, para. 18; in discrimination cases: C-381/99, *S. Brunnhofer v. Bank der österreichischen Postsparkasse AG* [2001] ECR I-4961, paras 52–62; C-427/11, *Kenny and Others v. Minister for Justice, Equality and Law Reform and Others* EU:C:2013:122, paras 18–20.

procedural law, as far as the principles of equivalence and effectiveness are not infringed.[319]

§2. Standard of Proof

145. A subject matter less treated in the literature, and not at all touched upon in the judgments, is the issue of *standard of proof.*[320]

That is, how conclusive must the provided evidence be or what degree of probability must have been shown to assess the proof of a fact. The law of evidence in the Member States varies. Here, private law delivers the most elaborated information.[321] Common law and Scandinavian laws apply the standard of preponderance of evidence. Many continental European laws adhere to a standard of (very) high probability.[322] German law, in addition, varies the standard of proof: (very) high probability for the ground of liability and clear preponderance for the amount of damages.[323]

If mentioned at all, authors opine that the standard of proof required in the procedures before the European courts is 'very high',[324] or that the applicant has 'to convince the Court'.[325] No sources for substantiation were given. The courts are regularly confined to communicate that the plaintiff failed to show the evidence of damage or causation.

146. Cases of *scientific uncertainty* concerning the causal relationship seem to have not yet shown up before the European courts. After hearing of evidence, it might be uncertain whether a concrete industrial activity, chemical substance or pharmaceutical has had adverse effects on the health of human beings. National courts show a non-uniform tendency to either lower the standard of proof or to shift the burden of proof to the defendant enterprise.[326] As has been said, an analogous development of the law cannot be stated for EU non-contractual liability law. But

---

319. Joined Cases C-310 and 406/98, *Hauptzollamt Neubrandenburg v. Leszek Labis and Sagpol SC* [2000] ECR I-1797, para. 29; Case C-228/98, *C. Dounias v. Ypourgio Oikonomikon* [2000] ECR I-577, paras 68–72. *See also* G. Wagner, *Europäisches Beweisrecht*, ZEuP 2001, 441.

320. *See* generally L. Tichý, *Die Wahrscheinlichkeit und das Beweismaß im Schadensersatzrecht*, in *Festschrift U. Magnus* 709 (Sellier 2014); M. Redmayne, *Standards of Proof in Civil Litigation* (1999) 62 MLR 167.

321. Criminal law internationally has its own rules of law of evidence, which can be neglected here.

322. Compare M. Brinkmann, *Das Beweismaß im Zivilprozess aus rechtsvergleichender Sicht* (Heymanns 2005).

323. §§ 286, 287 Act on Civil Procedure (Zivilprozessordnung – ZPO). Compare Brüggemeier, *Common Principles of Tort Law,* pp. 246 et seq.

324. *See*, e.g., A.G. Toth, *The Concepts of Damage and Causality as Elements of Non-Contractual Liability*, in *The Action for Damages,* 179, at 184 (Heukels & MacDonnell eds, KLI 1997).

325. Lenaerts, Arts & Maselis, *Procedural Law of the European Union* 400 (Sweet & Maxwell 2006).

326. Compare A. Porat & A. Stein, *Tort Liability under Uncertainty* (OUP 2001); *see also* C. Foster, *Science and the Precautionary Principle in International Courts and Tribunals: Expert Evidence, Burden of Proof and Finality* (CUP 2011); M. Faure, *Causal Uncertainty, Joint and Several Liability and Insurance*, in *Liber Amicorum Pierre Widmer* 79 (H. Koziol & J. Spier eds, Springer 2003).

EU institutions or Member States' authorities, as potential defendants before the European courts, can also be confronted with similar case scenarios. Scenarios are imaginable where scientific uncertainty functions as the ground on which a decision to withdraw or not to withdraw a marketing authority, e.g., for a pharmaceutical product, has to be taken.[327]

---

327. Compare the *Artegodan* case complex (fn. 267). *See* generally *Integrating Scientific Expertise into Regulatory Decision-Making – National Experiences and European Innovations* (C. Joerges, K.H. Ladeur & E. Vos eds, Nomos 1997).

Part II. Liability of Member States

Chapter 1. Various Types of Member State Liability

147. A common misunderstanding identifies Member States' liability with the *Francovich* doctrine. The first and broadest area of application, however, comprises the vertical effect cases, in the tradition of *van Gend en Loos*. Originally, these cases concerned the levying on private parties by national authorities of charges and levies incompatible with EU law. The plaintiffs claim unequal treatment and bring actions for damages seeking a compensation equivalent to the amount allegedly paid unduly. This variant of Member States' liability was already launched by the Court in 1960 with *Humblet*, a case under ECSC law.[328] Another field of application became discrimination law (*Marshall*). The *Francovich*-like liability of Member States covers a rather restricted scope. It correlates with the absence of horizontal direct effect of EU directives. Instead it grants aggrieved private parties the path of damages actions when Member States failed to implement directives correctly in time or in content. Additionally, there are two special cases of liability of Member States – breach of a State's duty to protect the Internal Market, and States' liability for their judicial bodies of last instance. Each type of Member States' liability has its own profile.

Finally, the question is raised of whether a vicarious liability of Member States for breach of EU law by their public servants exists.

§1. State Liability I: Vertical Direct Effect Cases

I. Protective Rule, Direct Effect, Supremacy and Effectiveness

148. In contrast to the liability of the Union, the Treaties do not contain any express legal basis for non-contractual liability of Member States for breach of EU law by their authorities and 'emanations' With regard to the former the ECJ fleshed out in its case law the arguably 'common principles' contained in Article 215(2) TEEC/Article 340(2) TFEU. The Member States' liability was autonomously created by the ECJ having recourse to the principles supposedly inherent in the EU legal system. Central conditions for such an action for damages are that the

328. Case 6/60, *Humblet v. Belgium* [1960] ECR 559 (claim of an ECSC official for compensation of unduly paid Belgian tax).

infringed provisions of EU law have a *protective* and *direct* effect on private parties. Direct effect of EU law constitutes the fundamental element in the supranational architecture of the Union's multi-level legal system of protection of individual rights.

149. Complementing principles for the elaboration of this concept of Member States' liability are the *supremacy* of EU law and the loyalty doctrine enshrined in Article 4(3) TEU. The Union and the Member States are, 'pursuant to the principle of sincere cooperation', bound to assist each other in carrying out tasks which flow from the Treaties. *Supremacy* means that EU law norms render automatically inapplicable any conflicting provision of Member States' law. National courts are under a duty to give full effect to the provisions of EU law even if in conflict with norms of domestic law. The *effectiveness* of EU law and the protection of rights conferred on private parties would be seriously impaired if allegedly aggrieved private parties could not invoke directly effective EU law norms before the national courts.[329]

150. Though this monograph is dedicated to tort law in the European Union, it is indispensable, in the following paragraphs, to sketch rather briefly these general doctrines of protectiveness, direct effect, supremacy and effectiveness, developed in the 'foundational period' of the EU legal order. The realm of Member States' liability for breach of EU law would remain incomprehensible without this excursus.

II. Protective Rule (*Schutznorm*)

151. The allegedly infringed provision of EU law must be a protective rule, i.e., it must aim to protect a conferred right or a legitimate interest of a private party. Protectiveness and conferral of rights are two sides of the same coin. Here, the same rules apply as for Union liability for breach-of-law.[330]

152. Rights are prominently conferred on private parties by rules of the Treaties, namely the *four economic freedoms* of the TFEU,[331] and by *general principles*

329. Compare Case 26/62, *N.V. Allgemene Transport- en Expeditie Onderneming van Gend en Loos v. Nederlandse Administratie der Belastingen* [1963] ECR 1; Case 6/64, *F. Costa v. Ente Nazionale Energia Elettrica (ENEL)* [1964] ECR 585; Case 11/70, *Internationale Handelsgesellschaft mbH v. Einfuhr- und Vorratsstelle für Getreide und Futtermittel* [1970] ECR 1125; Case 106/77, *Amministrazione delle finanze dello Stato v. Simmenthal SpA* (*Simmenthal II*) [1978] ECR 642. *See, inter alia*, B. de Witte, *Direct Effect, Primacy, and the Nature of the Legal Order*, in *The Evolution of EU Law* 323 (Craig & de Búrca eds, OUP 2011); *Direct Effect – Rethinking a Classic of EC Legal Doctrine* (J.M. Prinssen & A. Schrauwen eds, European Law Publ. 2002); J.H.H. Weiler, *The Transformation of Europe* (1991) 100 Yale L.J. 2403.

330. *See supra* text.

331. Free movement of goods (Art. 28 TFEU), employees (Art. 45), services (Art. 56) and capital (Art. 63); *see* in greater detail, C. Barnard, *The Substantive Law of the EU – The Four Freedoms* (OUP 2013). Free flow of data in the EU can be considered as a fifth freedom. Compare Directive 95/46/EC, OJ 1995 L 281/31, and General Data Protection Regulation. *See infra* text (Part VIII, Ch. 3).

of EU law,[332] e.g., the principles of equality, proportionality and protection of legitimate interests. For compliance with the principle of proportionality, it must be ascertained whether the means which the legal rule employs are suitable for the purpose of achieving the pursued objective and whether they do not go beyond what is necessary to achieve it. Other examples are the principle of the protection of legitimate expectations,[333] and the precautionary principle.[334]

153. Though Article 34 TFEU is in principle recognized to confer rights on private parties, the case of *Danske Slagterier* delivers an impressive example of how unforeseeable the outcome of a decision on grant of rights can be, even in this field of law. Here, two directives had exhaustively harmonized the export of male pig meat. Therefore, the only acceptable grounds to justify obstacles to free movement were to be found in the directives. Germany, however, introduced additional veterinary checks, which it considered appropriate for the health of its consumers, and was in delay with the implementation of the second directive. The Commission initiated a Treaty infringement procedure and the ECJ stated a breach of secondary EU law by Germany.[335] The plaintiff, an industry association of Danish slaughterhouse companies, sued Germany for compensation of a loss of at least DEM 280 million. For this damages action to be successful, the infringed directives regulating the pig meat market must confer rights to the slaughterhouses and pig farmers. On this question, brought to Luxembourg via reference for preliminary ruling by the German Federal Court of Justice,[336] the Court and the AG disagreed.[337] The AG denied protective effect, arguing that the two directives aim exclusively at regulation of the pig meat market.[338] The ECJ confirmed this primary goal of promoting free movement of male pig meat. But it also held that in fields exhaustively harmonized Member States are prevented from inventing additional obstacles to free movement. Therefore an incorrect transposition or application of directives allows the impeded parties to refer directly to Article 34 TFEU. In other words: The individual right is conferred by Article 34. This right is only defined in its content and given concrete expression by those directives. These rights can be enforced against Member States also by producers (slaughterhouses and pig farmers) who are not themselves exporters.[339]

154. This *Danske Slagterier principle* applies to all directives exhaustively harmonizing market sectors, provided that these directives do not themselves affirm the element of third party protection. Protection in favour of the manufacturers is for

332. *See* T. Tridimas, *The General Principles of EU Law* (OUP 2005); X. Groussot, *General Principles of Community Law* (Europa Law Publisher 2006); compare also N. Reich, *General Principles of EU Civil Law* (Intersentia 2014).
333. *See* Joined Cases C-104/89 and 37/90, *J.M. Mulder and Heinemann v. Council and Commission (Mulder II No 1)* [1992] ECR I-3061; Case T-336/94, *Efisol SA v. Commission* [1996] ECR II-1343.
334. Compare Craig, *EU Administrative Law* 641 (OUP 2010).
335. C-102/96, *Commission v. Germany* [1998] ECR I-6871.
336. Bundesgerichtshof, 12 Oct. 2006, NVwZ 2007, 362.
337. C-445/06, *Danske Slagterier v. Germany* [2009] ECR I-2119.
338. C-445/06, *Danske Slagterier*, AG Trstenjak, Opinion [2009] ECR I-2119, para. 73.
339. C-445/06, *Danske Slagterier*, Judgment, paras 23 and 24.

example acknowledged for the set of so-called New Approach or vertical product safety directives.[340] According to this legislation all State measures are prohibited which are capable of hindering, directly or indirectly, actually or potentially, intra-Union trade and fall within the scope of these directives.[341] – The *Danske Slagterier* case itself witnessed a dramatic fate. Initiated in December 1999, the ECJ delivered its judgment in 2009. After two follow-up decisions of the German Federal Court,[342] the case is eighteen years later [!] still pending before the Superior Regional Court of Cologne (as of Nov. 2017).[343]

155. Another telling example of protective effect litigation is the Austrian case of *Leth*.[344] Ms *Leth* was the owner of a property situated within the security zone of Vienna-*Schwechat* airport. She lived in the house built on that property. The Austrian authorities consented and completed several projects relating to the development and extension of the airport. However, no environmental impact assessments, as prescribed by Directive 85/337/EEC,[345] were carried out. Ms *Leth* sued the Austrian State for compensation of the decrease in the value of her property and for declaration that the defendants will be liable for any future material damage, e.g., health impairments by increase of noise. On request for preliminary ruling by the Austrian Supreme Court, the ECJ had to decide whether environmental impact assessments also serve to protect individuals against pecuniary damage.

156. The Court confirmed that the EIA Directive confers a right to have the environmental effects of a project examined. Whether this conferral gives rise to an individual right to an action for damages remained ambiguous:

> The answer is therefore that Article 3 of the Directive cannot be interpreted as meaning that the environmental impact assessment, … , does not include the assessment of effects which the project under examination has on the value of material assets. However, pecuniary damage, in so far as it is the direct economic consequence of the effects on the environment of a public or private project, is covered by the objective of protection pursued by the Directive. The fact that an environmental impact assessment has not been carried out, in breach of the requirements of the Directive, does not, in principle, by itself according to European law, and without prejudice to rules of national law, … , confer on an individual a right to compensation for purely pecuniary damage

340. Including machines, toys, etc. *See* on this in greater detail the website 'New Approach Standardization in the Internal Market'. For Art. 4(1) Directive on machinary, *see* ECJ, Case C-470/03, *A.G.M.-COS.MET* [2007] ECR I-2798, para. 79.
341. For the famous Dassonville-formula, *see* Case 8/74, *Procureur du Roi v. B. and G. Dassonville* [1974] ECR 837.
342. BGH, 4.6.2009, BGHZ 181, 199; BGH, 12.12.2013, III ZR 102/12, juris.
343. Oberlandesgericht Köln, 7 U 29/04.
344. C-420/11, *J. Leth v. Austria and Land Niederösterreich* EU:C:2013:166.
345. Directive 85/337/EEC on the assessment of the effects of certain public and private projects on the environment, OJ 1985 L 175/40, as amended (EIA Directive).

> […]. However, it is for the national court to determine whether the requirements of European law applicable to the right to compensation, … , have been satisfied.[346]

Curia locuta, causa finita? A central element of the requirements of European liability law is causation. The omission of having not carried out an environmental impact assessment procedure must have caused the pecuniary loss. The EIA Directive, however, does not preclude the implementation of a project even in the case where the environmental impact assessment establishes that there are significant negative effects on the environment.[347] Therefore, a causal link between breach of law and damage is missing, and the question of whether the EIA Directive confers a right to compensation for purely economic loss is immaterial for the decision of this case.

157. In the case of *Peter Paul*, the Court has stated that the various directives harmonizing the law of the financial industry[348] do not grant any rights to private parties. The *Paul* case concerned the directive on deposit-guarantee schemes.[349] The Court held that the banking directives only serve to establish an effective inter-state banking supervisory system.[350] – In *Enichem*, too, the Court took the view that the purpose of the Council framework directive on waste[351] was solely to harmonize the legislation of the Member States and not to create rights for private parties.[352] The protection of private parties should be ensured by waste liability directives.[353]

158. For a long time *human rights* have been acknowledged as enshrined in the general principles of EU law producing protective effect, though this was not provided for in the texts of the Treaties.[354] At the EU summit in Nice, December 2000, a Charter of Fundamental Rights, combining in a single text the civil, political, economic and social rights, was solemnly proclaimed. After the failure of the Treaty Establishing a European Constitution (TEC), the Charter of Fundamental Rights of

---

346. C-420/11, *Leth*, para. 48. On the EIA Directive compare also C-201/02, *D. Wells v. Sec'y of State for Transport, Local Gov. and the Regions* [2004] ECR I-723. For a critical commentary, *see* B.A. Koch & T. Thiede, *European Tort Law* 2013, 706 et seq. (E. Karner & B. Steininger eds, de Gruyter 2014).
347. Correctly stated by AG J. Kokott, Opinion, C-420/11, *Leth*, EU:C:2012:701, para. 42.
348. Based on Art. 64(2) TFEU.
349. Directive 94/19/EC, OJ 1994 L 135/5.
350. Case C-222/02, *Peter Paul and Others v. Germany* [2004] ECR I-9460. For annotations *see*, *inter alia*, M. Tison, *Do Not Attack the Watchdog* (2005) 42 CML Rev 639; J.H. Binder, *Cutting Back State Liability for Regulatory Negligence* (2005) Banking and Ins. L. Rev. 133.
351. Directive 75/442/EEC on waste, OJ 1975 L 194/47.
352. Case 380/87, *Enichem Base and Others v. Commune di Cinsello Balsamo* [1989] ECR 2491.
353. On this *see infra* text (Part VIII, Ch. 1).
354. Since Case 29/69, *E. Stauder v. Stadt Ulm* [1969] ECR 419, para. 7; Case 11/70, *Internationale Handelsgesellschaft mbH v. Einfuhr- und Vorratsstelle für Getreide und Futtermittel* [1970] ECR 1125 and Case 4/73, *Nold KG v. Commission* [1974] ECR 491, paras 12 et seq. Compare, *inter alia*, J.H.H. Weiler & N.J.S. Lockhart, *'Taking Rights Seriously': The European Court of Justice and its Fundamental Rights Jurisprudence I* (1995) 32 CML Rev 51/*'Taking Rights Seriously'* II (1995) 32 CML Rev 579.

the European Union (ChFR) entered into force in 2009.[355] The level of protection provided by the EU-ChFR must be at least as high as that of the ECHR (Article 53 ChFR). Additionally, the human rights of the ECHR are now explicitly recognized as general principles of EU law (Article 6(3) TEU). From 2009 onwards, the ChFR is binding law for the Union institutions and bodies when acting in the scope of their competences.[356] Member States are only bound by Charter rights when they 'implement' Union law (Article 51(1) ChFR).[357] This narrow interpretation of the scope of application has been confirmed by judicial authority,[358] but a wider applicability is sought by legal academia, so that EU citizens generally can invoke an infringement of Charter rights by measures of their Member States' authorities when national law fails.[359]

To monitor the compliance with Charter rights by the Member States, a Fundamental Rights Agency (FRA) was established in 2007 in Vienna.[360]

III. Vertical Direct Effect: *van Gend en Loos* and Supremacy: *Costa* v. *ENEL*

159. The protective nature of a provision of EU law does not matter towards Member States unless it additionally has a *direct effect*.[361] The ECJ articulated the

355. As a commentary, *see* S. Peers, T. Hervey, J. Kenner & A. Wards, *The EU Charter of Fundamental Rights* (Hart 2014).
356. Recently EU Charter rights are increasingly used to scrutinize surrender procedures between Member States under the Framework Decision on the EU arrest warrant (OJ 2002 L 190/1). *See* Case C-399/11, *S. Melloni v. Ministerio Fiscal* EU:C:2013:107 (execution of a sentence pronounced in absentia); Case C-168/13 PPU, *Jeremy F. v. Premier ministre* EU:C:2013:358; Joined Cases C-404/15 and C-659/15 PPU, *Aranyosi and Other v. Generalstaatsanwaltschaft Bremen* EU:C:2016:198. – At strife is the question of whether Member States' courts are exempted from exercising this control by applying national constitutional rights. Compare German Federal Constitutional Court, 15.12.2015, BVerfGE 140, 317.
357. Protocols of Poland and the UK contain Charter opt-outs (concerning social rights).
358. Compare Case C-617/10, *Åklagaren v. Åkerberg Fransson* EU:C:2013:280. This judgment itself, however, raises questions about the scope of applicability of EU law. *See* E. Hancox, *The Meaning of 'Implementing' Union Law under Art. 51(1) of the Charter* (2013) 50 CML Rev 1411.
359. A. von Bogdandy et al., *Reverse* Solange – *Protecting the Essence of Fundamental Rights Against EU Member States* (2012) 49 CML Rev 489. The title refers to two famous judgments of the German Federal Constitutional Court holding that '*as long as*' the level of protection of human rights by EU law is equivalent to the protective standard under the German Constitution, the test of constitutionality of EU law is not admissible to the German Constitutional Court. Compare BVerfG, 22 Oct. 1986, BVerfGE 73, 339 (*Solange* II), repealing BVerfG, 29.5.1974, BVerfGE 37, 271 (*Solange* I/Internationale Handelsgesellschaft) which claimed competence for national constitutional courts to decide on the constitutionality of secondary EU law. – Actually, after the Treaty of Lisbon, the national constitutional courts refer increasingly to their national constitutional identity (Art. 4(2) TEU) and insist on their prerogative to undertake an 'identity review' of EU acts. Compare, *inter alia*, German Federal Constitutional Court, 15.12.2015, BVerfGE 140, 317; F.X. Millet, *L'Union européenne et l'identité constitutionelle des États members* (Lextenso & Rodier 2013).
360. Regulation (EC) 168/2007 on the establishment of an agency of the European Union for Fundamental Rights, OJ 2007 L 53/1.
361. Compare, *inter alia*, *Direct Effect – Rethinking a Classic of EC Legal Doctrine* (J.M. Prinssen & A. Schrauwen eds, European Law Publ. 2002).

idea of vertical direct effect in the ground-breaking case of *van Gend en Loos*.[362] The often told story cannot be suppressed in this monograph, though formally it was not a damages case. The plaintiff, a Dutch transport company, imported a chemical product (*Kunststoffharz*) from Germany into the Netherlands. It was charged by the Dutch Revenue Authorities with increased customs duties. This increase was based on a law that had been passed in the three Benelux States after the entry into force of the EEC Treaty. The company alleged an infringement by the Netherlands of Article 30 TFEU,[363] and it brought an action against the Dutch authorities for annulment of the decision. Upon request by the Dutch Administrative Court (*Tariefcommissie*) to the ECJ for preliminary ruling, the question was whether a private party can invoke the Treaty's prohibition of customs duties (Article 30) as an individual right to be protected by national courts against an infringement by a Member State.

160. The Court first stressed the difference of the (then new) EU law to traditional public international law, stating that the Treaty is more than an agreement among Signatory States creating only mutual obligations between the contracting States. By the (then) EEC the Member States have limited their sovereign rights and have thus created a special legal system which became an integral part of their domestic laws. Against the interventions of the governments of Belgium and the Netherlands and opposite to the opinion of AG Roemer, the Court by a close vote then found:

> Community law … not only imposes obligations on individuals but is also intended to confer them rights which become part of their legal heritage … The wording of [now Art. 30 TFEU] contains a clear and unconditional prohibition which is not a positive but a negative obligation. This obligation, moreover, is not qualified by any reservation on the part of States, which would make its implementation conditional upon a positive legislative measure enacted under national law. The very nature of this prohibition makes it ideally adapted to produce direct effect in the legal relationship between Member States and their subjects.[364]

161. Thus, *van Gend en Loos* clarified that Article 30 (the same holds true for the other economic freedoms) is not only directly *applicable* in the way, for example, EU regulations are directly applicable in Member States' law. It is also vertically directly *effective*. That is, private parties can straightforwardly address the national courts if measures of their national authorities infringe their EU rights. Hence, Union legislative and administrative branches do not need the intermediary

362. Case 26/62, *N.V. Allgemene Transport- en Expeditie Onderneming van Gend en Loos v. Nederlandse Administratie der Belastingen* [1963] ECR 1, at pp. 12 and 13; *see also* Case 6/64, *F. Costa v. Ente Nazionale Energia Elettrica (ENEL)* [1964] ECR 585 and Case 57/65, *A. Lütticke GmbH v. Hauptzollamt Saarlouis (Lütticke I)* [1966] ECR 293.

363. Article 30 TFEU: 'Customs duties on imports and exports and charges having equivalent effect shall be prohibited between Member States.'

364. Case 26/62, *van Gend en Loos v. Nederlandse Administratie der Belastingen* [1963] ECR 1, at pp. 12 and 13; *see also* Case 6/64, *Costa v. ENEL* [1964] ECR 585 and Case 57/65, *Lütticke I* [1966] ECR 293.

of the Member States, as is the position in general public international law, to reach private parties as objects and subjects of EU law. In other words, directly effective EU law norms are self-executing.

162. One year later, another landmark judgment complemented the *van Gend en Loos* approach. In *Costa v. ENEL* the plaintiff was an Italian citizen who owned shares in an electricity company and opposed the nationalization of the electricity industry in Italy. Therefore Mr *Costa* refused to pay his electricity bill claiming that the nationalization violates EC law and the Italian Constitution. The Italian trial judge referred the case first to the Italian Constitutional Court and then to the ECJ. The *Corte constituzionale* upheld the Italian provisions.[365] The ECJ, however, found in its preliminary ruling that the law stemming from the Treaty because of its independent, special and original nature cannot be overridden by domestic norms of Member States' laws without being deprived of its character as Community law and without the legal basis of the Union itself being called into question.[366] Overriding domestic law 'however framed', meant that EU law norms, independent of their character as primary or secondary law, claim supremacy over national law, including Member States' constitutional law.[367]

163. The practical consequences of EU law's supremacy have been worked out in the *Simmenthal* litigation.[368] In principle, ordinary Member States' courts are not authorized to invalidate formal statutes passed by national Parliaments. The German Constitution, as but one example, reserves this privilege exclusively for the Federal Constitutional Court.[369] How then to proceed with domestic legal provisions conflicting with EU law? The *Simmenthal II* judgment offers as a solution: '*inapplicability*' instead of '*invalidity*'. If any (amending or supplementary) interpretation of the law is of no further support, the Court states in *Simmenthal II* first that any domestic law contradictory to EU law norms is at least inapplicable by national courts (and authorities), and second that the national legislature is hindered of adopting any subsequent contradictory law, and third that it is not necessary for the national court to request or await the prior setting aside of the domestic law provision by the legislature or a constitutional court.[370]

164. Both unrestricted supremacy of EU law and general competence of national courts to decide on the applicability of domestic law, have been criticized as an

365. Italian Constitutional Court, 5.3.1964, *Costa v. ENEL e soc. Edinsonvolta*, Foro it. 1964 I, 465.
366. Case 6/64, *F. Costa v. Ente Nazionale Energia Elettrica (ENEL)* [1964] ECR 585.
367. Explicitly stated in Case 11/70, *Internationale Handelsgesellschaft mbH v. Einfuhr- und Vorratsstelle für Getreide und Futtermittel* [1970] ECR 1125, para. 3: 'Therefore the validity of a Community measure or its effect within a Member State cannot be affected by allegations that it runs counter to either fundamental rights as formulated by the Constitution of that State or the principles of a national constitutional structure.'
368. *See* especially Case 106/77, *Amministrazione delle Finanze dello Stato v. Simmenthal SpA (Simmenthal II)* [1978] ECR 629.
369. Article 100(1) Federal Constitution (Grundgesetz).
370. Casa 106/77, *Simmenthal II*, paras 21–24.

'over-constitutionalisation' of EU law and raised questions of democratic legitimacy of this judicial regime.[371] It is nevertheless settled case law of the Court and established doctrine of EU law.[372]

165. The direct effectiveness of a legal provision is just one side of the coin. The other side requires an addressee. Towards whom is it effective? In *van Gend en Loos* and *Costa*, the focus was on the relationship between a Member State and a private party, business or citizen. Hence, the concept of direct effect has long been identified with *vertical* direct effect. It was but until recently that the *horizontal* dimension of direct effect came to the fore.[373]

166. The *van Gend en Loos* judgment made an additional important qualification. The conditions for direct effect are that the EU law norm must be *sufficiently clear, precise, and unconditional* (no time-limit or reservation) and leave no room for the exercise of discretion for the Member States when implementing the respective obligations by EU law. As far as general principles of EU law are concerned, they must therefore be concretized by secondary law (regulations, directives). Directives are binding upon each Member State to which they are addressed as to the result to be achieved but leave to national authorities the choice of form and methods of their transposition.[374] A general principle of vertical direct effect can be formulated as follows: 'Provisions of binding (primary or secondary) EU law which are sufficiently clear, precise and unconditional to be considered justiciable can be invoked and relied on by private parties before national courts.'[375]

167. Vertical direct effect rules are not restricted to relationships between State institutions and private parties. The German case of *G. Fuß* is but one telling example for the application of vertical direct effect (of directives) in a *public* employer-*public* employee relationship.[376] The case concerned a firefighter in a municipality whose working time extended the maximum weekly forty-eight hours prescribed by Article 6(b) of the Directive 2003/88/EC.[377] In its preliminary ruling, the Court held that the provisions of the domestic law contrary to the Directive were inapplicable by the German courts (supremacy of EU law). With respect to the

371. Compare, *inter alia*, D. Grimm, *Constitutionalism: Past, Present, and Future*, chap. 14 (OUP 2016).
372. *See* references in fn. 367.
373. On this in greater detail, *see infra* text.
374. Article 288(3) TFEU.
375. Direct effect of directives has first been acknowledged in Case 41/74, *Y. van Duyn v. Home Office* [1974] ECR 1337 (refusal to take up employment in the UK as a secretary with the Scientology Church). *See also* Case 8/81, *Becker v. Finanzamt Münster-Innenstadt* [1982] ECR 53 (directive not implemented); Case 152/84, *Marshall v. Southampton and South-West Hampshire Area Health Authority (Marshall No. 1)* [1986] ECR 723; Case 103/88, *Fratelli Costanzo SpA v. Commune di Milano* [1989] ECR 1839, paras 28-–33.
376. Compare Case C-243/09, *G. Fuß v. Stadt Halle (Fuß No. 1)* [2010] ECR I-9849, and Case C-429/09, *G. Fuß v. Stadt Halle (Fuß No. 2)* [2010] ECR I-12167. On the English *Marshall* case *see infra* text and fn. .
377. Directive 2003/88/EC concerning certain aspects of the organization of working time, OJ 2003 L 299/9.

plaintiff's claim for compensation of his losses, the national courts were referred to the principles of Member States' liability for breach of EU law, developed in the case law of the ECJ.[378] The Directive 2003/88/EC itself did not provide any sanctions in cases of non-compliance.

Together with the recognition of the independence of damages actions in the EEC legal system in 1971 (*Lütticke II*),[379] judgments such as *van Gend en Loos, Costa* and *Simmenthal II* formed the legal basis for effective compensation claims to be brought by private parties against Member States for breach of EU law.[380] Commentators annotated that by these landmark cases the EU law has been taken out of the hands of politicians and bureaucrats and been given 'to the people'.[381]

IV. Equivalence and Effectiveness

168. Legal protection of private parties against breach of EU law through Member States is characterized by a bifurcated system of justice. EU rights are enforced both by the ECJ and national courts. Damages actions against Member States, their institutional organs and other autonomous State 'emanations', for breach of protective and directly effective EU law must be brought before the national courts. The ECJ determines, often by means of preliminary rulings, the content of the respective EU law. The national courts then decide on the relevant breach of EU law by the domestic measure. The liability of the Member State has to be established on the basis of the domestic law of governmental liability.[382]

Not only was there no legal ground for Member States liability in the Treaties, *a fortiori* the EU law of the pre-*Francovich* phase did not provide any adequate legal remedies for enforcement. Starting with the question of 'relevant breach' of EU law, all conditions for liability, especially the requirement of fault, the nature and extent of damage and questions of causation, were left to the autonomy of national courts to determine under domestic law. That is the reason why the Court in so far had to refer to the remedies available in national law and, in so doing, postulated the principles of *equivalence* and *effectiveness*.[383] That is, first, the procedural conditions of national law governing the damages action for breach of EU law shall not be less favourable to the plaintiff than those relating to similar actions of a domestic nature

378. Case C-429/09, *Fuß (No. 2)*, paras 41 et seq.
379. Case 4/69, *Lütticke v. Commission (Lütticke II)* [1971] ECR 325. Compare *supra* text (Part I, Ch. 3, §1).
380. The *van Gend en Loos* case was settled out of court. After the decision of the ECJ, the Dutch government agreed to pay back the increase of the tariff *van Gend en Loos* had been unlawfully charged with.
381. G. Mancini & D.T. Keeling, *Democracy and the Court of Justice* (1994) 57 MLR 175.
382. Case 60/75, *C.A. Russo v. Azienda di Stato per gli interventi sul mercato agricolo (AIMA)* [1976] ECR 45, at 57.
383. Compare Case 33/76, *Rewe Zentralfinanz eG and Rewe Zentral AG v. Landwirtschaftskammer für das Saarland* [1976] ECR 1989 and Case 45/76, *Comet BV v. Produktschap voor Siergewassen* [1976] ECR 2043. On this in greater detail *see, inter alia, The European Court of Justice and the Autonomy of Member States* (H.W. Micklitz & B. de Witte eds, Intersentia 2011); compare also *The Influence of EU Law on National Private Law* (A.S. Hartkamp, C.H. Sieburgh et al. eds, Kluwer 2014).

(equivalence[384]), and second it shall not be made impossible in practice for the plaintiff to exercise rights which the national courts have a duty to protect (effectiveness[385]).

169. The risk of unequal treatment of injured parties under the various national legal systems remained. The EU courts were confronted with the necessity to work out principles upon which a more or less uniform and effective enforcement of Union rights could be established across the Member States. With *Francovich* (1991),[386] the Court of Justice began to invent genuine EU law remedies which brought a new momentum to the principle of effectiveness. National courts are now forced to develop their domestic law of damages to meet the new requirements. This is a complicated process which seems to be far from being completed.

This process got even more complex when from the mid-1990s onwards, with the *Brasserie du pêcheur* and *Hedley Lomas* judgments,[387] the Court of Justice undertook to consolidate on this basis the law of non-contractual liability of Union and of Member States, which also implied a convergence of remedies. This will be taken up later on in the text.

V. Addressees of Vertical Direct Effect or: Who to Sue

170. Damages cases founded on vertical direct effect cover a broad spectrum of public bodies. There are *Humblet* and *van Gend en Loos*-like claims against State financial or customs authorities for unlawfully charged fees.[388] In discrimination cases, public employers mostly are the addressees of damages actions. In *Marshall*, the dismissal of the female plaintiff by the regional Health Authority constituted discrimination on grounds of sex contrary to the Equal Treatment Directive 76/207/EEC.[389] She sued successfully for compensation.[390] In a subsequent proceeding, *Marshall No 2*, the House of Lords referred questions to the Court concerning the extent and nature of damages required by EU law under these circumstances.[391]

171. A very special issue of discrimination was raised by the *Pisciotti* and two other cases.[392] Do provisions in Member States' constitutions which reserve certain human rights exclusively to nationals generally constitute an infringement of the

384. Case 33/76, *Rewe*, para. 6; Case 45/76, *Comet*, para. 19.
385. Case 45/76, *Comet*, para. 16.
386. *See infra* text and fn 408.
387. *See infra* text and fns. 491 and 511.
388. Compare, *inter alia*, Case 60/75, *Russo v. AIMA* [1976] ECR 45; Case 199/82, *Amministrazione delle Finanze dello Stato v. SpA San Giorgio* [1983] ECR 3595.
389. Council Directive 76/207/EEC on the implementation of the principle of equal treatment for men and women as regards access to employment, vocational training and promotion, and working conditions, OJ 1976 L 39/40.
390. Case 152/84, *Marshall v. Southampton and South-West Hampshire Area Health Authority (Marshall No. 1)* [1986] ECR 723. *See also infra* text.
391. Case C-271/91, *Marshall v. Southampton and South-West Hampshire Area Health Authority (Marshall No. 2)* [1993] ECR I-4367.
392. C-191/16, *R. Pisciotti v. Germany*. Pending.

prohibition to discriminate on grounds of nationality (Article 18(1) TFEU)? In other words, must fundamental rights of nationals in Member States' constitutions be interpreted as fundamental rights of EU citizens? Article 16(2)(i) German Constitution (*Grundgesetz*) stipulates that no German citizen shall be extradited. Mr *Pisciotti*, an Italian citizen, in transit to Italy, was arrested on Frankfurt airport by the German police. The German authorities executed an American arrest warrant. Mr *Pisciotti* opposed the arrest and claimed violation of his right to free movement and contended discriminatory treatment. He fought without success against his extradition before many national and EU courts. With approval of the German courts,[393] finally he was extradited to the US. Back in Europe, after having served a prison sentence in Florida, he brought a damages action against Germany for breach of EU law (Article 18(1) TFEU) by his extradition.

172. The German courts argued that the prohibition of extradition of German nationals in the German Constitution is exempt from the scope of applicable EU law. This extradition problem has already been raised in the Latvian case of *A. Petruhhin.*[394] Here, a third State requested the extradition of an Estonian citizen who was charged with criminal offences by Latvia. The ECJ tried to strike a balance between EU citizens' right to free movement and the necessity to combat impugnity for criminal offences. It held that the Member State which received the extradition request has to inform the Member State of which the wanted person is a national and should surrender the person to it, provided that the accused person is there prosecuted for offences committed outside its national territory.[395] This Solomonic judgment, however, does not offer an answer to the damages claim. This case is pending at the Court for preliminary ruling.

173. In the Dutch case of *Dekker*,[396] the status of the defendant remained unclear. Ms *Dekker* applied for the post of instructor at a training centre for young adults. She gave notice before the committee dealing with the applications that she was three months pregnant. The committee nonetheless suggested her as the most suitable candidate for appointment. The centre, however, denied appointment for reason of financial costs. According to Dutch law, incorrectly implementing the Directive 76/207/EEC, the employer would not have been able to recoup the sick pay caused by her maternity absence. Ms *Dekker* sued the centre for damages for her financial loss. She addressed not the Dutch State for wrongful implementation, but she invoked her rights under the Equal Treatment Directive against the envisaged employer. The Court of Appeal Amsterdam dismissed her claim, considering the employer's decision to be justified. The *Hoge Raad* referred to the ECJ for a preliminary ruling. The Court held that the fact that the plaintiff was not appointed because of her pregnancy was a direct discrimination on the ground of sex which

393. Superior Regional Court (OLG) Frankfurt, 22.1.2014, 2 AuslA 104/13 and Federal Constitutional Court, 17.2.2014, 2 BvQ 4/14, NJW 2014, 1945.
394. C-182/15, *A. Petruhhin v. Latvijas Republikas Generalprokura*, EU:C:2016:630.
395. C-182/15, *Petruhhin*, para. 50.
396. Case 177/88, *Dekker v. Stichting Vormingscentrum voor Jong Volwassenen (VJV Centrum) Plus* [1990] ECR I-3941.

could not be justified because of financial costs.[397] Somewhat surprisingly, the Court neither focused at all on the central question of the status of the defendant employer – 'State emanation or not' –, nor did it cite any relevant case law.[398] As a matter of fact, the defendant centre in *Dekker* was a foundation of private law.[399] This did not exclude 'per se' the possibility of a State institution, since the centre could have been founded, financed and controlled by a public institution, e.g., the municipality. But there is no clarification to be found in the judgment.

174. In reality, it is often hard to decide whether a governmental function is exercised. The state may appear in various emanations of public authority, and this may vary from country to country and depend on the respective political ideology in vogue. For the affirmation of a vertical effect, the addressee must be 'the State', regardless of whether it is acting as employer or as public authority. The Court based its judgments on a broad interpretation of the notion of a 'State body'. It has held in a series of cases that unconditional and sufficiently precise provisions of a directive could be relied on against 'organisations or bodies which were *subject to the authority or control of the state or had special powers beyond those which result from the normal rules applicable to relations between individuals*'.[400]

§2. State Liability II: *Francovich Doctrine*

175. The case law connected with this label once caused considerable aggravation in legal academia when it came up in 1991. As late as in *Rewe v. Hauptzollamt Kiel* in 1981, the Court held that the EC Treaty 'was not intended to create new remedies'.[401] Ten years later the ECJ took a fundamentally different approach.[402] The Court was accused of running wild, crossing the boundaries of legitimate judicial law development. However, the Court instead sought to fill a lacuna in the system for safeguarding rights of private parties. Directives are the main regulatory instrument for the EU in private law matters. Provisions in directives become binding on private parties only from the time of and inasmuch as the national legislator has transposed them into domestic law. This led to the problem of how to protect a private party to whom rights have been sufficiently clear and unconditionally conferred in a directive when the concrete Member State fails to transpose the directive

397. Case 177/88, *Dekker*, para. 12. As Dutch follow-up decision compare Hoge Raad, NJ 1992, 225.
398. Especially not the *Costanzo* and *Foster* cases (compare fn. 400), just decided recently beforehand. The only judgment cited is *von Colson and Kamann* (compare fn. 611), which is in that respect not a case in point.
399. Information by Esther van Schagen, University of Groningen, at the author's request.
400. Case 103/88, *Fratelli Costanzo SpA v. Commune di Milano* [1989] ECR 1839; Case C-188/89, *A. Foster and Others v. British Gas plc* [1990] ECR I-3343, para. 18; listing examples in para. 19. *See also* V. Kvjatkovski, *What Is an 'Emanation of the State'? An Educated Guess* (1997) EPL 329; R.W. Davis, *Liability in Damages for a Breach of Community Law: Some Reflections on the Question of Who to Sue and the Concept of 'the State'* (2006) 31 EL Rev 69.
401. Case 158/80, [1981] ECR 1805, para. 44. *See also* Case 60/75, *Russo v. AIMA* [1976] ECR 45.
402. Possible reasons for this change of attitude are given by T. Tridimas, *General Principles* 501 (OUP 2005).

in due time or does it in an insufficient way. Thus, the Member State would violate its obligation under Article 288(3) TFEU.

176. Nevertheless, the frustrating fact remained that private parties aggrieved by breach of EU law by Member States had no realistic chance to invoke their rights against other private parties. The Court instead referred the injured parties to the Member States, their national courts and the diverse domestic laws of governmental liability. With a view to setting broad limits for the direct applicability of directives, the concept of the 'State' was understood in a broad sense, covering every State-controlled undertaking.[403] The results remained less satisfying.[404] Thus, it came as no surprise that a growing number of law scholars and practitioners opposed this restrictive policy of the Court. Two avenues to more effective protection for private parties in case of breach of EU law by non-transposition of directives by Member States were considered. One aimed, without success so far, at doing away with the *Marshall* doctrine of no horizontal direct effect of directives,[405] at least as far as protective rules were concerned.[406] The other finally led to the pragmatic compromises of two '*no horizontal direct effect but*' answers – the new *Francovich* type of Member States' liability, and the obligation on all Member States institutions to apply EU law by way of interpretation (so-called horizontal indirect effect): *Marleasing* and beyond.[407]

I. *Francovich and Bonifaci*

177. A. Francovich, D. Bonifaci and Others was an Italian case of male and female workers whose employer companies went bankrupt and became unable to pay wages to their employees.[408] The Community had passed in 1980 the Directive 80/987/EEC on the protection of employees in case of insolvency of the employer, containing a payment guarantee of wages of the last three months. The directive was to be implemented by the Member States till October 1983.[409] Towards the end of the 1980s, Italy had not yet transposed the directive in its domestic law. This led to a condemnation of Italy in a Treaty infringement procedure.[410] Mr *Francovich*, Ms *Bonifaci* and others sued the Italian State as supposed debtor of the sums guaranteed under the directive for payment and alternatively for compensation. Upon preliminary ruling requests by the Italian lower courts, the case came before the ECJ.

403. Compare Case C-188/89, *Foster and Others* [1990] ECR I-3313.

404. *See* from Case 6/60, *Humblet v. Belgium* [1960] ECR 559 to Case 60/75, *Russo v. AIMA* [1976] ECR 45 to Case 158/80, *Rewe v. Hauptzollamt Kiel* [1981] ECR 1805.

405. *See infra* text and fn. 605.

406. *See, inter alia*, AG Lenz, Opinion, Case C-91/92, *Faccini Dori* [1994] ECR I-3328, para. 54; AG van Gerven, Opinion, Case C-271/91, *Marshall No. 2* [1993] ECR I-4367, para. 12; AG Jacobs, Opinion, Case C-316/93, *Vaneetveld* [1994] ECR I-763, paras 15 et seq.

407. *See infra* text and fn. 612.

408. Joined Cases C-6 and 9/90, *A. Francovich, D. Bonifaci and Others v. Italy* [1991] ECR I-5403.

409. Directive 80/987/EEC on the approximation of the laws of the Member States relating to the protection of employees in the event of the insolvency of the employer, OJ 1980 L 283/23.

410. Case 22/87, *Commission v. Italy* [1989] ECR 143.

178. The Court first stated, consistently with its previous case law, that a non-transposed directive can exercise vertical direct effect against a Member State. Being sufficiently clear and unconditional with regard to the beneficiaries and to the content of the guarantee, the Directive 80/987/EEC gave no indication as to the institution which should assume the guarantee. This exempted *Francovich* et al. from the right to rely on the Directive 80/987/EEC against Italy before the national courts. The Court then took up the issue whether and how the Italian State 'as tortfeasor' could be made responsible for depriving its residents from a right conferred to them through a directive, unlawfully not transposed by the State. The Court considered the issue in the light of the general legal system of the Treaty and its fundamental principles. It ruled:

> The full effectiveness of Community rules would be impaired and the protection of the rights which they grant would be weakened if individuals were unable to obtain redress when their rights are infringed by a breach of Community law for which a Member State can be held responsible. The possibility of obtaining redress from the Member State is particularly indispensable where, as in this case, the full effectiveness of Union rules is subject to prior action on the part of the Member State and where, consequently, in the absence of such action, individuals cannot enforce before the national courts the rights conferred upon them by Community law.
> It follows that the principle whereby a State must be liable for loss and damage caused to individuals as a result of breaches of Community law for which the State can be held responsible is inherent in the system of the Treaty.[411]

179. A parallel case was *Wagner Miret*, where the Spanish authorities failed to implement the Directive 80/987/EEC concerning higher management staff.[412]

II. Consequences

180. AG *Mischo* made the proposal to transfer the established principles of the breach-of-law liability of the Union (Article 340(2)) to these cases of non-transposition of directives by Member States:

> In any event, the Court can thus hold that failure to implement a directive or its incorrect implementation constitutes an unlawful act which can give rise to liability on the part of the State if all other conditions [i.e. damage, causal link] are met.[413]

181. The Court hesitated to transpose the EU liability regime of Article 340(2) TFEU on this case scenario. Instead, it developed a supposedly new type of public liability, arguably *inherent* in the system of EU law, for Member States that violate

411. *Francovich*, paras 33–35.
412. Case C-334/92, *Theodoro Wagner Miret v. Fondo de garantia salarial* [1993] ECR I-6911.
413. Compare AG Mischo, Opinion, *Francovich*, ECR I-5371, para. 76.

their duty from Article 288(3) TFEU. This new EU *State liability regime* (type II) requires four conditions to be fulfilled:[414]

(i) Non-transposition of a directive within the prescribed time period. That is a clear-cut case of *plain breach* of EU law. State liability ensues automatically.[415] The discretion of the Member States is limited to the choice of means by which they intend to achieve the result required by the directive.
(ii) Conferral of rights on private parties by the directive in an unconditional and precise manner.
(iii) The beneficial private party must incur damage.
(iv) There must be a causal link between the breach and the damage sustained by the private party.

182. The situation can, however, be different when a directive has been transposed in due time but *incorrectly*. This distinction has been made by the Court in the case of *British Telecommunications*.[416] The United Kingdom had interpreted the Council Directive 90/531/EEC erroneously and hence implemented it improperly. Here, a serious breach may have to be established to trigger liability. Of special importance will be the degree of clarity and precision of the directive provisions.[417] This must normally be done by the national court taking into account all relevant circumstances of the case, in particular the 'factors' provided by the *Brasserie* judgment.[418]

183. The *Francovich* type of liability has its ground emphatically in the multilevel governance system of the Union, but it must be enforced before national courts in the framework of the domestic law of delict/torts. The various national laws on damages must not be less favourable than those relating to similar domestic claims and must not be so framed as to make it in practice impossible or excessively difficult to obtain compensation. In other words: The national law has to meet the conditions of equivalence and effectiveness.[419] Common law jurists analysed the '*Francovich* turn' of the Court as a principal move from an approach based on rights

414. *Francovich*, Judgment, paras 39, 40.
415. Confirmed, *inter alia*, by Joined Cases C-46 and 48/93, *Brasserie du pêcheur and Factortame III* [1996] ECR I-1131, para. 46; Joined Cases C-178, 179, 188–190/94, *Dillenkofer*, [1996] ECR I-4845, para. 29; Case C-319/96, *Brinkmann* [1998] ECR I-5255, para. 28.
416. Case C-392/93, *The Queen v. H.M. Treasury, ex p British Telecommunications* [1996] ECR I-1631 (no sufficiently serious breach). *See also* Case C-319/96, *Brinkmann Tabakfabriken GmbH v. Skatteministeriet* [1998] ECR I-5255 (no sufficiently serious breach) and Case C-140/97, *Rechberger and Others v. Austria* [1999] ECR I-3499 (question of seriousness left unanswered).
417. *See* already Joint Cases 106-120/87, *Asteris and Others v. Greece (Asteris II)* [1988] ECR 5515, para. 18.
418. *See infra* text and fn. 491.
419. *Francovich*, para. 43, following the line of the *Rewe* and *Comet* judgments of the 1970s (fn. 58). *See also*, *inter alia*, Case C-127/95, *Norbrook Laboratories v. Ministry of Agriculture, Fisheries and Food* [1998] ECR I-1531 (veterinary medicinal products).

to an approach based on remedies and welcomed the overdue adoption of the principle '*ubi ius, ibi remedium*' by EU law.[420]

184. Still today one can imagine that this judgment was quite a challenge to the community of lawyers in Europe, who were primarily trained in domestic law and mostly conservative by nature. Notwithstanding this, the ECJ unperturbedly oriented itself according to the core principles of EU law – supremacy and full effectiveness – and came back with an additional damages remedy to enhance the implementation of directives, alongside the right of the Commission to enforce Member States' obligations by Treaty infringement procedures.[421] The latter procedures, cumbersome by nature, were less helpful for the aggravated parties. They merely result in a declaratory judgment, and even the threat of pecuniary penalties does not guarantee compliance. In addition, public enforcement by other Member States under Article 259 TFEU is virtually never used.[422]

185. The *Francovich* line has been affirmed in follow-up decisions.[423] Nowadays, it is indeed a broadly acknowledged, 'inherent' element of EU law, which in the meantime is commonly, though incorrectly, used synonymously for Member State liability.

It has also been adopted by the EFTA Court of Justice for the EEA in a comparable case where an employee, after her employer had gone bankrupt, sued the State for damages alleging that Iceland had improperly implemented the Directive 80/987/EEC.[424]

§3. State Liability III: State Protective Duty

186. The Member States are bound by EU law to prevent breaches of effective protective provisions, regardless of whether they are committed by legislative or administrative measures[425] of its own public institutions, or by acts or omissions of *private parties*: individuals, businesses or other organizations, e.g., trade unions, NGOs, etc. The former are the vertical direct effect cases with damages actions brought against the Member State or any of its emanations, discussed *supra* in the text. – The latter are cases of breach of a State's affirmative duty to protect the functioning of the Internal Market. It is a principle recognized in international law that States may be responsible for the effects of the wrongful conduct of private parties

420. *See*, *inter alia*, T. Tridimas, *General Principles of EU Law*, 498 et seq. (OUP 2005); Tridimas, *Liability for Breach of Community Law* (2001) 38 CML Rev 301.
421. Articles 258, 259 TFEU.
422. Compare P. Wenneras, *Sanctions Against Member States under Art. 260 TFEU* (2012) 49 CML Rev 145.
423. Compare Joined Cases C-178, 179, 188, 189 and 190/94, *Dillenkofer and Others v. Germany* [1996] ECR I-4845 (directive on package travel); *see also* Case C-140/97, *W. Rechberger and Others v. Austria* [1999] ECR I-3499.
424. EFTA Court, Case E-9/97, *Sveinbjörnsdóttir v. Iceland* [1998] EFTA-CR 95. Compare also Aalto, *Public Liability in EU Law*, at pp. 66–67 (Hart 2011) with further references.
425. On judicial acts of State courts *see infra* text.

if they failed to take necessary measures to prevent those effects.[426] Prominent candidates to be protected against infringements by private parties are again the economic fundamental freedoms: free movement of goods, persons, services, capital (Articles 28 (30, 34), 35, 45 (56) and 63 TFEU),[427] and (as fifth freedom) the free movement of data.[428] The ECJ acknowledged a protective duty of a Member State against the detrimental effects of the wrongful conduct of private parties for the first time in *Commission v. France*. This supposedly plain legal situation turns complex when the Member State is simultaneously confronted with competing imperatives of equal importance as the economic freedoms. These imperatives are the fundamental rights of residents enshrined in national constitutions, in the ECHR and, since 2009, in the ChFR. The leading case in which the Court was confronted with the balancing of these two competing constitutional demands by Member States' authorities is *Schmidberger*.

I. *Commission* v. *France*

187. The story of an EU State protective duty began with the case *Commission v. France* in the so-called strawberry war.[429] For more than a decade, the Commission received complaints concerning the passivity of French authorities in face of violent acts committed by individuals and by protest movements of French farmers directed against agricultural products from other Member States. Those acts consist, *inter alia*, in the interception of trucks transporting such products in France and the destruction of their loads, violence against truck drivers, threats against French supermarkets selling agricultural products originating in other Member States. In 1993, the campaign was directed particularly at strawberries from Spain and tomatoes from Belgium. Though the French Government stressed to have adopted measures to combat the violence, these acts of vandalism continued in the subsequent years. The Commission finally filed a claim for declaration that France did not fulfil its obligations under the common organization of the markets in agricultural products and Article 34 TFEU. The Court, in plenary session, upheld the claim. It ruled:

> It is for the Member State concerned, unless it can show that action on its part would have consequences for public order with which it could not cope by using the means at its disposal, to adopt all appropriate measures to guarantee the full scope and effect of Union law so as to ensure its proper implementation in the interests of all economic operators. ...

---

426. Compare Draft Articles on Responsibility of States for Internationally Wrongful Acts, Yearbook of the International Law Commission, 2001 vol. II, Part Two (chap. ii). *See* in greater detail, J. Crawford, *The International Law Commission's Articles on State Responsibility* (CUP 2002); Crawford, *State Responsibility* (CUP 2014).
427. Compare C. Barnard, *The Substantive Law of the EU – The Four Freedoms* (OUP 2013).
428. Directive 95/46/EC on the protection of individuals with regard to the processing of personal data and on the free movement of such data, OJ 1995 L 281/31; replaced by the Data Protection Regulation (EU) 2016/679, OJ 2016 L 119/1. *See infra* text (Part VIII, Ch. 3).
429. Case C-265/95, *Commission v. France* [1997] ECR I-6959.

> Moreover, although it is not impossible that the threat of serious disruption to public order may, in appropriate cases, justify non-intervention by the police, that argument can, on any view, be put forward only with respect to a *specific incident* and not, as in this case, in a general way covering all the incidents [within more than 10 years].[430]

188. One outcome of this judgment was the adoption of a Council regulation providing, *inter alia*, that where serious disruption to the free movement of goods occurs in a Member State, the Member State concerned shall take all necessary and proportionate measures so that the free movement of goods is assured.[431]

The 'specific incident', mentioned in *Commission v. France*, came up in the case of *Schmidberger*.

II. *Schmidberger*

189. *Schmidberger* was a German transport undertaking operating various heavy goods vehicles. Its main activity was the transport of timber from Germany to Italy and steel from Italy to Germany. Its vehicles used the *Brenner Autobahn* as sole transit route from Germany to Italy and vice versa. From 11:00, Friday, 12 June 1998, to 15:00, Saturday, 13 June 1998, a demonstration was held on the Austrian side of the *Brenner Autobahn*. It was organized by an association 'to protect the biosphere in the Alpine region'. Its objective was to draw attention to the threat to the environment and public health posed by the constant increase in the movement of heavy goods vehicles on the *Brenner Autobahn*. This demonstration had been announced in due time to the regional authorities which decided to tolerate it. The demonstration resulted in the *Autobahn* being closed in this Austrian section to all traffic for thirty hours. *Schmidberger* could not operate its trucks for four consecutive days. It claimed an infringement of the EU law's right to free movement and transport of goods by the decision of the Austrian authorities not to ban the demonstration. It sued the Republic of Austria for damages, *inter alia*, for loss of profit.[432] Austria contended that the demonstration, limited in duration, was justified by the protesters' freedoms of expression and assembly.

190. On reference for preliminary ruling, the Court, in plenary session, stated that the specific aims of the demonstration are not in themselves material in legal procedures which seek to establish the *liability of a Member State* in respect of an alleged breach of Union law. This liability is to be inferred exclusively from the fact that *the national authorities* did not prevent an obstacle to transit traffic from being

430. Paragraphs 56 and 58.

431. Regulation (EC) 267/98 on the functioning of the internal market in relation to the free movement of goods among the Member States, OJ 1998 L 337/8.

432. Case C-112/00, *Eugen Schmidberger, Internationale Transporte und Planzüge v. Austria* [2003] ECR I-5659; *see also* Case C-36/02, *Omega Spielhallen- und Automatenaufstellungs-GmbH v. Oberbürgermeisterin von Bonn* [2004] ECR I-9609; Case C-244/06 *Dynamic Medien Vertriebs-GmbH v. Avides Media* [2008] ECR I-505.

placed on the *Brenner Autobahn*.[433] For the Austrian authorities, the case brought up the need to reconcile the requirements of the protection of a fundamental economic freedom enshrined in the Treaty on the one hand, with the respective freedom of expression and assembly enshrined in general principles of EU law (now Articles 11 and 12 ChFR), in Articles 10 and 11 ECHR and in the national Constitution on the other. The Court circumscribed this balancing:

> *First, whilst the free movement of goods constitutes one of the fundamental principles in the scheme of the Treaty, it may, in certain circumstances, be subject to restrictions for reason laid down in Art. 36 TFEU or for overriding requirements relating to public interest.*
> *Second, whilst the fundamental rights at issue ... are expressly recognised by the ECHR and constitute fundamental pillars of a democratic society, it nevertheless follows from the express wording of paragraph 2 of the Articles 10 and 11 ECHR that freedom of expression and freedom of assembly are also subject to certain limitations justified by objectives in the public interest, in so far as those derogations are in accordance with the law, motivated by one or more of the legitimate aims under those provisions and necessary in a democratic society.*
> *In those circumstances, the interests involved must be weighed having regard to all circumstances of the case in order to determine whether a fair balance was struck between those interests.*[434]

191. Having clarified the necessary approach, the Court finally accepted the balance struck by the Austrian authorities in this case. Hence, their decision not to ban the demonstration was not incompatible with Articles 34 and 35 TFEU.

§4. State Liability IV: Judicial Bodies of Last Instance

192. Established fields of Member State liability were legislative and administrative wrongs. A remarkable extension of the scope of liability for breach of directly effective EU law was brought about by the *Köbler* judgment. Though in the landmark *Brasserie* judgment of 1996 the Court had clarified that the principles of Member States liability for breach of EU law apply, 'whatever be the organ of the Member State whose act was responsible for the breach',[435] it was not without surprise, that with *Köbler*, for the first time, a Member State faced the risk of incurring liability for breach of EU law by a ruling of one of its courts of last instance.[436]

---

433. *Schmidberger*, para. 66.
434. Paragraphs 78, 79 and 81.
435. Joined Cases C-46 and 48/93, *Brasserie du pêcheur and Factortame III* [1996] ECR I-1131, para. 32; *see infra* text. After *Brasserie*, the issue of State liability for the judiciary was discussed by H. Toner, *Thinking the Unthinkable? State Liability for Judicial Acts* (1997) 17 YEL 165; G. Anagnostaros, *The Principle of State Liability for Judicial Breaches* (2001) 7 EPL 281.
436. Case C-224/01, *Gerhard Köbler v. Austria* [2003] ECR I-10239.

I. *Köbler*

193. Mr *Köbler*, a German national, had been a law professor at the University of Innsbruck, Austria, since 1986. In 1996, he applied for a length-of-service increment that was under Austrian law available to professors who had worked for at least fifteen years in Austrian universities. However, work done in universities of other Member States was not taken into account, and his request was denied by the Austrian authorities. Mr *Köbler* claimed a violation of the freedom of movement for employees (Article 45 TFEU). His claim was in the last instance dismissed by the Supreme Administrative Court of Austria. Mr *Köbler* then sued the Republic of Austria before the civil courts (*Landesgericht für Zivilrechtssachen Wien*) for damages.

194. On reference for a preliminary ruling, the ECJ first stated that the general principles on liability for breach of EU law also apply when the breach stems from a decision of a national court of last instance. Exempting these national judicial bodies from liability would call into question the full effectiveness of the provisions of EU law. The Court then specified the conditions for a relevant breach under these circumstances. In order to safeguard the authority of *res iudicata* of final decisions and thus the stability of law, Member State liability for a judicial decision can be incurred only in the exceptional case where the court has *manifestly* infringed directly effective EU law. In order to assess a manifest breach, the following factors have, *inter alia*, to be taken into account, 'the degree of clarity and precision of the rule infringed, whether the infringement was intentional, whether the error of law was excusable or inexcusable, … , non-compliance by the court with its obligation to make a reference for a preliminary ruling under Article 267 TFEU'.[437] In essence, these are the '*Brasserie* factors', listed in the *Brasserie du pêcheur* judgment to non-exhaustively define circumstances constituting a sufficiently serious breach by legislative acts.[438]

195. The judgment left behind mixed feelings. It is again one of those notorious triumphs of EU law but hollow victories for the claimants. The Court finally found an infringement of EU law but denied a *manifest* breach (in contrast to the Opinion of AG *Léger*[439]). After seven years of legal proceedings, Mr *Köbler* won his case but received neither damages nor the length-of-service allowance he applied for. Instead, other persons in a similar position would be able to benefit from the judgment.

The message unequivocally submitted is that Member States are responsible for manifest breach of directly effective EU law by decisions of their judicial bodies of last instance. This corresponds to the settled case law since *Brasserie*. In the literature four possible case scenarios for manifest breach by courts of last instance are listed: (a) where the national court fails to apply a clear and precise provision of EU

437. Case C-224/01, *Köbler*, para. 55. The last factor hints at the circumstance that the Austrian Supreme Administrative Court itself had already referred for preliminary ruling to the ECJ, but then misunderstood a notice of the Court and withdrew the reference.

438. *See* on this in greater detail *infra* text and fn. 501.

439. AG Léger, Opinion, *Köbler*, ECR I-10243.

law; (b) where it fails to abide by well-established ECJ case law; (c) where it refuses to make an obviously indicated reference for preliminary ruling; and (d) where it makes a reference but commits a flagrant error in applying the ruling of the ECJ.[440]

196. Another aspect has to be taken up. Among the criteria which supposedly constitute the manifestness of the breach, the Court took the ambiguous categories of personal fault among the '*Brasserie* factors' too seriously[441] and got on a wrong track. *Köbler* is *not* a case of individual responsibility of judges for a tort, but of State liability for gross malfunctioning of the institution judiciary (judicial bodies of last instance). The judiciary is more or less treated on the same footing as the other institutional organs of the State – legislature and executive. The wrong path towards personal tort liability is supported by another deficit in the multi-level governance structure. Most Member States' law of non-contractual public liability is conceptually not yet prepared for such an institutional breach-of-law liability approach. National State liability remained until recently attached to traditional vicarious liability, namely responsibility for individual torts of public servants, including judges. Both led to inconsistencies which came up again in the case of *Traghetti*.

II. *Traghetti*[442]

197. Traghetti del Mediterraneo SpA was an Italian maritime transport company in bankruptcy. It contended that the Italian *Corte di cassazione* had wrongly interpreted provisions of EU competition law when it dismissed *Traghetti's* damages claim against a competitor company. *Traghetti* sued the Italian State for compensation. Italian law restricts the (individual) responsibility of judges for damage caused in the exercise of their function to cases of intent and gross negligence/ serious misconduct,[443] as do the laws of most EU Member States.[444]

198. Traghetti is again a case of a Member State's liability for a decision of a court of last instance. The ECJ was asked to clarify the boundaries of the autonomy of domestic law in incidents of breach of EU law; that is, to what extent do the restrictions of the responsibility of judges in Italian law prevail. The Court held that the primacy of EU law precludes national legislation that limits State liability for judicial wrongs to cases of intentional fault or serious misconduct. The legitimate

440. Confirmed in Case C-168/15, *M. Tomášová v. Slovenská republika* EU:C:2016:602. *See also* Tridimas, *General Principles* 526 (OUP 2005).
441. Differently AG Léger, Opinion, *Köbler*, ECR I-10243, para. 154: 'I take the view that it is neither necessary nor appropriate to pay particular attention to the factor whether the breach of EU law was intentional or involuntary.'
442. Case C-173/03, *Traghetti del Mediterraneo v. Italy* [2006] ECR I-5177.
443. Law 117/88, Risarcimento dei danni cagionati nell'esercizio delle funzioni giudiziarie e responsabilità civile dei magistrate, Italian OJ 1988, n. 88.
444. *See*, e.g., § 839(2)(i) German BGB.

interest of Member States to privilege the position of courts of last instance had been acknowledged by the Court when requiring a *manifest* breach of EU law.[445]

199. But do the national rules on immunities for judges impede the application of superior EU law in a *Köbler*- and *Traghetti*-like case scenario? To cope with this question, another important aspect needs to be recalled. In cases of state responsibility for decisions of judicial bodies of the last instance, again the two clearly distinct types of *vicarious liability for torts* and *breach-of-law liability* of institutions with their different standards have to be distinguished:

> *The latter requires objective and grave inappropriateness of institutional processes and their outcomes (gross mal-jurisdiction). For Member State liability under EU law, it is the institution 'national court of last instance' and its defective outcome which is in the focus – not the individual judges who sat in the deciding chamber. Time to recall the definition of faute de service by G. Teissier of 1906: 'C'est le service public, c'est la machine gouvernementale ou administrative elle-même qui, … , est la cause du dommage.'*[446] *Neither judges nor courts are sued. The State is the defendant, represented by its executive, the government. In this regard, the situation is similar to the one under the international law of the European Convention of Human Rights. In several cases, the ECtHR in Strasbourg made a Contracting State responsible for an infringement of a fundamental right by its courts of last instance.*[447] *It ordered payment of just satisfaction without raising any question of personal responsibility (grades of fault) of the judges concerned. It is a non-issue.*
> *The former – vicarious liability for torts – requires personal fault for the responsibility of individual judges under national law, leading to vicarious liability of the State.*

200. This structural difference was seriously neglected by the *Traghetti* judgment. This failure was increased when the Commission in the sequel of *Traghetti* brought an action asking the Court to order Italy to readjust its law of immunities so that it would cope with the EU breach-of-law liability standards; and it was even exceeded when, after all, this action has been upheld by the ECJ.[448] *There was and still is no need for any readjustment.* The Italian Republic like any other Member State may face liability if its courts of last instance manifestly infringe EU rules. The ground for this State liability to arise is EU law! Article 4(3) TEU contains obligations of the Member States and its institutions to cooperate sincerely. This liability has then to be fleshed out under national law. The respective national substantive and procedural law has to secure equivalence and effectiveness. This is valid law

---

445. Case C-173/03, *Traghetti*, para. 42, with reference to Case C-224/01 (*Köbler*).
446. G. Teissier, *La responsabilité des pouvoirs publics* 49 (1906) (compare fn 349).
447. Compare ECtHR, 26 Apr. 1979, *Sunday Times v. UK* 2 EHRR 245; 21 Mar. 2000, *Dulaurans v. France* 33 EHRR 1093; 24 Jun. 2004, *von Hannover v. Germany I* 40 EHRR 1. – In *Köbler*, the ECJ expressly referred to this jurisdiction of the ECtHR to support its reasoning. *See* Case C-224/01, *Köbler*, para. 49.
448. Case C-379/10, *Commission v. Italy* EU:C:2011:775.

since *Köbler*.[449] Evidence that the Italian law of governmental liability might not meet these conditions has not been adduced.[450]

201. By no means does this have implications on the *personal responsibility* of judges when they decide legal cases *under national law*. Judges of the 'CJEU' are immune from any legal proceedings.[451] Judges of the national courts of the Member States are *in their personal capacity* only liable under similar conditions as they are exemplarily provided for in the Italian law of 1988, that is, e.g., only for intentional breach of law in German law[452] and for intentional and gross negligent conduct in Austrian law.[453] Their individual liability is then mostly absorbed vicariously (and exclusively) by the Member State.

202. Personal liability of judges under national law and Member States' breach-of-law liability for their judicial bodies of last instance under EU law are separate and different subjects. They are not mutually exclusive; they coexist next to one another. – A realignment of national law, however, is indicated when its provision expressly excludes any liability for decisions of national courts of last instance. Austria, e.g., bars explicitly any claim for compensation resulting from judgments of its judicial bodies of last instance, i.e., the Austrian Constitutional Court, Supreme Court of Justice and Supreme Administrative Court.[454] *Köbler*-like damages actions against the Republic of Austria for breach of EU law by judgments of its Supreme Courts are to be heard and determined by the Constitutional Court.[455]

§5. State Vicarious Liability: Breach of EU Law by Public Servants?

203. Can Member States' officials themselves commit a breach of EU law by their concrete activities and thus trigger vicarious liability of the respective public law body as well as of the Member State? This question was explicitly raised in the reference for preliminary ruling by the Regional Court Düsseldorf in the *Haim* case.[456] The Court ignored this aspect of the referred questions completely. It contended itself with stating that independent public law bodies can be individually

449. *See supra* text and fn. 436.
450. Compare Tribunale di Roma, 28 Jun. 2001, Giurisprudenza di merito 2002, 360: State liability for breach of EU law by the Corte di cassazione. On this in greater detail, *see* G. Comandé & L. Nocco, *Italy*, in *The Liability of Public Authorities in Comparative Perspective* 251 (K. Oliphant ed., Intersentia 2016).
451. Compare Art. 3(1) of the Protocol on the Statute of the Court of Justice of the EU.
452. §839(2)(i) BGB.
453. §3(1) Amtshaftungsgesetz (Act on liability of public authorities), Austrian Federal Law Gazette I No. 122/2013.
454. §2(3) Amtshaftungsgesetz.
455. Article 137 Act on the Federal Constitution. Compare B.A. Koch, *Austria*, in *The Liability of Public Authorities in Comparative Perspective* 19, at 44 (K. Oliphant ed. Intersentia 2016).
456. C-424/97, *S. Haim v. Kassenzahnärztliche Vereinigung Nordrhein (Haim II)* [2000] ECR I-5148, para. 24.

liable in addition to the Member State itself. In the Finnish case of *A.G.M.-COS.MET.*[457] the Court was again confronted with this complex legal problem and this time again the Court refused to give this problem serious thought.

I. Case Scenario of *A.G.M.-COS.MET.*

204. Mr *Lehtinen*, an expert official of the Finnish Ministry of Social Affairs and Health, uttered in public media statements that the vehicle lifts, manufactured by the Italian company *A.G.M*, were unsafe and dangerous in specific situations, even though the lifts had been certified as compliant with the applicable Directive 98/37 EC on machinery safety and given the CE marking of conformity.[458] The Directive 98/37/EC is one of the product safety directives under the 'New Approach to technical harmonization',[459] which provides that Member States shall not prohibit, restrict, or impede the marketing of products which presumably comply with the EU health and safety requirements. The Finnish Government had taken no official measures. It stressed that Mr *Lehtinen* acted deliberately and contrary to his Ministry's official position and that the Ministry made this clear to the public. The official argued that his statements were covered by his right to freedom of expression. *A.G.M.* sued the Finnish State and Mr *Lehtinen* jointly and severally for compensation of loss of profits allegedly suffered in Finland and elsewhere in Europe.

205. At first regard, it looks like a clear-cut domestic case under Finnish State liability law. But the right to free movement of goods (Article 28(1) TFEU) has a vertical direct effect. The Italian manufacturer *A.G.M.* claims to be infringed in its economic freedom by the statements of Mr *Lehtinen* acting as an official of the Finnish State. This case 'raises questions concerning principally the liability of a State for acts of its officials', stated AG *Kokott* in her Opinion.[460] That means the liability of the Finnish State in this case is grounded on principles of EU liability law, as they were developed in the ECJ case law. Herein are the intricacies of this case: It combines both pillars of Union liability under Article 340(2) TFEU – vicarious liability and breach-of-law liability – in a Member State liability scenario. Thus,

457. C-470/03, *A.G.M.-COS.MET Srl v. Suomen valtio and T. Lehtinen* [2007] ECR I-2798. *See* N. Reich, *A.G.M.-COS.MET, or: Who Is Protected by EC Safety Regulation* (2008) EL Rev 85; S. de Vries, *Case Annotation* (2008) 45 CMLRev 569.

458. Directive 98/37/EC on the approximation of the laws of the Member States relating to machinery, OJ 1998 L 207/1 (amended 2006).

459. The 'New Approach' was set out in Council Resolution of May 1985 laying down a new approach to technical harmonization and standards, OJ 1985 C 136/1; complemented in 1989 by the 'global approach to conformity assessment', OJ 1990 C 10/1. *See* on this in greater detail the website 'New Approach Standardization in the Internal Market'.

460. AG Kokott, Opinion, *A.G.M.-COS.MET* [2007] ECR I-2753, para. 1. Her opinion remained not free of contradictions. On the one hand: 'In any event, Union law does not impose liability on national officials' (para. 49); on the other hand: 'Whether Union law requires or permits liability to be imposed on national public officials is a question that requires an interpretation of substantive Union law' (para. 53).

A.G.M.-COS.MET is a State vicarious liability case for breach of EU law by an individual public servant.[461]

II. Critique of the ECJ Judgment

206. On the basis of the foregoing, one would expect that the Court proceeds correctly and scrutinizes whether Mr *Lehtinen* committed with his 'single-handed' public statements a tort towards *A.G.M.*, i.e., an unjustified infringement of the latter's right to free movement of its products, for which the Finnish State would then be vicariously responsible. This would imply a thorough legal analysis of Mr *Lehtinen's* conduct. As a State official, on the one hand, he is addressee of vertical direct effect (doctrine of indivisibility of the State). On the other hand, (Union or State) officials enjoy freedom of expression under EU law, even in areas falling within the scope of the activities of their institution and regardless of whether the expression in question dissents from or conflicts with opinions held by the employing institution.[462] This freedom of opinion would then have to be weighed and fairly balanced with *A.G.M.*'s freedom to market its products throughout the EEA. In cases of statements of facts, the plain proof of truth may in principle exonerate. If evidence for lack of safety had been shown, an *illegal* infringement of *A.G.M.*'s right to pursue its business may not have existed. However, duties of confidentiality and loyalty may then have stood in the way. Lack of safety proven or not, Mr *Lehtinen* may lastly resort to a right to 'protected disclosure' established by his freedom of expression.[463] These aspects will be taken up in greater detail *infra* the text in the section on conflicting fundamental freedoms and fundamental rights.

207. The Court had ignored all this. Its reasoning was quite straightforward but thoroughly narrowed down to EU product safety law.[464]

(a) The EU wants products benefitting from the free movement of goods in the EEA to fulfil requirements providing a high level of protection of public interests such as health and safety in general, while ensuring that the free movement of products is not restricted to any greater extent than that which is allowed under EU harmonization legislation. The *A.G.M.* vehicle lifts in question bore the 'CE' marking of conformity. Hence, they were presumed to comply with the health and safety

---

461. Brüggemeier, *EU Product Safety Law, Whistleblowers, and Member State Liability for Acts of Officials* (2015) 2 EJCL 212.

462. Article 11 ChFR: compare ECJ, C-274/99 P, *Connolly v. Commission* [2001] ECR I-1611, para. 43. Art. 10 ECHR: *see* ECtHR, 26 Feb. 2009, *Kudeshkina v. Russia (No 1)* hoduc (2009); 26 Sep. 1995, *Vogt v. Germany* A 323 (1995); 21 EHRR 205.

463. That is the so-called legitimate whistle-blowing. Compare Parliamentary Assembly of the Council of Europe, Resolution 1729 (2010) 'On the protection of "whistleblowers"'. *See also* ECtHR, 21.7.2011, *Heinisch v. Germany* hoduc (2011), and *infra* text.

464. Compare, *inter alia*, Hodges, *European Regulation of Consumer Product Safety* (OUP 2005); Falke & Schepel, *Legal Aspects of Standardisation in the Member States* (Luxembourg 2000).

requirements of the Directive 98/37/EEC on safety of machinery[465] and the respective EN standard. This presumption is refutable, but only under the formal conditions laid down in the Directive. Member States must initiate a safeguard clause procedure according to Article 7(1) Directive, which means that Member States are required to take all appropriate measures to withdraw machinery from the market if their competent authorities ascertain that the machinery in question endangers the safety of persons, domestic animals or property.[466] In such an event, Member States have to inform the Commission immediately of any such measure and indicate the reasons for their decision. Any form of State product warning outside the market supervision procedures provided for by the Directive would constitute a breach of EU law. As the New Approach directives grant third party protection in favour of the manufactures,[467] a claim for State liability would be well-founded.

208. (b) In the case before the Court, State authorities did not intervene. It was an unauthorized, single-handed action of an individual official. No State action, no breach of EU product safety law. Therefore, the ECJ sought to construe a State action. It tried to 'attribute' the statements of the official ('with the authority of his office') to the Finnish State. This changes the focus completely. It is no longer an issue of vicarious liability, i.e., the State absorbing the liability for a wrongful act (tort) of its official. It is now *an act or omission of the State*. The supposed illegality of a State's act becomes subject of judicial scrutiny, that is, whether the State with *its* statements infringes EU law. The settled programme of 'breach-of-law liability' has taken over, and the well-known formulae[468] are applied. As an act of the State, the statements are in breach of EU law because Finland was restricted to take the appropriate measures under the formal conditions laid down in the machinery safety directive.[469]

209. (c) If one follows the Court's questionable path of 'attribution' of Mr *Lehtinen's* statements to the Finnish State, than assumedly three variants of governmental liability exist:

(i) Vicarious liability, where no acts were attributed to the State, but liability for the *tort* of the public servant is absorbed by the State.
(ii) Cases of executive officers, where no acts were attributed, but *torts* of organs are imputed to the States or other incorporated entities as their own wrongs.[470] This is not feasible with acts by officials of lower or lowest level.[471]

---

465. Directive 98/37/EC, OJ 1998 L 207/1.
466. Article 7(1) Directive.
467. Case C-470/03, *A.G.M.-COS.MET*, para. 79.
468. *See* in greater detail *infra* text (next section).
469. So-called safeguard clause procedure. Compare Decision No. 768/2008/EC on a common framework for the marketing of products (and repealing Council Decision 93/465/EEC), OJ 2008 L 218/82. *See also* European Commission, *Vademecum on European Standardization*, Part II, Ch. 6 'Procedure for Formal Objections against Standards'.
470. On this *see supra* text.
471. Compare also AG Kokott, Opinion, Case C-470/03, *A.G.M-COS.MET* [2005] ECR I-2753, para. 79.

(iii) In these cases of non-executive officials, the Court now seems to have introduced a new hybrid form of semi-vicarious liability into EU law without any equivalent in the law of the Member States. That is, the Court attributes the plain act of the official to the State and the question of illegality (and fault) of the act is then answered from the perspective of a State's measure.[472]

210. (d) Also, a presumed analogy to the international law of the European Convention for the Protection of Human Rights and Fundamental Freedoms (ECHR)[473] is less than helpful. Under the ECHR, the Signatory States are responsible for every infringement of human rights committed in their territory by its institutions or officials. But here again, the breach has to be assessed for the institution or the person accused of it. That is, possible restrictions of rights and justifications of infringements provided for under the ECHR have to be taken into account,[474] opposing principles (rights and freedoms) have to be weighed and balanced. It is only the *unjustified* infringement of human rights by its institutions or officials for which the Signatory State is in charge. The hypothetical question whether the act, had it been committed by State authorities, would constitute an infringement is a non-issue in the law of the ECHR and in international law generally.[475]

211. (e) It remains to be recalled that governmental liability law by its basic structure grants only two paths to establish liability of a State, be it the Union or a Member State: for unlawful acts of public institutions (legislation, executive, judiciary) in fulfilling sovereign tasks – and for torts of public servants in performing their official duties. This corresponds to the structure of ex-Article 40 TECSC and Article 340(2) TFEU. As an unlawful act of a Finnish public institution could not be found in this case, the only possibility left was *vicarious liability* for wrongful acts (torts) of public servants. The basic question, however, of whether Mr *Lehtinen* committed a tort towards *A.G.M.* 'in the performance of his official duties' remained unanswered throughout the whole judgment; what is more, it was not even raised. The intricate tort of Mr *Lehtinen* in this case might exist in a *wrongful breach of EU law*. This will be taken up *infra* the text dealing with conflicts of fundamental freedoms and fundamental rights in the context of liability of private parties.

212. *The hybrid third path of semi-vicarious liability*, which the Court invented and sought to pursue in EU product safety law, *does not exist*. The fundamental question whether EU law recognizes a State's vicarious liability for wrongful breach of EU law by Member States' officials remained unanswered.

---

472. It is obvious that the State does not enjoy a right to freedom of expression. Compare *A.G.M-COS.MET*, paras 72 and 73.

473. Compare the Report by the European Commission of Human Rights of 25 Jan. 1976, quoted by AG Kokott, Opinion, *A.G.M.-COS.MET*, para. 85, fn. 33.

474. Compare Art. 10(2) ECHR.

475. Compare J. Crawford, *State Responsibility* (CUP 2014); *The Law of International Responsibility* (J. Crawford, A. Pellet et al. eds, OUP 2010).

Chapter 2. Once More on Causation: *Brinkmann* and *Leth*

213. Breach of EU law by the Member State must cause the purported loss or damage. The general principles of causation apply.[476] The onus of proof falls on the plaintiff. Interesting questions of causation were raised in the cases of *Brinkmann* and *Leth*.

214. *Brinkmann* was a German manufacturer of cigarette tobacco.[477] Next to regular cigarettes, it pressed tobacco into rolls which were enveloped in porous cellulose and packed into packets like normal cigarettes. These rolls still had to be wrapped into cigarette paper before they could be smoked. *Brinkmann* exported these rolls, *inter alia*, to Denmark. The dispute arose of whether they were to be taxed at the higher rate of cigarettes or at the lower rate of smoking tobacco. In Germany, the rolls were taxed as smoking tobacco; in Denmark, the authorities taxed them as cigarettes. The EU had passed a directive dealing with taxation of manufactured tobacco.[478] *Brinkmann* contended that the rolls had to be classified and taxed as smoking tobacco. It sued the Danish authorities for compensation of the unduly paid taxes and for breach of EU law because Denmark had not implemented the Directive 79/32/EEC.

215. On preliminary ruling before the ECJ, the Court made clear that under the taxation directive the rolls have to be classified as smoking tobacco. Thus, at first sight, there was a plain breach of EU law – non-transposition of a directive – which caused concrete loss to the plaintiff.

At second regard, however, things looked differently. Notwithstanding the non-transposition into domestic law, the Danish authorities had applied the respective provisions of the directive. Therefore, the plain breach through formal non-implementation could not any longer be considered the cause of the loss. But whilst applying the directive, the authorities interpreted the provisions incorrectly. It is now the improper application of the not transformed directive which seems to have caused the purported loss. A supposed question of causation turned out to be a problem of breach of law. Does this comportment of the Danish authorities constitute a relevant breach? The answer of the Court was in the negative: The interpretation given by the Danish authorities to the relevant definitions was not *manifestly* contrary to the wording or to the aim pursued by the directive.[479] This ruling is in line with the case law to incorrectly implemented directives (*British Telecommunications*).[480]

---

476. *See supra* text.
477. C-319/96, *Brinkmann Tabakfabriken v. Skatteministeriet* [1998] ECR I-5255.
478. Directive 79/32/EEC on taxes other than turnover taxes which affect the consumption of manufactured tobacco, OJ 1979 L 10/8.
479. C-319/96, *Brinkmann*, para. 31.
480. Compare *supra* text and fn 416.

216. In the Austrian case of *Leth*, it was the other way around. Normative questions of breach of law and infringement of rights displaced the aspect of causation.[481] Ms *Leth* lived in the vicinity of the Vienna-*Schwechat* airport. The Austrian authorities had completed several projects relating to the extension of the airport. However, no environmental impact assessments, as prescribed by Directive 85/337/EEC,[482] had been carried out. Ms *Leth* sued the Austrian State and the regional authorities for compensation of the decrease in the value of her property. The ECJ ruled that the directive confers on the public concerned a right to have the effects of the relevant project on the environment assessed and to express their opinion thereon. But the Court struggled with the problem of whether or not the EIA Directive grants an individual right to claim compensation for purely economic loss resulting from environmental effects.[483] Prior to this, the issue of causation should have been addressed. Any action for damages requires a causal link. However, did the breach of law, i.e., the omission of not carrying out an environmental impact assessment, cause the decrease in the value of Ms *Leth's* real estate? The answer can only be in the negative. It is settled law that the EIA Directive does not preclude the implementation of a project even in the case where the environmental impact assessment establishes that there are significant negative effects on the environment.[484] Ms *Leth's* situation would probably not be different if an assessment procedure had been carried out. Her damage is a secondary pecuniary loss resulting from environmental effects (increase of noise) caused by the enlargement of the airport. Responsibility of the Austrian authorities has to be determined under Austria's domestic law of State liability.

481. C-420/11, *J. Leth v. Austria and Land Niederösterreich,* EU:C:2013:166.
482. Directive 85/337/EEC on the assessment of the effects of certain public and private projects on the environment, OJ 1985 L 175/40, as amended.
483. *See supra* text and fn. 346.
484. Compare AG Kokott, Opinion, C-420/11, *Leth,* EU:C:2012:701, para. 42.

Chapter 3. Procedural Autonomy of Member States Law and Its Limits

217. Member States' liability for breach of EU law has to be enforced before national courts. EU primary law does not provide for any overarching enforcement system. It is dependent on the national rules of remedies and procedure. In this regard, Member States were said to possess a 'procedural autonomy'. This national procedural autonomy, however, is limited. It applies as long as the substantive and procedural conditions for reparation of loss and damage laid down by the domestic law are not less favourable than those relating to similar national claims and do not render the exercise of Union rights 'virtually impossible or excessively difficult'.[485] That is, the national rules on remedies and procedure must comply with the *principles of equivalence* and *effectiveness.*[486] Concerned are substantive provisions on cause of actions and remedies, damages and causation, period of limitation, procedural rules on standing to sue, etc.

218. In *Factortame Ltd I*, the Court demonstrated its willingness to force national courts to set aside domestic procedural rules even if the rule in question was based on important policies of the Member State, namely the missing power of courts under English law to issue an injunction against the Crown.[487]

219. But before the enforcement by means of domestic procedural remedies, the principles of EU liability law have to be transferred into national law. The ground of liability, i.e., the criteria of *relevant breach of EU law* – no-fault, institutional fault, gross maladministration – must, via conform interpretation, be incorporated into the respective corpus of national law of governmental liability.

220. N. Reich proposed as a possible general ground for EU breach-of-law liability in the law of delict/torts of the Member States the 'tort' of *breach of a protective statute* (*Schutzgesetzverstoß/ violation des dispositions impératives*).[488] As a genuine EU induced national head of damages for breach-of-law liability law, it must be separated from fault. Hence, it is in principle the illegal legislative, administrative or judicial act that triggers liability. 'Breach of statute' fits quite well for this purpose. Many national laws recognize already *de lege lata* a presumption of

---

485. *See*, *inter alia*, Case 33/76, *Rewe-Zentralfinanz eG and Rewe-Zentral AG v. Landwirtschaftskammer für das Saarland* [1976] ECR 1989, para. 5; Joined Cases C-6/90 and C-9/90, *Francovich and Bonifaci v. Italy* [1991] ECR I-5403, para. 43; and as more recent case law, Case C-432/05 *Unibet (London) Ltd and Unibet (International) Ltd v. Justitiekanslern* [2006] ECR I-2271, para. 61, and Case C-445/06, *Danske Slagterier v. Germany* [2009] ECR I-2119, para. 31.
486. For a case, applying the principle of equivalence, compare C-118/08, *Transportes Urbanos v. Administración del Estado* [2010] ECR I-635. On this in greater detail, *see The European Court of Justice and the Autonomy of Member States* (H.W. Micklitz & B. de Witte eds, Intersentia 2011).
487. Case C-213/89, *The Queen v. Sec'y of State for Transport, ex parte Factortame (Factortame I)*[1990] ECR I-2433. *See also* as English sequel *Factortame Ltd v. Sec'y of State for Transport* [1990] UKHL 7.
488. N. Reich (2007) 44 CML Rev 705, 708 et seq.

fault, rebuttable or non-rebuttable. Even the English law, well known for its aversion for no-fault liability rules in common law, is here open for adaptation.[489] 'If strict liability is rare at common law, it is relatively common by statute.'[490]

The same would hold true, *inter alia*, for heads of pre-contractual liability (*iniuria in contrahendo*).

489. Under traditional UK State liability, the plain illegality of the administrative act 'without more' regularly does not give a cause of action. Compare *Three Rivers District Council v. Bank of England (No 3)* [2000] 2 WLR 1220. 'What more' depends on the specific tort. In greater detail *see* C. Harlow, *State Liability and Beyond* (OUP 2004).
490. T. Weir, *Tort Law* 93 (2d ed., OUP 2006).

Part III. Consolidation of Liability of Union and Member States for Breach of EU Law

221. The development of non-contractual liability for breach of EU law by public authorities of the Union and the Member States entered a new stage with the cases of *Brasserie du pêcheur* and *Hedley Lomas* in 1996, and the case of *Bergaderm* in 2000.

§1. Legislative Acts: *Brasserie du Pecheur* and Factortame III[491]

222. Brasserie du pêcheur SA was an Alsatian brewing company which exported beer to Germany. The German authorities prohibited the further import because the French beer did not meet the German production requirements for beer – the so-called *Reinheitsgebot* (purity requirement). Already in 1987, however, the ECJ had ruled that the application of the *Reinheitsgebot* to impede the import of French beer was an infringement of the right to free movement of goods.[492] This basic economic freedom has vertical direct effect. *Brasserie SA* sued the Federal Republic of Germany for loss of profits.

223. Factortame Ltd was a Spanish fishing company, located in England, which applied for registration of its Spanish ships in the UK to get access to the British fishing quota (so-called quota-hopping). The British authorities on the basis of their domestic law denied registration. In a first preliminary ruling, initiated by the English High Court, the ECJ had decided (*Factortame II*) that the UK, with their 'Registration of Fishing Vessels Regulations' on the basis of the Merchant Shipping Act 1988, violated the freedom of establishment (Article 49 TFEU).[493] Thereupon

491. Joined cases C-46 and 48/93, *Brasserie du pêcheur SA v. Germany/The Queen v. Secretary of State for Transport, ex parte: Factortame Ltd and Others (Factortame III)* [1996] ECR I-1131. As follow-ups *see, inter alia*, Case C-127/95, *Norbrook Laboratories Ltd v. Ministry of Agriculture, Fisheries and Food* [1998] ECR I-1531; Case 352/98 P, *Laboratoires Pharmaceutiques Bergaderm and Goupil v. Commission* [2000] ECR I-5291; Case C-282/05 P, *Holcim (Deutschland) AG v. Commission* [2007] ECR I-2973.

492. Case C-178/84, *Commission v. Germany* [1987] ECR I-1227.

493. Case C-221/89, *The Queen v. Sec'y of State for Transport, ex parte Factortame* (*Factortame II*) [1991] ECR I-3905. – *Factortame I* concerned a procedural aspect. *See supra* text and fn. 487.

Factortame Ltd sued the British government for damages. The English High Court (QBD) referred to the Court for a second preliminary ruling.[494]

224. With the judgment in these joined cases, the ECJ set about the supposedly impossible mission of 'bridging the unbridgeable'.[495] *Brasserie* and *Factortame* were cases of State liability for acts and omissions of national legislature contravening EU law. The Court of Justice tried to harmonize the then three main fields of non-contractual liability of public authorities for legislative wrongs: Union's breach-of-law liability under Article 340(2), Member States' liability I (vertical effect cases), and Member States' liability II (*Francovich*). It summarized the state of the law:

> (t)he condition under which the State may incur liability for damage caused to individuals by a breach of Community law cannot, in the absence of particular justification, differ from those governing the liability of the Community in like circumstances. The protection of rights which individuals derive from Community law cannot vary depending on whether a national authority or a Community authority is responsible for the damage.[496]
>
> …
>
> The strict approach taken towards the liability of the Community in the exercise of its legislative activities is due to two considerations. First, even where the legality of measures is subject to judicial review, exercise of the legislative function must not be hindered by the prospect of actions for damages whenever the general interest of the Community requires legislative measures to be adopted which may adversely affect individual interests. Second, in a legislative context characterized by the exercise of a wide discretion, which is essential for implementing a Community policy, the Community cannot incur liability unless the institution concerned has manifestly and gravely disregarded the limits on the exercise of its powers.[497]
>
> That said, the national legislature – like the Community institutions – does not systematically have a wide discretion when it acts in a field governed by Community law. Community law may impose upon it obligations to achieve a particular result or obligation to act or refrain from acting which reduce its margin of discretion, sometimes to a considerable degree.[498] … Art. 189 TFEU places the Member States under an obligation to take, within a given period, all the measures needed in order to achieve the result required by a directive. In such a case, the fact that it is for the national legislature to take the necessary measures has no bearing on the Member State's liability for failing to transpose the directive.

494. On the *Factortame* case complex, compare D. Vaughan, *Factortame and After: A Fishy Story* (2005) EBLRev 511.
495. W. van Gerven, *Bridging the Unbridgeable: Community and National Tort Laws after Francovich and Brasserie* (1996) 45 ICLQ 507.
496. Joined Cases C-46 and 48/93, *Brasserie*, para. 42.
497. *Brasserie*, para. 45, reference made to *HNL*; *see supra* text and fn 219.
498. Paragraph 46; reference made to *Francovich*; *see supra* text and fn 408.

> In contrast, where a Member State acts in a field where it has a wide discretion comparable to that of the Community institutions in implementing Community policies, the conditions under which it may incur liability must, in principle, be the same as those under which the Community institutions incur liability in a comparative situation.[499]

225. In such circumstances, EU law:

> *grants a right to reparation where three conditions are met:*
>
> – the rule of law infringed must be intended to confer rights on individuals;
> – the breach must be sufficiently serious; and
> – there must be a direct causal link between the breach of the obligation resting on the State and the damage sustained by the injured parties.[500]

(Unlike in earlier judgments, the Court in this landmark decision failed to list damage as an independent fourth condition of liability.)

226. Afterwards, this paragraph 51 turned into a phrase of quasi-eternal validity, relentlessly repeated by the two European Courts in each non-contractual liability case and often used regardless of the conditions under which it had been coined. *Brasserie* introduced the formula of a 'sufficiently serious breach' of EU law in cases of wide discretion of national legislatures (*manifest and grave disregard*). Its determination depends on the circumstances of the case. As regards the latter, the Court formulated a non-limitative catalogue of factors, in the sequel commonly called '*Brasserie* factors':

> (t)he clarity and precision of the rule breached, the measure of discretion left by that rule to the national or Community authorities, whether the infringement and the damage caused was intentional or involuntary, whether any error of law was excusable or inexcusable, the fact that the position taken by a Community institution may have contributed towards the omission, and the adoption or retention of national measures or practices contrary to Community law.[501]

227. Whether this catalogue of factors is very helpful to concretize the conditions of a sufficiently serious breach is not beyond doubt; especially the question whether the reference to categories of personal fault makes sense in the context of institutional liability for unlawfulness remains unanswered.[502] Instead, the first factor shall be commented on here briefly. The lack of 'clarity and precision of the rule breached' developed into a welcome defence tool for EU institutions and Member

499. Paragraphs 46 and 47.
500. Paragraph 51.
501. Paragraph 56.
502. *See* on this in greater detail *supra* text.

States to escape liability (particularly because EU legislation is generally not very well known for its clarity and precision). Cases of legal provisions lacking clarity and precision have fast been identified with broad discretion.[503] But it is less the Member States discretion that is at stake under these circumstances, rather the methodological question of interpretation and application of the respective provision. In other words: The problem lies in assessing the breach! Whether the assessed breach was 'excusable' or not then depends on other factors. In recent case law, this factor is called 'high complexity', and the liability seems to depend on institutional fault of the public authority concerned.[504] The situation is different, however, if the European legislator intended the provision not to be specific but more general. This would grant the public authorities in charge a margin of discretion to fill in the details of a regulation.

228. Using the example posed by the joined cases *Brasserie and Factortame III* – liability for *legislative acts*[505] – the Court took the advanced state of the respective Union law, developed especially in the case of *Bayerische HNL*, and transferred its principles to Member States' liability. It established State liability for breach of EU law by legislative measures as a principle as fundamental as that of primacy of EU law and direct effect.

This extension of the breach-of-law liability of Member States parallel to the *Francovich* line, though irrespective of any transposition of directives, comes without great surprise. The Court's reasoning is nevertheless not free from contradiction. The Court of Justice states correctly the basis of its adjudication:

> Since the Treaty contains no provision expressly and specifically governing the consequences of breaches of EU law by Member States, it is for the Court, … , to rule on such a question in accordance with generally accepted methods of interpretation, in particular by reference to the fundamental principles of the Union legal system and, where necessary, general principles common to the legal systems of the Member States.[506]

229. Only two paragraphs later, the Court said that the principle of non-contractual liability, laid down in Article 340(2) TFEU, was simply 'an expression of the general principle *familiar to the legal systems of the Member States* that an *unlawful act or omission* gives rise to an obligation to make good the damage

---

503. Compare, *inter alia*, Case C-278/05, *Robins and Others v. Secretary of State for Work and Pensions* [2007] ECR I-1054, para. 73; Case C-221/10 P, *Artegodan GmbH v. Commission* EU:C:2012:216.

504. *See* on this *supra* text.

505. In the *Brasserie* case the plaintiff could finally not recover (compare BGH, 24 Oct. 1996, BGHZ 134, 30: lack of a sufficiently serious breach); in the *Factortame* case the company lastly succeeded (compare *R v. Sec'y of State for Transport, ex p Factortame Ltd (Factortame IV)* [2000] 1 AC 524 (HL): the House of Lords applying directly the *Brasserie* conditions of liability. – For an assessment of ultimate Member States' liability before national (English and German) courts, compare T. Lock, *Is Private Enforcement of EU Law Through State Liability a Myth?* (2012) 49 CML Rev 1675.

506. *Brasserie*, para. 27 (emphasis added).

caused'.[507] First, this does not fit to the above quoted central statement in paragraph 27 or to the reasoning of the *Francovich* judgment ('inherent in the system of the Treaty'[508]). And second, it is simply wrong: (1) Article 340(2) does not contain one principle of non-contractual liability but two: torts (fault) of servants and wrongful acts of the State (maladministration).[509] (2) In the first case of vicarious liability, common principles exist. In the latter case, addressed by the Court, the legal systems of the Member States are heterogeneous and especially no general principle of liability for unlawful legislative measures can be derived from them. The basis of State liability for legislative acts contrary to EU law has its foundation directly in the multi-level governance structure of the Union and the primacy of EU law.[510]

§2. Administrative Acts: *Hedley Lomas*

230. Although not expressly mentioned in *Brasserie*, the implicit conclusion was that the same process of approximation should occur in the field of public liability for *administrative wrongs*. This was indeed carried out through the case of *Hedley Lomas*.[511] *Hedley Lomas*, a shepherd in Northern Ireland, applied for an export licence for a quantity of live sheep intended for slaughter in a Spanish slaughterhouse. The licence was not issued by the British Ministry, even though, according to the information obtained by Mr *Lomas*, the slaughterhouse in question had been approved since 1986 and was complying with EU directives on animal welfare.[512] Mr *Lomas* claimed a violation of his rights under Article 35 TFEU and brought damages proceedings against the British Ministry of Agriculture before the English High Court.

231. Both AG *Léger* and Court of Justice were oriented towards the well-known distinction between the *Lütticke* and *Schöppensted* formulas from EU liability law under Article 340(2) TFEU. For the ECJ it was a case of an administrative wrong committed by a State authority which had only considerably reduced or even no discretion. Under these conditions, the mere infringement of Union law is considered to be sufficient to establish a relevant breach.[513] It remains for the national court under its domestic law to assess the damage and to determine whether there is a

507. Paragraph 29.
508. *Francovich*, para. 35. This formula has also been repeated countless times in follow-up decisions; *see* for references AG Léger, Opinion, *Köbler*, ECR I-10243, para. 35 fn 25.
509. Compare in greater detail *supra* text.
510. Correctly stated by AG Léger, Opinion, Case C-5/94, *Hedley Lomas* [1995] ECR I-2556, para. 95.
511. Case C-5/94, *The Queen v. Ministry of Agriculture, Fisheries and Food, ex parte Hedley Lomas* (Irland) Ltd. [1996] ECR I-2553; for a case annotation, *see* P. Oliver (1997) 34 CML Rev. 666.
512. Directive 74/577/EEC on stunning animals before slaughter, OJ 1974 L 316/10. The refusal of the British authorities to grant export license was based on the conviction that a certain number of Spanish slaughterhouses were in fact nor complying with the requirements of the directive and on the fact that the directive did not lay down any monitoring procedure.
513. *Hedley Lomas* [1995] ECR I-2604, para. 28.

(direct) causal link between the breach and the damage purportedly sustained by the plaintiff.[514]

§3. Towards Conversion: *Bergaderm*

232. *Bergaderm* was a case where it was questionable whether a Commission directive could be deemed to be administrative rather than legislative in character.[515] The Court ruled that this distinction no longer mattered for the applicable standard to determine unlawfulness in an action for damages. The limits of the discretion enjoyed by the institution have become the decisive criteria. They have to be established regardless of the general or individual nature of the measure in question, that is, independent of whether it is a legislative or administrative measure.[516] Though *Bergaderm* was an EU liability case, its ruling became generally valid for Union (Article 340)2) TFEU) and Member States liability for breach of EU law. In one of the next cases, *Camar and Tico*, the ECJ applied the test of manifest and grave disregard – until recently restricted to legislative acts – for the first time to an administrative measure of a public institution.[517]

233. Solely the liability of private parties for breach of EU law has so far been left out – the controversial issue of horizontality. This will be taken up in the next section.

---

514. Paragraph 30.
515. Case C-352/98 P, *Laboratoires Pharmaceutiques Bergaderm SA and Gouplin v. Commission (Bergaderm)* [2000] ECR I-5291; compare also *supra* in text. *See* as follow-up decisions Case C-312/00 P, *Commission v. Camar and Tico* [2003] ECR I-11355; Case C-472/00 P, *Commission v. Fresh Marine* [2003] ECR I-7541 and Case C-198/03 P, *Commission v. CEVA and Pfizer* [2005] ECR I-6392.
516. *Bergaderm*, para. 46. *See* already beforehand, *inter alia*, AG Léger, Opinion, *Hedley Lomas* [1996] I-2556, para. 172.
517. Case C-312/00 P, *Commission v. Camar and Tico* [2003] ECR I-11355. The ECJ overruled the decision of the EGC which still pursued the pre-*Bergaderm* approach according to which plain breach of law in cases of administrative acts constituted unlawfulness/relevant breach which may trigger liability.

Part IV. Liability of Private Parties for Breach of EU Law

Chapter 1. Various Types of Liability

§1. Horizontal Direct Effect

234. Necessary requirements for a private party to bring a damages action against another private party for breach of EU law are the *protective* character and the horizontal *direct* effect of the arguably infringed provision of EU law. The conditions to be met for a protective rule to exist are the same as developed *supra* in the text concerning the liability of public authorities. The concept of horizontality, however, is of a rather complex nature.[518] It covers two aspects: (i) The *horizontal direct effect* of provisions of the Treaties and of secondary EU law developed alongside the settled lines of verticality. The first time the ECJ envisaged a horizontal direct effect was in the case of *Walrave.* (ii) The second aspect raises intricate questions of third party effects of *fundamental rights* of the EU Charter. This problem came up with the cases of *Viking* and *Laval.*

I. *Walrave* and *Koch*

235. Walrave and *Koch* were two Dutch professional cyclists. They felt impeded in the exercise of their professional sport by general rules laid down by the International Union of Cyclists (IUC). The IUC rules govern comprehensively the cycling sport and the working conditions for professional cyclists. *Walrave* and *Koch* sued the IUC and two other cycling federations for declaration that the incriminated rules were void, because they were arguably infringing Article 45 (free movement of workers) and Article 56 (free movement of services) TFEU.[519] The question which came before the ECJ therefore was: Can general rules adopted by a private organization be an infringement of rights conferred on individuals by

518. Compare the contributions of Hartkamp & van Leuken, in *The Influence of EU Law on National Private Law*. 57/73 (A.S. Hartkamp, C.H. Sieburgh et al. eds, Kluwer 2014).
519. Case 36/74, *B.N.O. Walrave and L.J.N. Koch v. Association Union Cycliste Internationale* [1974] ECR 1405.

Articles 45 and 56 of the Treaty? The Court drew an analogy to legislation by the State. The prohibition laid down in Articles 45 and 56 does not only apply to general rules of public authorities, 'but extends likewise to rules of any other nature aimed at regulating *in a collective manner* gainful employment and the provision of services'.[520] It was the similarity of regulatory functions and characteristics between the cycling association and a public body that served as justification for the ECJ that Article 45 could be infringed by collective arrangements of private organizations. Therefore, commentators qualified this judicial achievement as a sort of *semi-horizontal direct effect*.[521]

The fact that it is private associations that exercise a regulatory task and have quasi-legislative powers in these cases later led to qualify this case law as *regulatory effect doctrine*.

236. *Walrave* was followed up by similar decisions. In *Bosman*,[522] the Court invalidated rules laid down by football organizations, in *Deliège*[523] (rules of a judo league), and in *Lethonen*[524] (those of basketball associations).

237. This type of semi-horizontal direct effect has recently been extended to the field of standardization and certification by private non-profit bodies like Association française de la normalisation (AFNOR), British Standards Institution (BSI), DIN, CEN and others. In *Fra.bo SpA*, an Italian producer of copper fittings for gas and water piping sued the oldest German certification body, the Deutsche Vereinigung des Gas- und Wasserfaches e.V. (DVGW) of 1859.[525] A certificate of the DVGW is conditional for distributing products of the gas and water sector in Germany, and the DVGW had withdrawn the certificate for the plaintiff's construction products. A harmonized European technical standard was lacking for these products, and *Fra.bo* fulfilled the Italian requirements for distribution of its copper fittings. On preliminary ruling before the Court, the question was whether DVGW as a private law association was bound by the provisions governing the free movement of goods. The Court applied the *regulatory effect doctrine*. Due to the regulatory powers entrusted by the German State to DVGW, the activities of the latter have the effect of giving rise to restrictions on the free movements of goods 'in the same manner as do measures imposed by the State'.

---

520. Paragraphs 17–19. *See also* Case 13/76, *Gaetano Donà v. Mario Mantero* [1976] ECR 1333.
521. M. Quinn & N. McGowan, *Could Article 30 Impose Obligations on Individuals?* (1987) 12 EL Rev 163.
522. Case C-415/93, *Union royale belge des sociétés de football association and Others v. Bosman and Others* [1995] ECR I-4921.
523. Joint Cases C-51/96 and C-191/97, *C. Deliège v. Ligue francophone de judo et disciplines associées* [2000] ECR I-2595.
524. Case C-176/96, *J. Lethonen and Castors Canada Dry Namur-Braine ASBL v. Fédération royale belge des sociétés des basket-ball ASBL (FRBSB)* [2000] ECR I-2681.
525. Case C-171/11, *Fra.bo SpA v. Deutsche Vereinigung des Gas- und Wasserfaches e.V. (DVGW)* EU:C:2012:453.

II. *Defrenne II*

238. After *Walrave* and *Bosman,* it remained unclear whether horizontal effect would also apply in the relationship between employees and individual private employers. This issue came up soon afterwards in the case of *Defrenne II.*[526] Ms *Defrenne* had worked as an air hostess for the Belgian airline *Sabena SA*. She alleged that during her employment she received lower wages than her male colleagues who did the same job. She claimed an infringement of the right to equal payment under Article 157 TFEU by her employer *Sabena*. Article 157(1) reads: '*Each Member State* shall ensure that the principle of equal pay for male and female workers for equal work or work of equal value is applied.' Ms *Defrenne* brought an action against her employer before the Belgian Labour Courts claiming compensation for loss of salary.

239. The ECJ in its preliminary ruling held:

> [31] Indeed, … , the fact that certain provisions of the Treaty are formally addressed to the Member States does not prevent rights from being conferred at the same time on any individual who has an interest in the performance of the duties thus laid down. …
>
> [38] Furthermore it is not possible to sustain any objection that the application by national courts of the principle of equal pay would amount to modifying independent agreements concluded privately or in the sphere of industrial relations such as individual contracts and collective labour agreements.
>
> [39] In fact, since Art. 157 TFEU is mandatory in nature, the prohibition on discrimination between men and women applies not only to the action of public authorities, but also extends to all agreements which are intended to regulate paid labour collectively, as well as to contracts between individuals.[527]

240. There it is: the *horizontal direct effect* of the principle of equal pay. Grand result, poor legal reasoning. The court progressed from the category of vertical direct effect (paragraph 31) to indirect horizontal effect (paragraph 38) to end up with horizontal direct effect, simply by adding to the *Walrave* formula the words 'as well as to contracts between individuals'.[528] This apodictic phrase is used word-by-word in subsequent decisions.[529] Here is not the place to engage more deeply in a critique of the *Defrenne II* judgment. The result that legal provisions of EU law can

526. Case 43/75, *Gabrielle Defrenne v. Sabena SA* (*Defrenne II*) [1976] ECR 455. (*Defrenne I* concerned an action for annulment of rules governing rights to pensions by air crews: Case 80/70, *Defrenne v. Belgium* [1971] ECR 445).

527. Paragraphs 31, 38, 39.

528. It is worth mentioning though that the *Walrave* judgment was neither cited nor quoted in *Defrenne II*.

529. Compare Case C-94/07, *A. Racanelli v. Max-Planck-Gesellschaft* [2008] ECR-I 5939, para. 45 and Case C-172/11, *G. Erny v. Daimler AG* EU:C:2012:399, para. 36.

have horizontal direct effect nevertheless has widely been accepted.[530] An interesting follow-up decision in an equal-pay employment case was *Macarthys Ltd v. Smith*. Here, Lord Denning, against the majority of the Court of Appeal, insisted that directly effective EU law has priority over English law. After the preliminary ruling of the ECJ,[531] the Court of Appeal unanimously dismissed the appeal of the defendant employer.[532]

III. Consequences

241. A prominent and undisputed field of horizontal direct effect is EU competition law (Articles 101 and 102 TFEU).[533] The prohibitions on restricting or distorting competition are explicitly addressed to private enterprises, in contrast to the free movement rules. Respective agreements are automatically null and void (Article 101(2)). Breach of EU competition rules is sanctioned primarily with penalties issued by the Commission and Member States' authorities.[534]

Due to the lack of any harmonized law of damages for infringement of EU competition law, the regime for determining the compensation was afforded by the various national laws under the procedural autonomy of the Member States. Damages actions for violation of EU rules on competition had to be developed in the Member States' domestic tort law. This turned out to be a troublesome undertaking, especially in most of the civil law countries. In English law, again Lord Denning tried to pave the way straightforwardly. He referred to the case law of the ECJ[535] and held in 1974:

> So we reach this important conclusion. Articles 85 and 86 [EEC] are part of our law. They create new torts or wrongs. Their names are 'undue restriction of competition within the common market', and 'abuse of dominant position within the common market'. Any infringement of those articles can be dealt with by the English courts. It is for our courts to find the facts, to apply the law, and to use the remedies which we have available.[536]
>
> *In the end, however, the results of these national realignments proved to be 'diverse and totally underdeveloped'.*[537]

---

530. As far as the fundamental freedoms are concerned, *see infra* text.
531. Case 129/79, *Macarthys Ltd v. W. Smith* [1980] ECR 1275.
532. *Macarthys Ltd v. Smith* [1980] EWCA Civ 7.
533. ECJ, Case 127/73, *BRT and Others v. SABAM* [1974] 51, para. 16, and follow-up decisions.
534. Compare Council Regulation (EC) No. 1/2003 on the implementation of the rules on competition laid down in Arts 81 and 82 of the Treaty, OJ 2003 L 1/1.
535. Especially to Case 127/73, *Belgische Radio en Televisie (BRT) v. SV SABAM and NV Fonior (BRT No 1)* [1974] ECR 52, and Case 127/73, *BRT No. 2* [1974] ECR 313.
536. *Application des Gaz S.A. v. Falks Veritas Ltd.* [1974] 3 All ER 51, at 58 (CA). The landmark case in English law became, ten years later, *Garden Cottage Foods Ltd v. Milk Marketing Board* [1984] 1 AC 130 (HL).
537. *See* the comparative report for the EU by D. Waelbrook, D. Slater & G. Even-Shoshan, *Study on the Conditions of Claims for Damages in Case of Infringement of EC Competition Rules* (Ashurst 2004).

242. With the consolidation of the rules on public liability of Union and Member States in the mid-1990s, juristic academics and practitioners therefore demanded also a readjustment in the field of liability of private parties. The consolidated rules of public breach-of-law liability after *Brasserie and Factortame III* should, *mutatis mutandis*, be transposed to the competition law and function there too as a harmonized basis for compensation between private parties. Spokesman of this movement was, *inter alia*, AG *van Gerven*. In his seminal Opinion in *Banks & Co v. British Coal Corp.*,[538] under the competition rules of the ECSC Treaty, he argued:

> The general basis established by the Court in the Francovich judgment for State liability also applies where an individual infringes a provision of Community law to which he is subject, thereby causing loss and damage to another individual. ... Once again, the full effect of Community law would be impaired if the former individual or undertaking did not have the possibility of obtaining reparation from the party who can be held responsible for the breach of Community law – all the more so, evidently, if a directly effective provision of Community law is infringed.[539]

§2. COMPETITION LAW: *COURAGE LTD* AND *MANFREDI*

243. This position was finally adopted by the ECJ in the English case of *Courage Ltd v. Crehan*.[540] The facts of the case related to an exclusive purchase obligation in a twenty-year lease contract between a pub tenant and a brewing company. When *Courage Ltd* brought an action to recover unpaid supplies of beer, Mr *Crehan* argued that the beer tie was infringing Article 101 TFEU and counter-claimed damages. Under English law, however, a party to an illegal contract cannot claim damages from the other party (so-called principle of *pari delicto*). For preliminary ruling before the ECJ, the Court restated again that Articles 101 and 102 TFEU are fundamental provisions for the functioning of the internal market. They produce direct effects in relations between private parties and confer rights on individuals which national courts must safeguard. The Court went on to hold:

> (t)he full effectiveness of Art. 101 TFEU and, in particular, the practical effect of the prohibition laid down (in its first paragraph) would be put at risk if it

538. AG van Gerven, Opinion, Case C-128/92, *Banks & Co v. British Coal Corporation* [1993] ECR I-1212.
539. van Gerven, Opinion, para. 43.
540. Case C-453/99, *Courage Ltd v. B. Crehan and B. Crehan v. Courage Ltd and Others* [2001] ECR I-6297. For comments *see* K. Havu, *Horizontal Liability for Damages in EU Law* (2012) 18 ELJ 407; S. Drake, *Scope of Courage and the Principle of 'Individual Liability' for Damages* (2006) 31 EL Rev 841; N. Reich, *The 'Courage' Doctrine: Encouraging or Discouraging Compensation for Anti-Trust Injuries?* (2005) 42 CML Rev 35; A. Komninos, *New Prospects for Private Enforcement of EC Competition Law* (2002) 39 CML Rev 447.

> were not open to any individual to claim damages for loss caused to him by contract or by conduct liable to restrict or distort competition.[541]

This implies:

> that any individual can rely on a breach of Article 101(1) TFEU before a national court even where he is party to a contract that is liable to restrict or distort competition within the meaning of that provision.[542]

244. The statement of the ECJ as to liability itself left the question of further conditions for liability rather open. One can recognize requirements of damage and causation, next to a breach of an EU law provision granting rights to individuals. The usual procedural autonomy dictum followed.[543] In *Manfredi*, too, the obligation of Member States to enforce EU competition law and secure full compensation is emphasized.[544] As to conditions and scope of liability, *Courage* and *Manfredi* have opened the discussion.

245. Both judgments, backed by follow-up decisions,[545] served as a legal basis and an incentive for the Commission to take action to harmonize the national law of damages for breaches of EU antitrust law. Most victims of antitrust infringements, particularly small and medium enterprises (SMEs) and consumers, rarely obtain reparation for their losses suffered. The amount of compensation that these victims are foregoing is estimated by the Commission in the range of several billion euros a year.[546] Therefore, the European Commission has taken a number of steps since 2004 to stimulate the debate on that topic and elicit feedback from stakeholders on a number of possible options which could facilitate antitrust damages actions. Based on the outcomes of several public consultations, the Commission has suggested specific policy choices and measures in a White Paper of 2008.[547] On 17 April 2014,

---

541. Paragraph 26.
542. Paragraph 24. Tridimas, *General Principles*, p. 543 (OUP 2005), stresses parallels to US law and makes reference to a similar judgment of the US Supreme Court by which the principle of *pari delicto* in US antitrust litigation has been repealed. Compare *Perma Life Mufflers Corp. v. Intern'l Parts Corp.*, 392 US 134 (1968).
543. Mr Crehan's damages claim was dismissed by the High Court which could not find anti-competitive conduct: *Crehan v. Inntrepreneur Pub Company and Brewman Group Ltd* [2003] EuLR 663. – In an important earlier case, breach of statutory duty had been established as a cause of action for a competitor's damages claim. Compare *Garden Cottage Foods v. Milk Marketing Board* [1984] 1 AC 130 (HL).
544. Joined Cases C-295–298/04, *Manfredi and Others v. Lloyd Adriatico Assicurazioni* [2006] ECR I-6618, paras 59 and 60 (repeating the formulas of *Courage*).
545. Case C-360/09, *Pfleiderer AG v. Bundeskartellamt* [2011] ECR I-5161; Case C-199/11, *Europese Gemeenschap v. Otis NV and Others* EU:C:2012:684; Case C-536/11, *Bundeswettbewerbsbehörde v. Donau Chemie AG and Others* EU:C:2013:67; Case C-557/12, *Kone AG and Others v. ÖBB Infrastruktur AG* EU:C:2014:1317 (umbrella pricing).
546. White Paper on Damages actions for breach of EC antitrust rules, COM(2008) 165 final, at p. 2 with reference to s. 2.2. of the Impact Assessment Report.
547. White Paper, COM(2008) 165 final; *see also* Green Paper on damages actions for breach of EC antitrust rules, COM(2005) 672 final.

the European Parliament passed the text of a directive on antitrust damages actions; on 10 November 2014, the directive was adopted by the Council.[548]

246. Member States needed to implement the Directive 2014/104/EU in their national legal systems by 27 December 2016. The directive seeks to optimize the relationship between private enforcement of EU antitrust law through damages actions and public enforcement of antitrust rules by the Commission and national competition authorities. It focuses primarily on procedural aspects such as easier access to evidence, rebuttable presumption of damage and clear limitation periods. The provisions on liability confine themselves to stipulate a right to full compensation and to refer to the general principles of effectiveness and equivalence.[549] The central question of whether compensation is conditional on the infringer's fault (with or without reversal of the burden of proof) or no-fault, i.e., plain breach of antitrust rules, remains unanswered.[550] Envisaged collective actions by consumer associations, to facilitate the enforcement of scattered damages,[551] have also not been taken up.

247. An important recent case in this context is the European truck cartel. In July 2016, the EU Commission found that *MAN, Volvo/Renault, Daimler, Iveco* and *DAF* had broken EU antitrust rules. These truck manufacturers had colluded for fourteen years, from 1997 until 2011, on truck pricing and on passing on the costs of compliance with stricter emission rules. The Commission imposed a record fine of EUR 2.9 billion. The companies acknowledged this involvement and agreed to settle the case. – In 2017, more than 200 businesses which had purchased or leased trucks during the relevant period brought actions for damages running into hundred millions against the truck manufacturers.

§3. Implied Rights of Action: Muñoz SA

248. A remarkable extension of private litigation for breach of EU law has been brought by the *Muñoz* judgment of the ECJ.[552] Background of the case was EU law on the common organization of the markets of agricultural products, in particular

548. Directive 2014/104/EU on certain rules governing actions for damages under national law for infringements of the competition law provisions of the Member States and of the European Union, OJ 2014 L 349/1. Compare, *inter alia*, N. Dunne, *Courage and Compromise: The Directive on Antitrust Damages Actions* (2015) 40 EL Rev 581; J. Kortmann, *The Draft Directive on Antitrust Damages Actions and its Likely Effects on National Law*, in *The Influence of EU Law on National Private Law* 661 (Hartkamp et al. eds, Kluwer 2014). *See* generally I. Lianos, P. Davis & P. Nebbia, *Damages Claims for the Infringement of EU Competition Law* (OUP 2015).
549. Articles 3 and 4 Directive 2014/104/EU.
550. On the fault requirement, compare White Paper (2008), at pp. 6/7. Instead, the directive repeats the odd mantra of effectiveness and equivalence (Art. 4).
551. Compare Green Paper COM(2005) 672 final, at p. 8 (Protection of Consumer Interests); *see also* S. Keske, *Group Litigation in European Competition Law* (Intersentia 2010).
552. Case C-253/00, *A. Muñoz y Cia SA and Superior Fruiticola v. Frumar Ltd and Redbridge Produce Marketing Ltd* [2002] ECR I-7289.

fruit and vegetables. A Commission regulation laid down quality standards, applicable, *inter alia*, to table grapes, intending the products to be delivered fresh to the consumers.[553] *Muñoz SA* was a Spanish producer of high-quality white table grapes, marketing them under the variety name 'Superior Seedless' in the United Kingdom and elsewhere. The defendant *Frumar* was an English fruit import company selling table grapes contrary to the requirements of the EU quality standards. Several complaints of *Muñoz* to the competent British supervisory authority failed. *Muñoz* finally sued *Frumar* and its parent company for declaration that they breached EU law.

249. The case raised the essential question under what circumstances a private party may seek from national civil courts an order that another private party should comply with EU law, where under public law there is a supervisory authority which sees no reason for prosecuting an infringement of EU law. This meant, *inter alia*, that an answer must be given to the question concerning the extent to which national procedural law has to afford rights of actions to private parties concerned who have suffered loss as a result of the breach of EU law by another person or undertaking. The English High Court found an infringement of EU rules on quality standards by the defendants, but denied a right of *Muñoz SA* to bring a civil action against a competitor based on non-compliance with EU regulations.

250. With reference to the Court, the ECJ's answer is remarkably unambiguous and straightforward. After having stressed once more the principal starting point, that national courts within their jurisdiction must ensure that the provisions of EU law take full effect,[554] it went on to hold:

> (A)s is apparent [from the Regulation] the purpose of applying common quality standards is to keep products of unsatisfactory quality off the market, to guide production to meet consumers' requirements, and to facilitate trade relations based on fair competition. …
> Accordingly, the full effectiveness of the rules on quality standards … imply that it must be possible to enforce that obligation [of the Regulation] by means of civil proceedings instituted by a trader against a competitor.
> The possibility of bringing such proceedings strengthens the practical working of the Community rules on quality standards. As a supplement to the action of the authorities designated by the Member States to make the checks required by those rules it helps to discourage practices, often difficult to detect, which distort competition. In that context actions brought before the national courts by competing operators are particularly suited to contributing substantially to ensuring fair trading and transparency of markets in the Community.[555]

553. Commission Regulation (EEC) 1730/87 laying down quality standards for table grapes, OJ 1987 L 163/25 (2.5 Defending consumer interests), and Council Regulation (EC) 2200/96 on the common organization of the markets in fruit and vegetables, OJ 1996 L 297/1.
554. Case C-253/00, Muñoz, para. 28, citing Case 106/77, *Simmenthal II* [1978] ECR 629; Case C-213/89, *The Queen v. Sec'y of State for Transport (Factortame I)* [1990] ECR I-2433, and Case C-453/99, *Courage* [2001] ECR I-6297.
555. Paragraphs 29–31.

251. The *Muñoz* judgment means no less than a reconstruction of the edifice of legal governance in the EU. Up to then, the dual vigilance principle had been in force: compliance with EU law was enforced by actions of EU institutions and Member States, and by claims of private parties under the conditions of conferred rights and direct effect (*van Gend en Loos*).[556] With *Muñoz,* another cornerstone has been brought into the system of EU law: a private action as a means to enforce EU economic policy rules.[557] That is, private actions for injunction or damages no longer serve only to rectify infringed individual rights, *but to protect EU institutions and their effectiveness.* The justification delivered by the Court is that the workability of the complex regulatory architecture of the Single Market demands additional instruments of monitoring and enforcement of directly applicable EU law. The instrument introduced by *Muñoz* is a sort of 'implied tort' doctrine, as it is called in American corporation and antitrust law.[558] The infringement of a codified prohibition by an undertaking is a breach of law and hence a tort, and aggrieved private parties can sue. Their claims fulfil an important public law function.

252. At the same time, the judgment raises new questions, especially concerning the scope of legitimate applicants. It is common opinion that an *actio popularis* against infringements of EU law should be avoided.

Alongside this evolution in competition law and beyond, in the meantime central provisions of the Treaties and the Charter of Fundamental Rights also entered the realm of horizontality. This challenging new field of law will be treated in the next section.

---

556. Case 26/62, *van Gend en Loos* [1963] ECR 1, at p. 13: '[t]he vigilance of individuals concerned to protect their rights amounts to an effective supervision in addition to the supervision entrusted by articles 258, 259 TFEU to the diligence of the Commission and of the Member States'.

557. Compare already R.M. Buxbaum, *Die private Klage als Mittel zur Durchsetzung wirtschaftspolitischer Rechtsnormen* (Müller 1972).

558. Buxbaum, p. 30.

Chapter 2. Fundamental Freedoms Versus Fundamental Rights

§1. Horizontality

I. Horizontal Effect of Fundamental Freedoms

253. There is almost no other subject of constitutional EU law to which so much scholarly writing has been dedicated to as to these two topics. Therefore, it must be stressed here once more that this is a monograph on EU *tort law*, which can touch these subjects only in a very cursory way, and, as necessary, cases on horizontal liability for damages are discussed at the end of this section.

It should be noted at the outset that the fundamental principle of free movement enshrined in Articles 45, 49, 56 and 63 TFEU is drafted in general terms and is not specially addressed to the Member States. *Walrave* and follow-up decisions[559] have held that the prohibition of impediments of the four freedoms does not only apply to actions of public authorities but also to general rules by private bodies aimed at regulating gainful employment in a collective manner (so-called regulatory effect doctrine). Subsequent case law went a step further and made it clear that the horizontal reach of the prohibition of discrimination is not restricted to situations where private actors regulate employment collectively. Prohibition of discrimination on grounds of nationality, as regards pay and conditions of employment, or on gender, as regards equal pay of men and women, now includes relevant discrimination by any individual employer.[560]

254. The first case to acknowledge the horizontality of an economic freedom itself (here: free movement of workers – Article 45 TFEU) was *Angonese*.[561] It concerned the concrete denial of access to a recruitment competition for a post in a private bank in Bolzano. Mr *Angonese* was a Southern Tyrolean of Italian nationality whose mother tongue was German. The *Cassa di Risparmio* made the participation in the recruitment competition conditional on the possession of a specific certificate of bilingualism, issued by the provincial authorities. Though not in possession of such a certificate, Mr *Angonese* was perfectly bilingual and had other diplomas to witness that. He was nevertheless refused to participate in the competition. Mr *Angonese* claimed a violation of freedom of movement for workers (Article 45 TFEU) and sued the bank for loss of opportunity. The Court in its preliminary ruling referred to its *Walrave* and *Defrenne II* judgments[562] and then held:

---

559. Compare *supra* text and fns 519 et seq.
560. Compare Case 43/75, *Defrenne II* [1976] ECR 455 (on Art. 157 TFEU: equal pay). On this in greater detail, *see* M. de Mol, *Horizontal Direct Effect of Union Prohibitions of Discrimination*, in *The Influence of EU Law on National Private Law* 219 (Hartkamp et al. eds, 2014).
561. Case C-281/98, *R. Angonese v. Cassa di Risparmio di Bolzano SpA* [2000] ECR I-4161.
562. *See supra* text and fns 519 and 526.

> Such considerations must, a fortiori, be applicable to [Article 45 TFEU], which lays down a fundamental freedom and which constitutes a specific application of the general prohibition of discrimination contained in [Article 18 TFEU]. ... In that respect, ... , it is designed to ensure that there is no discrimination on the labour market.
>
> Consequently, the prohibition of discrimination on grounds of nationality laid down in [Article 45 TFEU] must be regarded as applying to private persons as well.[563]

The Court found that making the access to the recruitment process conditional on the possession of one particular diploma was a significant breach of Mr *Angonese's* right to free movement of persons.

255. Similar considerations apply in principle to the other freedoms to establish, to provide services, and to move capital under Articles 49, 56, 63 TFEU.[564] This will be taken up in greater detail *infra* this section.

II. Third Party Effect of Fundamental Rights[565]

256. Since the coming into force of the 'Charter of Fundamental Rights of the European Union' (ChFR), EU citizens have been under a threefold protective umbrella of fundamental rights: rights guaranteed by the national constitution, rights provided for by the ECHR, and, last but not least, the fundamental rights of the EU Charter.[566] The overarching political objective is to establish a space with unconditional access to equal constitutional protection under the three human rights regimes throughout the EU. The Charter enshrines political, social and economic 'rights', 'freedoms' and 'principles' for EU citizens and residents. The Charter's distinction between 'fundamental rights' and 'fundamental principles' is a political one. Some Member States wanted to impede that judges could interfere with 'areas of significant budgetary importance' by using the economic and social 'rights' of the Charter. Hence, Article 52(5) ChFR stipulates:

---

563. Paragraphs 35 and 36.

564. On this in greater detail, *see* D. Wyatt, *Horizontal Effect of Fundamental Freedoms and the Right to Equality after Viking and Mangold* (2008) 4 CYELP 1; and R. van Leuken, *Direct Horizontal Effect of the Fundamental Freedoms*, in *The Influence of EU Law on National Private Law* 73 (Hartkamp et al. eds, 2014).

565. *See*, *inter alia*, D. Leczykiewicz, *Horizontal Application of the Charter of Fundamental Rights* (2013) 38 EL Rev 479; and C. Mak, *Unchart(er)ed Territory: EU Fundamental Rights and National Private Law, in The Influence of EU Law on National Private Law* 323 (Hartkamp et al. eds, 2014).

566. The distinction between Charter 'rights' and Charter 'principles' itself is ambiguous, because the aforesaid fundamental *rights* themselves are open-textured *principles*. As such they are opposed to clear-cut 'claim rights' in the Hohfeldian sense, which imply enforceable duties towards someone. Compare W.N. Hohfeld, *Some Fundamental Legal Conceptions as Applied in Judicial Reasoning*, in *id.*, *Fundamental Legal Conceptions as Applied in Judicial Reasoning and Other Legal Essays* (Yale Univ. Press 1919).

> [t]he provisions of [the] Charter which contain principles may be implemented by legislative and executive acts taken by institutions, bodies, offices and agencies of the Union, and by acts of the Member States when they are implementing Union law, in the exercise of their respective powers. They shall be judicially cognisable only in the interpretation of such acts and in the ruling on their legality.

257. The realm of fundamental rights in this tort law context is restricted to the 'classical' or 'first generation rights' of Title II of the Charter: Fundamental Freedoms (privacy and data protection, freedom of opinion, etc.). Hence, the aforesaid political distinction between Charter 'rights' and Charter 'principles' is immaterial for the discussion in this section.

With respect to the Charter rights, their spatial reach is expressly confined to the area of application of EU law and the group of addressees is restricted to EU institutions and Member States' authorities exclusively (Article 51(1) ChFR). This has been confirmed by judicial authority. In *Åkerberg,*[567] the Grand Chamber of the Court affirmed the applicability of EU law in a presumably clear domestic case where the Swedish law provided administrative and criminal sanctions for the failure of its residents to comply with tax obligations.[568] It examined the compatibility of Swedish law with the constitutional prohibition of *ne bis in idem* (Article 50 ChFR).[569] The Court restated its established position:

> The Court's settled case law indeed states, in essence, that the fundamental rights guaranteed in the legal order of the European Union are applicable in all situations governed by European Union law, but not outside such situations … That definition of the field of application of fundamental rights of the European Union is borne out by the explanations relating to Art. 51 of the Charter, which, in accordance with the third subparagraph of Art. 6(1) TEU and Art. 52(7) of the Charter, have to be taken into consideration for the purpose of interpreting it. … According to those explanations, 'the requirement to respect fundamental rights defined in the context of the Union is only binding on the Member States when they act in the scope of Union law'.[570]

258. A fully fledged *vertical direct effect doctrine* of EU fundamental rights as a core element of legal governance would indeed imply that EU citizens can invoke any breach of fundamental rights by Member States' public authorities, independent of the scope of Union law. That is, that they can invoke violation of these fundamental rights before the national courts when their domestic law fails. This has been claimed in the juristic academia by various scholars.[571] A ground-breaking

567. Case C-617/10, *Åklagaren v. Åkerberg Fransson* EU:C:2013:105.
568. Sufficient to assume applicability of EU law was the plain existence of Directive 2006/112/EC on the common system of value added tax (vat), OJ 2006 L 347/1, for inter-Member States transactions.
569. Compare also Art. 4 Protocol No. 7 to the ECHR.
570. Case C-617/10, *Åkerberg*, paras 19–20.
571. Compare, *inter alia*, A. von Bogdandy et al., *Reverse* Solange – *Protecting the Essence of Fundamental Rights Against the EU Member States* (2012) 49 CML Rev 489.

decision of the Court of Justice à la *van Gend en Loos* concerning the universality of the vertical direct effect of fundamental rights of the Charter throughout the EU, however, is yet to come. Hopefully, this will not turn into a 'Waiting for Godot' process.

259. A completely different aspect is the *third party effect* (*Drittwirkung*) of fundamental rights.[572] It is obvious that the horizontal dimension of EU fundamental rights has not been envisaged by the drafters of the Charter and the authors of the Explanations. They adhered to the restrictive path taken exemplarily in 1948 by the drafters of the West German Constitution (*Grundgesetz*). Pursuant to Article 1(3) *Grundgesetz* exclusively the three State powers legislature, executive and judiciary shall be bound by the fundamental rights of the Constitution. This interest in taming State powers and in a defensive function of fundamental rights was historically understandable in post-war Germany against the backdrop of the totalitarian system of National Socialism. Nearly thirty years later the Portuguese constitution of 1976 pursued a decisively more liberal approach. Article 18(1) reads: 'This Constitution's provisions with regards to rights, freedoms and guarantees shall be *directly applicable to and binding on public and private persons and bodies*.' Would this be the wording of Article 1(3) *Grundgesetz*, it would change practically nothing. The actual German law and practice would be in complete accordance with this hypothetical command of the Constitution.[573]

260. Be that as it may, the lesson to be learned from sixty years of practical experience with adjudicating fundamental rights under, e.g., the *Grundgesetz* and the ECHR,[574] provides evidence that *Drittwirkung* of fundamental rights is an incontestable fact.[575] It follows from the supremacy of constitutional law, which mandates that all law, including private law, is subject to the Constitution. This does not render private actors bound by the Constitution, but it does mean that in governing their legal relations with one another, constitutional rights have a significant

572. I prefer this term, as traditionally connected with horizontal effect of fundamental rights in the constitutional law of the Member States. That may help to keep the two subjects separated – the broader EU law horizontality issue and the more specific fundamental rights aspect.

573. A representative of this thesis of 'outcome-neutrality' is M. Kumm. Compare Kumm, *Who's Afraid of the Total Constitution? Constitutional Rights as Principles and the Constitutionalization of Private Law* 7 GLJ 341, 352 et seq. (2006).

574. On 'Drittwirkung' of European Convention rights and freedoms compare D. Spielmann, *The European Convention on Human Rights. The European Court of Human Rights*, in *Human Rights and the Private Sphere: A Comparative Study* 427 (D. Oliver/J. Fedtke eds, Routledge 2007); Spielmann, *L'effet potentiel de la Convention européenne des droits de l'homme entre personnes privées* (Nemesis/Bruylant 1995); *Droit civil et Convention européenne des droits de l'homme* (F. Werro ed., Schulthess 2006).

575. Compare the materials collected in *Fundamental Rights and Private Law in the European Union* 2 vols (G. Brüggemeier, A. Colombi Ciacchi & G. Comandé eds, CUP 2010): comprising EU, England, France, Germany, Italy, The Netherlands, Poland, Portugal, Spain and Sweden; *see also Human Rights and the Private Sphere: A Comparative Study* (D. Oliver & J. Fedtke eds, Routledge-Cavendish 2007).

impact on them. This holds true for national law, for the international law of the ECHR, and this will be true under EU law.[576]

261. That is precisely what the German Federal Constitutional Court expressed in its famous *Lüth* judgment:

> (F)ar from being a value-free system the Constitution erects an objective system of values in its section on basic rights … This system of values, centering on the human being to develop in society, must apply as a constitutional axiom throughout the whole legal system: it must direct and inform legislation, administration, and judicial decision. It naturally influences private law as well; no rule of private law may conflict with it, and all such rules must be construed in accordance with its spirit.[577]

Whether this third party effect is qualified as direct or indirect is an obsolete academic dispute which belongs to legal history.[578] *Drittwirkung* can take various forms: conform interpretation of legal rules and contracts, disapplication of non-constitutional provisions, further judicial development of private law so that it copes with the fundamental rights, etc. A famous example of the latter has been from 1950 onwards in Germany the ‘invention’ of personality rights and their incorporation into the architecture of the civil code’s law of delict and damages of 1896.

262. Concerning the fundamental rights of Title II of the EU Charter, it has to be recalled that according to settled case law of the European courts the fact that provisions of the Treaty are formally addressed to the Member States does not prevent rights from being conferred at the same time on private parties who have an interest in compliance with the obligations thus laid down.[579] Article 6(3) TEU ascribes the Charter the same legal status as the TEU and the TFEU with its economic freedoms. Article 2 TEU clarifies additionally that the EU is a ‘union of values’, and the ECJ has held that the Union has ‘not only an economic but also a social purpose’.[580] Against this background, the little that can be said is that in horizontal direct effect cases under EU law, where economic freedoms are not absolute but open-textured principles, fundamental rights can be utilized as restrictions of the

576. For US American law *see*, *inter alia*, S. Gardbaum, *The Horizontal Effect of Constitutional Rights* (2003) 102 Mich L. Rev. 388–459.
577. Federal Constitutional Court, 15 Jan. 1958, BVerfGE 7, 198, at 205.
578. Influential was the attempt to do away with any horizontal effect and replace it with the instrument of State duties to protect private parties. Compare C.W. Canaris, *Grundrechte und Privatrecht. Eine Zwischenbilanz* (de Gruyter 1999). That State protective duties do exist, is free from doubt. But the Federal Constitutional Court, requested by a party of a private law suit to give a constitutional law ruling, is *not* assessing a state court’s failure to protect a private party (and thus giving reason for a claim for state liability) but is *determining the constitutional influence on the rules of private law* governing the concrete case. For criticism *see*, *inter alia*, Brüggemeier, *Horizontal Effects of Fundamental Rights. A Critical View on the German Cathedral*, in *Constitutionalisation of Private Law* 59 (T. Barkhuysen & S. Lindenbergh eds, Brill 2008).
579. Compare Case 43/75, *Defrenne v. Sabena (Defrenne II)* [1976] ECR 456; Case C-281/98, *Angonese v. Cassa di Risparmio di Bolzano* [2000] ECR I-4161.
580. Case C-438/05, *Viking Line* (fn.), para. 79.

freedoms to movement.[581] This urges courts then to weigh the equivalent but competing legal principles and strike a fair balance between fundamental rights and fundamental freedoms; or, in the meanwhile classic words of German constitutional law, to bring them into a *practical concordance* (K. Hesse).[582]

§2. Balancing Competing Principles: Fundamental Freedoms Versus Fundamental Rights

263. The Court, sitting in Grand Chamber, has recently been confronted with this task in three cases. In the judgments *Viking* and *Laval*, dealing with collective actions by trade unions against 'social dumping', it tackled this problem of balancing in a formally appropriate way, though the substantive outcome may not be free from critique. In the third case of a State official's disclosure of safety risks of products (*A.G.M.-COS.MET*), the Court avoided this balancing completely.

I. *Viking*

264. In *Viking*, the defendants were a large Finnish passenger ferry operator, *Viking Line ABP*, and its Estonian subsidiary, *OÜ Viking Line Eesti*.[583] *Viking Line* operated several vessels, including '*Rosella*', which under the Finnish flag plies the Tallinn-Helsinki route between Estonia and Finland. The company wished to 'reflag' *Rosella,* that is, to change its place of establishment to Estonia in order to benefit from the lower wages and to provide its services from there. The Finnish Seamen's Union (FSU), of which the crew of *Rosella* were members, sought to prevent this from happening. The FSU, supported by its mother association, the International Transport Workers' Federation (ITF) with seat in London, threatened strike action and boycotts if *Viking Line* were to relocate '*Rosella*' without maintaining its

581. Another relevant field concerned is the conflict between free flow of personal data and the protection of privacy. Compare Directive 95/46/EC and *see* in greater detail *infra* text (Part VIII, Ch. 3).

582. K. Hesse, *Grundzüge des Verfassungsrechts der Bundesrepublik Deutschland* (20th ed., Müller/Hüthig 1999). R. Alexy reformulated this axiom on a more generalized level: the distinction between (private law) rules and fundamental rights principles. According to him, principles are optimization requirements which are subject to factual and legal constraints, whilst rules can only be fulfilled or not and contain fixed points in the field of the factually and legally possible. That means, if rules collide there are meta-rules that apply (e.g., lex posterior derogat legi priori, lex specialis derogat legi generali) causing the exclusion of one at the expense of the other. However, if two principles compete, the resolution is not to declare one of them invalid but to determine which of the two prevails under the circumstances. Compare R. Alexy, *Theorie der Grundrechte* 71 (2d ed. Suhrkamp 1994; in English: Alexy, *A Theory of Constitutional Rights* (OUP 2009)).

583. Case C-438/05, *International Transport Workers' Federation and Finnish Seamen's Union v. Viking Line ABP and OÜ Viking Line Eesti* [2007] ECR I-10806. – A parallel case was C-341/05, *Laval un Partneri Ltd v. Svenska Byggnadsarbetareförbundet and Others* [2007] ECR I-11767. The text *supra* concentrates on the *Viking* case where horizontality is in the focus. On both cases *see*, *inter alia*, C. Barnard (ed.), *'Viking' and 'Laval': Workshop Papers from 1 Feb. 2008*, (2008–2009) 11 CYELS; A. Hinarejos, *Laval and Viking: The Right to Collective Action versus EU Fundamental Freedoms* (2008) 8 HRL Rev 714; N. Reich, *Free Movement v. Social Rights in an Enlarged Union – the Laval and Viking Cases before the ECJ* (2008) 9 GLJ 125–160.

current wage levels. *Viking Line* brought an action before the Commercial Court in London, seeking *declaratory and injunctive relief* against the threatened boycotts by ITF and FSU. After the relief was granted, ITF and FSU filed an appeal before the English Court of Appeal. The Court of Appeal referred 'an extensive series of meticulously worded questions'[584] to the ECJ for preliminary ruling.

265. AG *Maduro* condensed this dispute as follows:

> (a)t the heart of the matter lies the following question: does the Treaty imply that, in order to ensure the proper functioning of the common market, the provision on freedom of movement protects the rights of market participants, not just by limiting the powers of the authorities of the Member States, but also by limiting the autonomy of others?[585]

He proposed an answer in the affirmative.

266. The Court followed the proposal of its AG but ruled only on the concrete collective union action at stake in this proceeding. It stated that Article 49 TFEU is capable of conferring rights on a private undertaking which may be relied on against a trade union and that boycott actions such as those threatened by ITF and FSU constitute a restriction on freedom of establishment. It concluded:

> (t)hat Art. 49 TFEU is to be interpreted to the effect that collective action such as that at issue in the main proceedings, which seeks to induce an undertaking whose registered office is in a given Member State to enter into a collective work agreement with a trade union established in that State and to apply the terms set out in that agreement to the employees of a subsidiary of that undertaking established in another Member State, constitutes a restriction within the meaning of that article. This restriction may, in principle, be justified by an overriding reason of public interest, such as the protection of workers, provided that it is established that the restriction is suitable for ensuring the attainment of the legitimate objective pursued and does not go beyond what is necessary to achieve that objective.[586]

267. The consequence of this judgment is no less than the clarification that the Treaty articles on freedom of movement apply directly to *any private action* that is capable of *effectively* restricting other private parties from exercising their rights of freedom of movement. A justification of the restriction is possible if the criterion of *proportionality* is met.[587] Whether the concrete trade unions' actions in *Viking* were

584. Formulation by AG Maduro, Opinion, Case C-438/05, *Viking*, ECR I-10784, para. 12.
585. Paragraph 36.
586. ECJ, ECR I-10806, para. 90.
587. For European lawyers and labour lawyers it is questionable whether the plain application of the principle of proportionality appropriately takes into account the societal relevance of 'social rights' in the process of European integration. Compare, *inter alia*, C. Joerges & F. Rödl, *Formalised Law and the 'Social Deficit' of the EU* (2009) 15 ELJ 1.

proportionate or disproportionate was up to the English Court of Appeal to determine.[588]

268. Another question raised is how to assess whether a measure is effectively restricting the freedom to movement?[589] The Court avoided an answer to this question. Sensible considerations have been contributed by *Derrick Wyatt*.[590] To determine the horizontal reach of the fundamental freedoms, he focused, *inter alia*, on one important aspect:

> Normal market behaviour designed to improve the market position or market returns of one economic operator should not in principle be held to amount to a restriction on the fundamental freedom of another market operator. The concept of a restriction on a fundamental freedom rather implies action which is external to the market, or which at any rate falls outside the range of normal competitive market behaviour designed to increase market returns or improve the market position of enterprises vis-à-vis their competitors, supplier or customers.[591]

II. *A.G.M.-COS.MET. v. Lehtinen* Reloaded

269. In *Schmidberger*,[592] it was the defendant Austrian State which was confronted with two conflicting objectives of its protective duty: (i) to impede the disruption of free movement of goods on the Brenner transit route by private actors, and (ii) to secure the freedom of opinion and assembly of its citizens (under national, international (ECHR) and EU law). Its authorities decided not to ban the demonstration, though it was an effective infringement of the right of *Schmidberger's* transport company under Article 28 TFEU. This administrative measure was upheld by the Court because it was justified as proportionate.

In his *Viking* Opinion, AG *Maduro* indulged himself in a hypothetical reflection: If *Schmidberger* had brought a private lawsuit against the demonstrators and/or their organization, the Court (on preliminary ruling) still would have had to weigh the right of free movement of the former against the right to demonstrate of the latter. But the AG missed one decisive difference: In *Schmidberger*, the Court aptly stated that account must be taken only of the action or omission by the State. The specific aims of the demonstration are not in themselves material in a legal proceeding which seeks to establish the breach-of-law liability of a Member State.[593]

---

588. The case has finally been settled out of court.
589. The question was already brought up by AG Maduro; compare Opinion, *Viking*, ECR I-10784, para. 43.
590. D. Wyatt, *Horizontal Effect of Fundamental Freedoms and the Right to Equality after Viking and Mangold* (2011–2012) 14 CYELS 1, at 11.
591. (2011–2012) 14 CYELS 1, at 11/12.
592. *See supra* text and fn 432.
593. Case C-112/00, *Schmidberger*, ECR I-5694, paras 66 and 67.

270. The situation is different in a private lawsuit. With the action in *A.G.M.-COS.MET*, AG *Maduro's* hypothetical case has come close to reality. *A.G.M.*, an Italian manufacturer of vehicle lifts, sued Mr *Lehtinen* for damages. Mr *Lehtinen*, an official of the Finnish Government, had publicly criticized the safety of *A.G.M.'s* products and thus allegedly caused a reduction in sale in Finland and elsewhere. The case has already been discussed at length *supra* in the text. Although it is lastly an incident of vicarious liability of the Finnish State, it is here, in the context of horizontality, the right place to develop systematically the appropriate arguments. Did Mr *Lehtinen* commit a tort of breach of EU law?

271. At the outset, it must be said that it seems to be free from doubt that Mr *Lehtinen* has effectively infringed the Italian company's right to free movement of its products. His action is behaviour external to the market but interfering considerably in the operations of *A.G.M.* to market its products, which were in compliance with EU safety requirements. Hence, EU law is touched and, as already pointed out *supra* in the text,[594] the question has to be answered whether Mr *Lehtinen's* action was a tort or can be justified by reference to EU and/or ECHR fundamental rights.

272. Mr *Lehtinen* uttered publicly, but single-handedly, his personal view which was contrary to the official position of his Ministry, that the vehicle lifts of *A.G.M.* were unsafe. Thus, his conduct falls under the reach of freedom of expression as enjoyed by any public servant under EU law[595] as well as under ECHR law,[596] be s/he an EU civil servant or Member State official. This general freedom of public servants is restricted by duties of loyalty and confidentiality as they are provided for on EU level by Article 339 TFEU and Articles 11 and 12 of the Staff Regulations. These duties are intended to preserve the relationship of trust which must exist between the institution and its officials or other employees. They apply regardless of whether the facts that have been disclosed were true or untrue. This may lead to a presumption of unlawfulness of Mr *Lehtinen's* conduct.

273. A counter justification for this breach of confidentiality could exist when exceptionally the conditions of a special variant of freedom of expression are met, those of protected disclosure of facts. Conditions of legitimate whistle-blowing have been elaborated by the ECtHR under Article 11 ECHR. These rules are transposable to the EU Charter law. Its Article 52(3) stipulates that identical rights, such as freedom of expression under Article 11 CFR and under Article 10 ECHR, enjoy the same protection under EU law as they enjoy under the ECHR.

---

594. Compare paras 204–212 and Brüggemeier, *EU Product Safety Law, Whistleblowers, and Member State Liability for Acts of Officials* (2015) 2 EJCL 212.

595. Article 11 ChFR. Compare Case C-274/99 P, *B. Connolly v. Commission* [2001] ECR I-1638, paras 43 et seq.

596. Compare ECtHR, 26 Feb. 2009, *Kudeshkina v. Russia (No 1)* hudoc (2009); 26.9.1995, *Vogt v. Germany* A 323 (1995); 21 EHRR 205.

274. In *Heinisch v. Germany*,[597] the applicant, a geriatric nurse, was dismissed because she made public serious shortcomings in the daily care provided by her employer, a geriatric nursing home operated by a State-owned undertaking. The German courts[598] upheld her dismissal. On application to the ECtHR, the Court referred first to Resolution 1729 (2010) of the Parliamentary Assembly of the Council of Europe 'On the protection of "whistle-blowers"'.[599] It contained under No. 6.2.4 the following 'guiding principle':

> Any whistle-blower shall be considered as having acted in good faith provided he or she has reasonable grounds to believe that the information disclosed was true, even if it later turns out that this was not the case, and provided he or she did not pursue any unlawful or unethical objectives.

275. The ECtHR held that the dismissal was an interference with the applicant's right to freedom of expression and went on to scrutinize its justification by reasons given in Article 10(2) ECHR: whether the dismissal is 'prescribed by law', 'pursues a legitimate aim', or is 'necessary in a democratic society'. In addressing the last criterion 'necessary in a democratic society' the Court developed as applicable principles for the case, *inter alia,* the following:

> Consequently, in the light of [an official's] duty of loyalty and discretion, disclosure should be made in the first place to the person's superior or other competent authority or body. It is only where this is clearly impracticable that the information can, as a last resort, be disclosed to the public. In assessing whether the restriction on freedom of expression was appropriate, the Court must therefore take into account whether the applicant had any other effective means of remedying the wrongdoing which he or she intended to uncover.[600]

Further criteria are the authenticity of the information disclosed, the damage suffered as a result of the disclosure, and the motive behind the action. In the *Heinisch* case, the ECtHR found that the German courts failed to strike a fair balance between the protection of the legitimate interests of the defendant employer and the applicant's right to freedom of expression. Germany was ordered to pay 'just satisfaction' to Ms *Heinisch.*

276. In the *Lehtinen* case, it is the obligation to pay damages which is the sanction for the disclosure of supposed safety lacks of *A.G.M.*'s vehicle lifts. The claim

597. ECtHR, 21 Jul. 2011, *Heinisch v. Germany* hudoc (2011).
598. Three Labour Courts (compare as last instance Federal Court of Labour, 6 Jun. 2007, AZR 264/06) and the Federal Constitutional Court, 6 Dec. 2007 (dismissal of constitutional review).
599. Guiding principle No. 6.1.1. delivers a definition of whistle-blowing: 'The definition of protected disclosures shall include all bona fide warnings against various types of unlawful acts, including all serious human rights violations which affect or threaten the life, health, liberty and other legitimate interests of individuals as subjects of public administration or taxpayers, or as shareholders, employees or customers of private companies.'
600. Paragraph 66.

is to be upheld if Mr *Lehtinen's* disclosure was a wrongful action, at least a negligent interference with *A.G.M.*'s business. The wrongfulness lastly depends on whether or not Mr *Lehtinen* can enjoy the privilege of protected disclosure under conditions of legitimate whistle-blowing. Though acting deliberately, an avoidable error about his justification would exclude intention and constitute negligence.[601] Thus, in the negative case there would be a tort of wrongful (negligent) breach of EU law by a public servant. Under Finnish law, his liability would then be absorbed 'vicariously' by the Finnish State.[602]

It is here not the place to discuss this in detail. That would have been the task of the Finnish courts, if correctly instructed by the ECJ.[603] In this monograph, the final outcome does not matter, it merely serves to demonstrate the right processing of this case with its intricate horizontal direct effect and *Drittwirkung's* dimensions.

---

601. This opens up two additional aspects: (i) If Mr *Lethinen's* error on the justification of his disclosure of the safety lacks was unavoidable, then negligence is missing and no liability exists. (ii) If liability exists, it is questionable whether the national private laws of the Member States provide a cause of action for negligent interference with business. This would require the creation of a new cause of action in national law in favour of the undertakings whose economic freedoms have been infringed.

602. The Finnish Tort Liability Act, Ch. 4, treats vicarious liability for private employees and public servants in the same manner. The servant is in his/her own capacity only liable if special reasons demand it and in cases of deliberate actions.

603. In Finland, the case was ultimately settled out of court.

Chapter 3. Horizontal Direct Effect of Directives?

277. This touches once more one of the most controversial topics of general EU law.[604] It has long been established law that, unlike e.g., the above-mentioned Treaty provisions, directives do not have *horizontal* direct effect. That is, no private party can invoke the provisions of an untransposed or not correctly transposed directive against another private party before the national court, as private parties are bound only by the national legislative act by which the directive has been transposed into national law. The main reason given for this lack of horizontal direct effect is that otherwise the clear distinction between regulations and directives would be blurred. Pursuant to Article 288(3) TFEU, directives exercise direct effect only between the Union and the Member States.

§1. *MARSHALL (NO. 1)*

278. This position has been principally supported by the ECJ in the British case of *Marshall (No. 1).*[605] Provisions of the UK Social Security Act 1975 required female employees to retire at 60 and male employees at 65. Ms *Marshall* was dismissed at 62. She sued her employer, a health authority, for compensation of the financial loss she sustained, arguing that her dismissal at the age of 62 violates the 1976 Equal Treatment Directive.[606] The Court held:

> With regard to the argument that a directive may not be relied upon against an individual, it must be emphasized that according to Art. 288 TFEU the binding nature of a directive, which constitutes the basis for the possibility of relying on the directive before a national court, exists only in relation to 'each Member State to which it is addressed'. It follows that a directive may not be relied upon as such against such a person.

279. The national health system in the UK is a publicly funded system created under the National Health System Act 1946.[607] Therefore, the Court could consider the defendant health authority to be an 'emanation of the State' and therefore addressee of the vertical effect of the Directive. Hence, *Ms Marshall* was entitled to invoke the rights provided by the directive against *AHA* and could recover.[608]

---

604. *See*, *inter alia*, P. Craig, *The Legal Effect of Directives: Policy, Rules and Exceptions* (2009) 34 EL Rev 349; T. Tridimas, *Black, Whites and Shades of Grey: Horizontality of Directives Revisited* (2002) 21 YEL 327.
605. Case 152/84, *M.H. Marshall v. Southampton and South-West Hampshire AHA (Marshall No. 1)* [1986] ECR 723.
606. Directive 76/207/EEC on the implementation of the principle of equal treatment for men and women as regards access to employment, vocational training and promotion, and working conditions, OJ 1976 L 39/40.
607. *See*, *inter alia*, G. Rivett, *From Cradle to Grave: 50 Years of the NHS* (Kingfisher Publ. 1998).
608. The amount of damages was assessed in Case C-271/91, *Marshall v. Southampton and South-West Hampshire Area Health Authority (Marshall No. 2)* [1993] ECR I-4367.

A couple of follow-up decisions, to name just the Danish *Hertz*[609] and British *Webb*[610] case, concern requests for interpretation of the national law implementing the Directive 76/207 in the context of private employment relationships and their termination.

§2. *MARLEASING* AND THE EMERGENCE OF INDIRECT HORIZONTAL EFFECT

280. Notwithstanding occasional irritations, the iron rule is still in force: Directives do not have horizontal direct effect. To compensate this deficit, on the one hand, the court developed the *Francovich*-like type of liability of Member States. On the other, it introduced a sort of *indirect horizontal effect*, leading to considerable uneasiness in the Member States and among juristic scholars. The latter means national courts are obliged to interpret domestic law in the light of the directive, implemented or unimplemented. This interpretative obligation was deduced from the Member States' legal duty to take all measures necessary to ensure compatibility with EU law (Article 4(3) TEU).

281. Based on decisions in the 1980s,[611] the new principle was officially inaugurated by the Spanish case of *Marleasing*.[612] The issue of this case was whether national law can provide for a judicial declaration of nullity of a company contract on grounds other than those exhaustively listed in an EU directive, however not yet implemented in national law. The Court ruled that a national court is required to interpret its national law, regardless of whether passed before or after the directive, '*in the light of the wording and purpose*' of the directive (doctrine of *interprétation conforme*), to preclude a result contrary to its objective. *Inter alia*, this judgment led to doubts how this new method of 'consistent interpretation' of national law fits in the traditional canon of interpretative methods. Is the wording of the national provisions a borderline or does *interprétation conforme* authorize national courts to *contra legem* interpretation, thus crossing the conventional limits of law setting and law interpretation?

282. Later on, the Court supported this position, stating that the national courts are generally obliged to apply domestic law in the light of EU law. If the objective of a directive cannot be achieved through interpretation, the national court shall assess whether the applicant can rely on direct effect, given that the defendant could be interpreted as an emanation of the State. If this option is also not possible, the aggravated private party should rely on *Francovich* to get compensation for any loss

609. Case 179/88, *Handels- og Kontorfunktionærernes Forbund v. Dansk Arbejdsgiverforening* [1990] ECR I-3979.
610. Case C-32/93, *C.L. Webb v. EMO Air Cargo (UK) Ltd* [1994] ECR I-3578.
611. Case 14/83, *von Colson and Kamann v. Land Nordrhein-Westfalen* [1984] ECR 1891.
612. Case C-106/89, *Marleasing SA v. La Commercial International de Alimentación SA* [1990] ECR I-4135; *see also* Joined Cases C-240–244/98, *Oceano Grupo Editorial v. Rocio Murciano Quintero* [2000] ECR I-4941 (unfair terms in consumer contracts).

arguably sustained. Also, failure of a national court of last instance to apply the *Marleasing* doctrine might give rise to liability.[613]

§3. *MANGOLD* AND BEYOND

283. This legal development took a special turn in cases concerning employer-employee relationships. In the case of *Mangold*,[614] the issue was whether a German national provision on fixed-term employment contracts was applicable although supposedly in contradiction to an EU directive. The transposition period for this directive had, however, not yet expired in Germany. The Court here explicitly made, surprisingly and for the first time, reference to a *general principle of non-discrimination on grounds of age*. It argued that the existence of this principle was supported by 'various international instruments and ... constitutional traditions common to the Member States', though not identifying these sources more precisely.[615] It was implemented by the Directive 2000/78/EC,[616] which had not yet been transposed into German law. In its ruling, the Court did not rely on this directive; it ruled that this general principle (sic!)[617] can be invoked in the horizontal relationship between private employer and employee. If a national rule, contrary to the directive, is perfectly clear and cannot be interpreted, then the national court has to disapply the domestic provision. Due to many reservations in juristic academia and legal practice, the *Mangold* doctrine is limited to situations where a directive gives sufficiently precise expression to the general principle concerned. This remains of relevance for fundamental rights/freedoms of the EU Charter which are qualified as non-rights but 'principles'.[618]

284. Notwithstanding the diverse epistemological difficulties raised by *Marleasing*, *Mangold* and follow-up decisions,[619] the obligation of national courts to interpret its domestic law in conformity with EU law has in the meantime been recognized as 'inherent' in the system of EU law.[620] This subject of indirect horizontal effect and the like does not, however, need to be further elaborated on in this monograph. As pointed out at the beginning, with all its intricacies, this issue

613. *See* Case C-224/01, *Köbler*, *supra* text and fn 436.
614. Case C-144/04, *W. Mangold v. R. Helm* [2005] ECR I-9981; *see also* Case C-555/07, *S. Kücükdeveci v. Swedex GmbH & Co KG* [2010] ECR I-365 (period of employment), Case C-282/10, *M. Dominguez v. Centre Informatique du Centre Ouest Atlantique and Préfet de la région Centre* EU:C:2012:33 (right to paid annual leave); Case C-176/12, *Association de médiation sociale v. Union locale des syndicates CGT and Others (AMS)* EU:C:2014:2.
615. Case C-144/04, *Mangold* [2005] ECR I-9981, paras 74 and 75. As a harsh critique compare, *inter alia*, R. Herzog & L. Gerken, *Stop the European Court of Justice*, euobserver, 10.9.2008.
616. Directive 2000/78/EC establishing a general framework for equal treatment in employment and occupation, OJ 2000 L 303/16.
617. Non-discrimination on grounds of age is now comprised by the fundamental principle of non-discrimination in Art. 21(1) ChFR.
618. On this *see supra* text.
619. Compare fn 614.
620. Joined Cases C-397–403/01, *Pfeiffer and Others v. Deutsches Rotes Kreuz* [2004] ECR I-8835.

belongs to general EU law.[621] The remaining legal deficits in non-transposition cases after *Francovich* and *Marleasing* are well presented in the cases of *Faccini Dori*[622] and *El Corte Inglés*,[623] where the Court once more refused in a decisive manner to give horizontal direct effect to directives.

621. On this *see*, *inter alia*, Craig & de Búrca, *EU Law*, 200 (OUP 2011).
622. Case C-91/92, *P. Faccini Dori v. Recreb Srl* [1994] ECR I-3325: Ms *Faccini Dori* concluded at Milan Central Railway Station a contract for an English language correspondence course. Some days later she cancelled her order. The Directive 85/577/EEC to protect the consumer in respect of contracts negotiated away from business premises had not yet been transposed by Italy. Thus, the verdict that Ms *Faccini Dori* had to pay the agreed sum with interest and costs was upheld. *See also* Joined Cases C-397–403/01, *Pfeiffer and Others v. Deutsches Rotes Kreuz* [2004] ECR I-8835.
623. Case C-192/94, *El Corte Inglés v. Blazquez Rivero* [1996] ECR I-1281 (consumer credit directive).

Chapter 4. Conditions of Liability, and Competent Jurisdiction

285. In principle, an action for damages against a private party for breach of EU law has the same *structure* as the action against the Union or a Member State under vertical direct effect. But the *conditions* are not necessarily equivalent. For a successful action, the plaintiff must adduce evidence for the infringement of a protective horizontally directly effective provision of EU law, the incurrence of damage and the causal link between infringement and damage.

286. Unlike the other cases of EU law-based *State* breach-of-law liability, it seems here not feasible to formulate general rules for a relevant breach by private parties. It is less convincing, too, that requirements formulated for controlling public authorities shall be equally applicable for private parties. The conditions must be more context-specific. The rules for breach of competition law differ from the conditions in the case scenarios of private restrictions on the right to free movement. There must be an unjustified, effective infringement of the economic freedom. Most importantly, the central category for determining public liability of EU institutions and State authorities, their respective *margin of discretion* is absent in these scenarios.[624] Private parties do not exercise any discretion. They have to comply with law. These provisos having been made, one can restate the structure, namely the four conditions required for the liability of a private party for breach of EU law:

- protective, horizontally directly effective provision of EU law;
- damage;
- causation;
- *relevant breach* – this fourth and decisive condition has to be determined context dependent.

287. In addition, a further operation is necessary for the completion of an action for damages. Like in the Member States liability cases, the interface between EU law and national remedies has to be mastered, namely the process of transposing the EU law ground of liability into the respective national law system of remedies and causes of actions allowing compensation.[625] This opens up another playground for conform interpretation of national private law. This classic problem of separation of Union law and national law has been intensively treated by the ECJ in the 'discrimination of access to employment' cases in the 1980s and 1990s on the basis of the equal treatment Directive 76/207 EEC.[626] In *von Colson*, the Court stated for

624. *See supra* text.

625. Compare N. Reich, *The Interrelation Between Rights and Duties in EU Law: Reflections on the State of Liability Law in the Multilevel Governance System of the Union* (2010) 29 YEL 112; Reich., *Horizontal Liability in EC Law: Hybridization of Remedies for Compensation in Case of Breaches of EC Rights* (2007) 44 CML Rev 705. *See also* K. Havu, *Horizontal Liability for Damages in EU Law – The Changing Relationship of EU and National Law* (2012) 18 ELJ 407.

626. From Case 14/83, *von Colson and Kamann v. Land Nordrhein-Westfalen* [1984] ECR 1891; Case 79/83, D. *Harz v. Deutsche Tradax GmbH* [1984] ECR 1921; Case C-180/95, *N. Draempaehl v. Urania Immobilienservice oHG* [1997] ECR I-2195 to C-407/14, *M.A. Arjona Camacho v. Securitas Seguridad España SA* EU:C:2015:831.

the first time that national rules may not be sufficient for the enforcement of Union measures.[627] In *Marshall (No. 2)*, it declared a national upper limit on the amount of compensation (in cases of gender-based discrimination) contrary to EU law.[628] In the meantime, the settled jargon in discrimination cases became that financial compensation under national law must be 'adequate' in that it must enable to make good the loss and damage sustained by discriminatory dismissal in full.[629] More generally, reference is made to the procedural autonomy of the national legal systems which must fulfil two requirements: the chosen remedies for breach of EU law must be equivalent to the solutions of the domestic law in similar cases, and the chosen sanctions must be effective.[630] In the German discrimination case *Egenberger* the Court has to address the problem of whether entities of Christian Churches have the privilege to exclude per se Non-Christians from participation in recruitment competitions for secular posts.[631]

288. Whereas in non-contractual liability cases under Article 340(2) the Union can only be sued before the European courts, for cross-border litigation between private parties the competent jurisdiction has to be determined under the law of the Brussels I Regulation.[632] According to Article 7(2) of the Regulation, the plaintiff has to sue the defendant at the courts of the EEA State where the harmful event occurred or may occur.[633]

627. Case 14/83, *von Colson and Kamann* [1984] ECR 1891.
628. Case C-271/91, *Marshall (No. 2)* [1993] ECR I-4367.
629. Case C-407/14, *Arjona Camacho* EU:C:2015:831, para. 32.
630. On the principles of equivalence and effectiveness *see* already *supra* text.
631. Case C-414/16, AG Tanchev, Opinion, pending.
632. Council Regulation (EU) 1215/2012 on jurisdiction and the recognition and enforcement of judgments in civil and commercial matters, OJ 2012 L 351/1. *See supra* text.
633. *See supra* text (General Introduction, §3, III).

Part V. Joint Liability and Consequences of Liability

Chapter 1. Joint Liability and Subsidiary Liability

289. Sometimes two separate damages actions are brought against the Member State and against the Union.[634] In cases where the cause of the damage can be traced back equally to an illegal act or omission on the part of the Member State and to one on the part of the Union, the liability may be borne by Member State and Union *jointly and severally*. As a matter of fact, in the wheat mill case complex (*E. Kampffmeyer)*,[635] the ECJ has recognized that the [now] Union and the West German State were jointly liable for the damage caused to the claimants. Here, the Commission had authorized West Germany to maintain protective measures which were contrary to EU law. In a recent case where the legislative authorization by the EU merely granted a power and did not require the Member State to take a specific measure, responsibility of the Union for the then illegal action of the Member State, due to a lack of causation, was denied.[636]

290. Under conditions of joint and several liability of Union (EU institutions) and Member State, the damaged private party can elect who to sue *in solidum*, the Union before the European Courts, or the Member State before its national courts. The private party can obviously recover only once. Therefore, it needs procedures of apportionment of damages between the jointly liable defendants if one of them fully compensates the claimant. If the Union has paid the damages and a Member State is the other liable party, by EU law the Member State is under an obligation to reimburse its share of the damages. If the State does not fulfil its obligation, the Commission may initiate a Treaty infringement procedure before the European courts. Thus, the ECJ will ultimately determine the apportionment of damages between EU and Member State.

Procedures for both, to sue the two defendants jointly (before a European or a national court?) and to have recourse to the other non-sued defendant, have until now not yet been established.[637]

634. *See* e.g., Case 30/66, *Becher v. Commission* [1967] ECR 387.
635. Joined Cases 5, 7 and 13–24/66, *E. Kampffmeyer and Others v. Commission (E. Kampffmeyer)* [1967] ECR 245 (interlocutory judgment).
636. Case T-146/01, *DLD Trading Co v. Council* [2003] ECR II-6009.
637. For a detailed discussion of this neglected issue, *see* P. Oliver, *Joint Liability of the Community and the Member States*, in *The Action for Damages* 285 (Heukels & McDonnell eds, KLI 1997).

291. Imaginable is also joint and several liability of the Union and a private party,[638] or of a Member State and a private party, each one in breach of EU law respectively. Here would then be brought forward to EU law the question of subsidiarity of State liability.[639] According to this principle, the Union or Member State would be under a duty to compensation only if the damaged claimant cannot recover from the private party. Subsidiarity of State liability in cases of joint liability with a private party is an established principle in German law of governmental liability.[640] The subordinate character of EU institutions' liability, if joined with the liability of a private party, is also recognized in ECJ case law. In several cases, the Court stressed that liability of the Union may be conditional on the exhaustion of national remedies, provided always that such national remedies are effective means of protection for the private parties concerned and are capable of resulting in full compensation of the damage alleged.[641] Subsidiarity is expressly addressed in the civil service law of the EU. Article 24(2) of Staff Regulations stipulates that the Union has only to make good a damage sustained by a public servant if s/he is unable to obtain compensation from the private party who caused the harm.

638. This case scenario is envisaged in the civil service law. Compare Art. 24(2) Staff Regulations.
639. In the concrete *Kampffmeyer* case, both ECJ and German courts originally attempted to refer to the principle of subsidiarity, that is, the establishment of liability was made conditional on the showing that compensation before the national courts or the ECJ respectively was not attainable. Compare Joined Cases 5, 7 and 13 to 24/66, *E. Kampffmeyer* [1967] ECR 245 (as opposed to AG Gand, Opinion [1967] ECR 269, at 279); – and LG Bonn, 28 Nov. 1967 (1 O 223/67); OLG Köln, 2 May 1968, EuR 1968, 405 with comment by Ipsen. – The ECJ has amended this position with Case 43/72, *Merkur-Aussenhandels-GmbH v. Commission* [1973] ECR 1056.
640. §839(1)(ii) BGB. Compare BGH, 12 Apr. 1954, BGHZ 13, 88.
641. *See, inter alia,* Case 175/84, *Krohn v. Commission* [1986] ECR 753, para. 27; Case 81/86, *de Boer Buizen v. Council and Commission* [1987] ECR 3677, para. 9.

Chapter 2. Consequences of Liability: Damages

292. Dealing to a large extent with governmental liability, of the Union or the Member States, the first thing to be stated at the outset is that the remedies available do not comprise any correction or annulment of the unlawful legislative or administrative measure taken by the public authorities. State liability law does *not* grant any right to an *actus contrarius*, it only allows actions for *monetary compensation*.[642] The annulment of public measures must be pursued with separate claims before the European courts or the administrative courts of the Member States. The original symbiotic relationship has long been abolished, and the action for damages been established as autonomous and independent claims.[643]

The symbiosis of administrative and damages claims is to a certain extent still alive in the staff cases.[644]

293. Civil liability has been utilized by the European Courts for two purposes: on the one hand for deterrence, in order to discourage Member States from circumventing EU law. This includes the quest that the compensation, when a civil law sanction has been chosen by the Member State for infringement of the objectives of an EU directive, must be an effective remedy to exercise preventive effects. The appropriateness of the sanctions has to be determined by reference to the objectives of EU law.[645] On the other hand, it serves to protect the economic and non-economic interests of private parties and to ensure the compensation of their losses. Only the latter purpose is discussed in this section.

294. The consequence of liability, established under the conditions featured *supra* in the text, is *monetary compensation* of material and immaterial harm, of economic and non-economic loss. Article 340(2) TFEU and Article 41(3) ChFR stipulate analogously that any damage caused by the EU institutions or its servants has to be 'made good'. This is unanimously interpreted as a right of the aggrieved party to full compensation.

§1. Vicarious Liability for Torts

295. In the tort cases of vicarious liability, predominantly the general principles common to the law of the Member States apply.

---

642. This principle is clearly expressed in §1(1) Austrian Amtshaftungsgesetz (compare fn. 453).
643. Compare the post-*Plaumann* case law; *see supra* text (paras 92 et seq.).
644. *See infra* text (Part VI, Ch. 2).
645. Compare, *inter alia*, Case 14/83, *von Colson and Kamann* [1984] ECR 1891; Case C-271/91, *Marshall (No. 2)* [1993] ECR I-4367; Case C-180/95, *Draempaehl* [1997] ECR I-2195.

I. Personal Injuries

296. If an accident occurred resulting in *personal injuries*, like in the *Sayag*, *Grifoni I*, and *Leussink* cases,[646] the victim can recover the damage arising directly out of the injury, i.e., primarily costs of necessary medical treatment, physiotherapy and care.

297. Compensation can also comprise consequential damages. In the *Grifoni (I No. 2)* case, the costs for the provision of a suitably adapted home were awarded.[647] A prominent incident of consequential damages is *loss of earnings*. This loss is in principle recoverable under EU law. Loss of future earnings presents particular problems of assessment in EU cases because the diversity of national laws in this respect makes it almost impossible to identify a 'common' approach. AG *Tesauro* in *Grifoni* presented three main different methods of calculation: the *in concreto* assessment practised in particular in Germany, the multiplier approach in force in the common law countries, and the use of actuarial tables based mainly on the degree of invalidity and on a coefficient to take account of life expectancy. In the Romanic countries in the last group, different coefficients are provided for in the actuarial tables used.[648]

298. AG *Tesauro* denied in way of compromise to calculate a weighted average of the results obtained under each of the three methods. In view of the difficulties inherent in any alternative approach, he proposed a solution by referring to principles of international private law:

> Reference should be made to the method in use in the country in which the event occurs (place of accident, nationality and residence of the injured party) in order to assess the loss in financial terms.[649]

Though it had completely ignored the AG's proposal with respect to the ground of liability in the *Grifoni (I No. 1)* case,[650] here the Court apparently adopted the wise proposal of the AG. In applying Italian law, Mr *Grifoni's* claim for loss of earnings was divided between a period of total temporary invalidity, a subsequent period of temporary partial invalidity, and finally permanent partial invalidity.[651]

646. *See supra* text and fns.174, and 182.
647. C-308/87, *Grifoni (I No. 2)* [1994] ECR I-341, para. 11.
648. AG Tesauro, Opinion, *Grifoni (I No. 2)* [1994] ECR I-341, para. 8.
649. *Ibid.*
650. *See supra* text and fn 174.
651. For further details compare C-308/87, *Grifoni (I No. 2)* [1994] ECR I-341, paras 20–35; *see also* K. Oliphant, *Nature and Assessment of Damages*, in *Tort Law of the European Community* 241, at 258 et seq. (Koziol & Schulze eds, Springer 2008).

II. Non-economic Loss

299. The victim of an accident must be compensated, irrespective of any financial loss, for any personal injury damage which comprises physical or mental suffering.[652] Hence, in principle, *pain and suffering* is recoverable under EU law.[653] The respective amounts awarded vary tremendously in the Member States.[654] Another Question is whether additionally loss of amenities of life and disfigurement or dismemberment are compensable in Member States' law. Here again, the decision to apply the conflict-of-laws rules on *lex loci delicti* seems to be an appropriate choice.[655] Having said this, it deserves note that the European courts developed genuine criteria for compensation of non-economic loss in the special field of staff cases.[656]

III. Wrongful Death

300. The availability of compensation for loss of financial dependency or other material damage suffered as a result of another person's wrongful death has not yet been considered by the European courts in the field of vicarious liability law. In each case, the general principles, as far as common to the Member States, have to be taken into consideration. At least loss of maintenance by the dependents is a commonly recognized damage recoverable in all private law regimes of the Member States.

301. With regard to 'bereavement damages', an extreme diversity of national laws prevails and excludes any commonality.[657] Some States have passed special statutes.[658] The Court touched this issue in a traffic accident insurance case,[659] where wife and daughter of a deceased traffic victim claimed from the liability insurer of the causer of the accident compensation for the immaterial damage caused through the loss of husband and father. The Court held that the notion of

652. *Grifoni (I No. 2)*, para. 37. On compensation of non-material damage in staff cases, *see infra* text (paras 353–355).
653. An imperfect piece of EU legislation in this respect is the product liability directive of 1985, which does not include pain and suffering awards in personal injury cases. *See infra* text (Part VII, Ch. 1).
654. *Compensation for Pain and Suffering. New Trends in Europe and in USA* (Munich Re-insurance Co. ed., MunichRe 2012); S.D. Sugarman, *Comparative Look at Pain and Suffering Awards* (2005) 55 DePaul L. Rev. 399.
655. For a comprehensive comparative account compare S.D. Sugarman, *Tort Damages for Non-economic Losses: Personal Injury* 323, in *Comparative Tort Law* (M. Bussani & A.J. Sebok eds, Cheltenham, Elgar 2015).
656. *See* in greater detail *infra* text (Part VI, Ch. 2).
657. Compare U.M. Magnus, *Unification of Tort Law: Damage*s 210/211 (KLI 2001).
658. *See* prominently the British Fatal Accident Act 1976, as amended by Administration of Justice Act 1982. In 2017, Germany passed a 'Gesetz zur Einführung eines Anspruchs auf Hinterbliebenengeld', BGBl. I 2017, p. 2421.
659. C-22/12, *K. Haasová v. R. Petrík and B. Holingová* EU:C:2013:692; *see also* C-277/12, *Vitalijs Drozdovs v. Baltikums AAS* EU:C:2013:685 and AG Jääskinen, Joined opinion EU:C:2013:471.

'personal injuries' in the sense of the Motor Insurance Directives[660] covers any type of damage, material and immaterial, resulting from personal injury. If provided for by the applicable national tort law in question, bereavement damages have to be compensated by liability insurers.[661]

IV. Loss, Destruction and Damage of Things

302. Impairments resulting from the loss, destruction or damage of things have since the *lex Aquilia* been a core element of every law of delict or torts. A question in dispute can only be the issue of the calculation of the damage. The concrete damage can be measured by the market value of the good, or on a cost-of-cure basis.

Also questionable is the recoverability of consequential damages, especially loss of use of the respective object. In this respect, little European judicial authority exists on these questions.[662]

§2. Breach-of-Law Liability

303. In principle, a private party who suffered harm caused by a breach of EU law is entitled to full compensation. Full compensation shall place the natural or legal person in a position in which that person would have been had the breach of law not been committed. The right to full compensation therefore covers redress of actual economic loss and loss of profit, plus payment of interest.

I. Economic Loss

304. The realm of liability for breach of EU law, covering Union, Member States' and private parties' liability, is primarily, if not exclusively, concerned with pure economic losses, mostly loss of profits. Insofar the Court ruled in *Brasserie:*

> Total exclusion of loss of profit as [an independent] head of damage for which reparation may be awarded in the case of a breach of Union law cannot be accepted. Especially in the context of economic or commercial litigation, such a total exclusion of loss of profit would be as to make reparation of damage practically impossible.[663]

660. Recently codified as Directive 2009/103/EC relating to insurance against civil liability in respect of the use of motor vehicles, and the enforcement of the obligation to insure against such liability, OJ 2009 L 263/11.
661. Compare fn. 659 and *see infra* text.
662. For a comparative stock-taking compare Magnus, *supra* fn. 657, at 213–216.
663. Joined Cases C-46 and 48/93, *Brasserie du pêcheur and Factortame III* [1996] ECR I-1131, para. 87.

Legislative or administrative measures implementing the various economic policies often have adverse financial effects on the enterprises operating in the respective economic sector. Actions were then brought by businesses claiming loss of profit. For this class of actions, the ECJ developed an additional criterion: the damage must be '*direct, certain and specific*'.[664] This criterion served to exclude the assumed normal and foreseeable financial risks inherent in the market conditions from the scope of compensable losses.

305. In litigation under EU competition law just the opposite is true. In *Courage* and *Manfredi,* the Court emphasized that 'any individual' should be able to claim damages as long as a causal link between the loss and the competition infringement can be established.[665] 'Any individual' comprises parties to the competition restriction and third parties like final customers of the products. This is one of the rare cases where expressly primary, secondary and tertiary victims are covered by the protective scope of liability under EU tort law.[666]

306. If this criterion has been met, then the courts have to assess the alleged damage. In accordance with the law of the Member States, the category of damage comprises *damnum emergens* and *lucrum cessans*.

Damnum emergens is an actual loss of assets by destruction or depreciation, or the loss of money spent for the reparation of damaged property. If provable in its concrete extent, this damage is completely recoverable under EU law.

Lucrum cessans is a future loss. It covers an increase of assets under hypothetical conditions: how things would have developed if the damage-causing incident would not have occurred. In restating its settled case law, the ECJ in *Manfredi* made clear once more that a total exclusion of loss of profit would be such as to make reparation of damage practically impossible.[667]

307. Lucrum cessans means primarily the *loss of future earnings or profits*. For an assessment of this damage, account has to be taken of the loss of earnings consisting in the difference between, on the one hand, the income which the applicants would have obtained in the normal course of events from the transactions they would have made and, on the other hand, the income which they actually obtained under the circumstances produced by the unlawful measure of the EU institution.[668] The very existence of the economic loss is not called into question by uncertainty as to its precise extent.[669]

---

664. Case 18/60, *Worms v. High Authority* [1962] ECR 195, at 206; Joined Cases 67–85/75, *Lesieur v. Commission* [1976] ECR 797, at 804–806.
665. Joined Cases C-295-298/04, *Manfredi* [2006] ECR I-6619, para. 62 (with reference to *Courage*).
666. For more details, *see* now the Directive 2014/104/EU, OJ 2014 L 349/1, on antitrust damages actions.
667. Paragraph 96.
668. Joined Cases C-295-298/04, *Manfredi* [2006] ECR I-6619, paras 92, 95–96.
669. Case C-611/12 P, *J.F. Giordano v. Commission* EU:C:2014:2282, para. 40. In this case, the Court nevertheless erroneously denied compensation. For a critique of this judgment, *see* Brüggemeier, *Revocation of Fishing Quotas* (2015) 2 JETL 304.

This damages calculation must also have regard to whether the loss through the unlawful measure has actually been passed on in the prices to the customers. Such a price increase would diminish or exclude a compensable loss.[670]

II. *Perte d'une chance*/Loss of a Chance

308. According to this concept, originally developed in France,[671] also the loss of a relevant chance to realize an increase of assets or to avoid a financial loss or an impairment of health can be qualified as a compensable damage. It leads to proportional compensation of damage corresponding to the opportunity lost. Some Member States recognize this approach in medical treatment cases in which a doctor made a mistake in his diagnosis or did not treat the patient in appropriate time. In the hypothetical case of correct comportment, the patient would have had a chance of x% to be cured or to survive. Then, x% of the concrete sustained damage could be recoverable from the hospital or medical staff. Other case scenarios are the excluded chances, by fault of another party, to participate in a competition or tournament, or to proceed with a judicial process due to one's attorney's failure to appeal in time.

309. Whether *perte d'une chance* is recognized in general EU law of damages is questionable.[672] The concept seemed, however, to be applied in staff cases.[673] The medical treatment case of *Nijmann* looks like a loss of a chance case, though not explicitly labelled as such.[674] Loss of opportunity has been treated as compensable damage cases of impeded participation in recruitment procedures.[675] A recent example is the case of *Girardot*. Ms *Girardot*, an EU official, by wrongful conduct of the Commission was barred from participating in a recruitment procedure for a vacant post within an EU institution. The ECJ, upholding the decision of the EGC, clarified that the damage sustained by the applicant is not the loss of earnings resulting from not being appointed to the post, but a percentage which intends to quantify the chance which Ms *Girardot* had of being recruited.[676]

---

670. Joint Cases 64 and 113/76, *Dumortier* [1979] ECR 3091, para. 15; Case 199/82, *Amministrazione delle Finanze dello Stato v. SpA San Giorgio* [1983] ECR 3595; Joined Cases 241, 242 and 245–250/78, *DGV and Others v. Council and Commission* [1979] ECR 3017. *See also infra* text: offsetting of advantages.
671. Cass Req, 17 Jul. 1889, Recueil Sirey 1891, 1, 399; compare G. Viney, P. Jourdain & S. Caval, *Traité de Droit Civil. Les conditions de la responsabilité*, nos 278–284, 370–373 (4th ed. L.G.D.J. 2013). On the French law in a comparative perspective, *see* R. Cardona Ferreira, *The Loss of Chance in Civil Law Countries* (2013) 20 MJ 56.
672. *See* the stock-taking by AG Villalón in his opinion on the *Giordano* case: ECJ C-611/12 P, *Giordano v. Commission*, EU:C:2014:195.
673. Compare V. Giacobbo-Peyronnel, *L'indemnisation de la perte de chance en droit de la function publique de l'Union européenne,* in *Contentieux de l'Union européenne – Questions choisies* (S. Mahieu ed., Larcier 2014).
674. *See infra* text and fn 757.
675. Compare T-20/89, *H.J. Moritz v. Commission (Moritz No. 2)* [1993] ECR II-1423; follow-up decision to Case-68/91 P, *Moritz v. Commission* [1992] ECR I-6849.
676. Compare Case T-10/02, *Girardot v. Commission* (*Girardot No. 1*) EU:T:2004:94; and *Girardot No. 2* EU:T:2006:148; Case C-348/06 P, *Commission v. Girardot* [2008] ECR I-833.

310. Angonese was a classical loss of a chance case,[677] but there the Court focused on horizontal direct effect and left the question of damage to the national Italian court. The product liability and medical treatment case of *Veedfald*[678] might be qualified as a loss of a chance case. It is, however, a secondary injury case. Both AG and ECJ did not address these issues.

III. Punitive/Exemplary Damages

311. Punitive damages which can complement the compensatory damages for economic and non-economic loss under certain circumstances are primarily awarded in overseas common law jurisdictions like USA, Canada and Australia. In the EU only the law of England, Wales, Northern Ireland, Ireland and the mixed jurisdiction of Cyprus in a more or less restricted form provide for this specific kind of damages (exemplary damages).[679] Concerning their availability in EU non-contractual liability law, the ECJ stated in *Brasserie:*

> In so far as [oppressive, arbitrary or unconstitutional] conduct [of public authorities] may constitute or aggravate a breach of Union law, an award of exemplary damages pursuant to a claim or an action founded on Union law cannot be ruled out if such damages could be awarded pursuant to a similar claim or action founded on domestic law.[680]

312. Nevertheless, in *Factortame IV* the English Divisional Court rejected the claim for exemplary damages. One of the arguments used was that the recognition of exemplary damages as recoverable in the UK under EU law would set English law apart from other Member States law where punitive damages mostly cannot be awarded. This would counteract efforts to develop a uniform set of EU liability law remedies.[681] In 2014, the EU legislator stipulates in the Directive on Antitrust Damages Actions: 'Full compensation under this Directive shall not lead to overcompensation, whether by means of punitive, multiple or other types of damages.'[682] A similar approach has been endorsed in discrimination cases. In *Arjona Camacho* the Court held that adequate financial remedies for discrimination on grounds of sex do not involve punitive damages which go beyond full compensation of loss and damage actually sustained.[683]

---

677. *See supra* text and fn 561.
678. *See infra* text and fn 805.
679. Compare on legal politics, *The Power of Punitive Damages – Is Europe Missing Out?* (L. Meurkens & E. Nordin eds, Intersentia 2012); *Punitive Damages: Common Law and Civil Law Perspectives* (H. Koziol & V. Wilcox eds, Springer 2009).
680. Joined Cases C-46 and 48/93, *Brasserie du pêcheur and Factortame III* [1996] ECR I-1131, para. 89; *see also* Joined Cases C-295-298/04, *Manfredi* [2006] ECR I-6618, paras 92, 93.
681. *R v. Sec'y of State for Transport ex parte Factortame Ltd (Factortame IV)* [1998] 1 CMLR 1353 (QBD).
682. Article 3(3), OJ 2014 L 349/1; *see also supra* text.
683. Case C-407/14, *M.A. Arjona Camacho v. Securitas Seguridad España SA* EU:C:2015:831, para. 34 (on the basis of the recasted equal treatment Directive 2006/54/EC).

§3. Interest

313. A claim for interest is in general admissible.[684] 'The award of interest, in accordance with the applicable national rules, must therefore be regarded as an essential component of compensation.'[685] Interest is payable on the amount of compensation as from a determined date to the date of payment. The annual rate will be fixed having regard to the respective conditions of the financial markets.

§4. Limitations of Damages

314. Four well-known elements of the liability law of the Member States limit or reduce the amount of damages: contributory negligence, avoidable consequences, offsetting of advantages (*Vorteilsausgleichung*), and assumption of risk.[686] All four elements are also applicable under EU law. 'It is a general principle common to the legal systems of the Member States that the injured party must show reasonable diligence in limiting the extent of the loss or damage, or risk having to bear the damage itself.'[687]

I. Contributory Negligence

315. Contributory negligence (*Mitverschulden/faute de victime*) of the claimant is the most important ground for limiting or denying liability of the defendant.[688] Under Roman law, continental *ius commune* and in English common law, the victim's own fault that contributed to the injury entirely exonerated the defendant from liability. Starting with the civil law codifications of the nineteenth century, this rule was thoroughly derogated from in the twentieth century in both legal systems of civil law and common law. The *rule of comparative fault* came into force. The existence and extent of compensation depend upon a balancing to determine whether and to what degree any fault of the damaged party has contributed to causing the damage. Contributory fault of employees/public servants is imputed to the employer or the public authority. If contributory negligence is established, it results in an apportionment of damage between the parties; e.g., in the 'tort' cases of *Adams*[689] and

684. Compare A. van Casteren, *Art. 215(2) EC and the Question of Interest*, in *The Action for Damages* 199 (Heukels & McDonnell eds, KLI 1997); P. Oliver, *The Right to Interest in Community Law*, EuZW 1998, 481.
685. *See, inter alia*, C-271/91, *Marshall (No. 2)* [1993] ECR I-4367, para. 31.
686. On this in greater detail, *see* Brüggemeier, *Common Principles of Tort Law* 220; W. van Gerven et al., *Tort Law* 689.
687. Joined Cases C-104/89 and C-37/90, *Mulder and Others v. Council and Commission (Mulder II)* [1992] ECR I-3061, para. 33; Joined Cases C-46 and 48/93, *Brasserie du pêcheur and Factortame III* [1996] ECR I-1131, para. 85.
688. For a comparative account *see Unification of Tort Law: Contributory Negligence* (U. Magnus & M. Martín-Casals eds, KLI 2004).
689. Case 145/83, *Adams v. Commission* [1985] ECR 3556, paras 53 and 54.

Grifoni[690] the Court determined a quota of 50% contributory negligence of the plaintiffs.

316. In cases of State liability, Union or Member States, contributory negligence can lead to the forfeiture of claims. Thus, national law often provides that actions for damages against the State are excluded if the damaged party failed to prevent the loss by appealing against a court decision or by contesting an administrative act before the competent courts.[691] This was early adopted for EU law.[692] In the *Brasserie* case, the Court mentioned this onus to exhaust in time all legal remedies available, but remained inexplicit about the consequences in case of failure.[693]

In *Transportes Urbanos,* a rule of Spanish law did not require that, in cases of unconstitutionality of Spanish legislation, all domestic remedies for challenging the validity of an administrative measure must be exhausted, before the plaintiff can bring an action for damages against the State. Here, the principle of equivalence precluded a similar requirement of exhaustion in cases of State liability for breach of EU law through national legislation.[694]

II. Mitigation of Damage

317. From the perspective of the law of damages, once the ground of liability is given, that is, upon determination of an attributable injury to a legally protected interest, of a *danno ingiusto*[695] or a damage per se,[696] a new situation arises. It implies a disadvantage for the claimant: as to the further consequences, he/she/it is now expected to remedy or limit the losses arising from the injury or primary damage. One speaks of a 'duty'[697] imposed by law or burden to mitigate the damage. Reasonably avoidable consequences cannot be recovered.[698] This avoidability-of-cost rule is recognized in EU law. In *Brasserie*, the ECJ made this clear for cases of breach of EU law before national courts:

> i)n order to determine the loss or damage for which reparation may be granted, the national court may inquire whether the injured person showed reasonable diligence in order to avoid the loss or damage or limit its extent … .[699]

---

690. Case C-308/87, *Grifoni (I No. 1)*, paras 16 and 17.
691. *See*, e.g., §2(2) Austrian Amtshaftungsgesetz; §839(3) German BGB.
692. Case 4/67, *Anne Muller (née Collignon) v. Commission* [1967] ECR 365.
693. *Brasserie*, para. 84.
694. C-118/08, *Transportes Urbanos y Servicios Generales SAL v. Administración des Estado* [2010] ECR I-635.
695. Article 2043 Italian Cod. civ.
696. Article 1382 French C. civ.
697. Strictly speaking, it is not a legal duty, since it cannot be enforced as such. Duty, burden, or onus are used here, as they often are, synonymously.
698. *Brasserie*, para. 85; Joined Cases C-104/89 and C-37/90, *Mulder and Heinemann (Mulder II No. 1)* [1992] ECR I-3061, para. 33.
699. *Brasserie*, para. 84.

III. Offsetting of Advantages

318. Payment of damages should not entail unjust enrichment of the recipients/ claimants. Therefore courts have to take account of the fact that unduly caused losses have been incorporated in the price of goods and thus passed on to purchasers. This passing-on defence is recognized in cases where EU institutions or Member States authorities levied duties in breach of EU law and claimants sued for repayment of these charges.[700] – Another field of application of the passing-on defence is antitrust damages law. In *Courage* and *Manfredi* the Court stated that EU law does not prevent courts from taking steps to ensure that the protection of rights guaranteed by Articles 101 and 102 TFEU does not lead to unjust enrichment of those who enjoy them.[701]

IV. Assumption of Risk

319. Another doctrine that mostly legitimates an exclusion of liability is assumption of risk. *Scienti non fit inuria.* The constitutive element is the necessary individual decision (reasonable or unreasonable) to accept a certain *known* risk as 'part of the bargain'. There must be knowledge of the risk and acceptance thereof, though such acceptance of risk may be either express or implied. The typical risks 'inherent in the respective sector of business', notoriously mentioned by the European courts,[702] can be interpreted as assumed financial hazards of running this business. Not assumed are the unknown, unforeseeable risks the enterprise is confronted with, which may lead to compensation.

In *Courage Ltd*, the ECJ ruled that being a party to the competition restricting agreement that has caused harm is not a valid reason to prevent the party from relying on the relevant provision in order to get compensation.[703]

320. In cases of minors, an assumption of risk is valid only if the condition of discernment, i.e., the capacity to comprehend the situation, is fulfilled. As far as can be seen, the European Courts have not yet had the opportunity to deal expressly with the doctrine of assumption of risk.

§5. Prescription/Period of Limitation

321. The Protocol on the Statute of the CJEU provides in Article 46(i): 'Proceedings against the Union in matters arising from non-contractual liability shall be

---

700. Case C-199/82, *Amministrazione delle Finanze dello Stato v. SpA San Giorgio* [1983] 3595; Case C-147/01, *Weber's Wine World Handels-GmbH and Others v. Abgabenberufungskommission Wien* [2003] I-11365.

701. Case C-453/99, *Courage Ltd* [2001] ECR I-6297, para. 30; Joined Cases C-295-298/04, *Manfredi and Others* [2006] ECR I-6618, para. 94. In greater detail, *see* C.A. Jones, *Private Enforcement of Antitrust Law in the EU, UK and USA* (OUP 1999); *Competition Damages Actions in the EU* (D. Ashton & D. Henry eds., Elgar 2013).

702. *See* references in fn 285.

703. Case C-453/99, *Courage Ltd* [2001] ECR I-6297, paras 28 and 36.

barred after a period of *five years* from the occurrence of the event giving rise thereto.'[704] This five-year period cannot begin before all the requirements governing an obligation to provide compensation for damage are satisfied and in particular before the damage to be made good has materialized. Accordingly, when the situations concerned are those in which the liability of the Union has its origin in a legislative measure, the period of limitation cannot begin before the injurious effects of the measure have been produced. All damages actions brought against the Union under Article 340(2) TFEU are covered.

322. The expiry of the limitation period must be raised by the defendant.[705] As in the laws of many Member States, the expiry of the limitation period cannot be raised by the Court on its own motion. Expiry cannot be pleaded against an applicant who was not aware in time of the event which gave rise to the damage and therefore did not have reasonable time to bring a claim in due time. The fact that the applicant was unaware must be excusable from the point of view of a normally prudent person.

323. Article 46 of the Statute of the Court of Justice also treats the interruption of the period of limitation. The five-year period of limitation is interrupted if proceedings are instituted before the Court or if prior to such proceedings an application is made by the aggrieved party to the relevant institution of the Union. In the latter case, a claim must be instituted within a period of two months.

324. Claims for breach of EU law directed against Member States or private parties fall under the prescription law of the respective Member State. In the *Factortame* litigation the English High Court held that *Factortame's* damages actions were 'founded on tort' and that consequently a six-year limitation period applied.[706] In this respect, it is the general message of the ECJ that reasonable national limitation periods are compatible with EU law requirements.[707] Whether this reasonability is given if the national period of limitation is shorter than the five-year period seems questionable. There is, however, as far as can be seen, no judicial authority as yet dealing with this question.

---

704. On this in greater detail, *see* A. Pereira, *Limitation Periods in EC Law*, in *Tort Law of the EC* 293 (Koziol & Schulze eds, Springer 2008); M. Broberg, *The Calculation of the Period of Limitation in Claims Against the European Community for Non-Contractual Liability* (2001) 27 EL Rev 275; M. Núnez Müller, *Die Verjährung außervertraglicher Schadensersatzansprüche gegen die EG,* EuZW 1999, 611; T. Heukels & A. McDonnell, *Limitation of the Action for Damages Against the Community*, in *The Action for Damages* 217 (Heukels & McDonnell eds, KLI 1997).
705. Case 20/88, *Roquette Frères v. Commission* [1989] ECR 1553; Lenaerts, Arts & Maselis, *Procedural Law* 405 (2006).
706. *R v. Sec'y of State for Transport, ex p. Factortame Ltd and Others (Factortame V)* [2001] 1 WLR 942.
707. Compare *Rewe* and *Comet*, *supra* fn 383.

Chapter 3. Summary and Commentary

§1. Three Heads of Liability for Breach of EU Law

I. Union's Breach-of-Law Liability

325. According to the settled case law on the Union's liability for damage caused to private parties by breach of EU law attributable to a Union institution or body, a right to an action for damages against the EU is afforded where four conditions are met:

(1) Availability of a protective provision of EU law; that is, the provision must not only impose an obligation on the EU institution, but must be intended to confer rights on private parties or to protect their legitimate interests in another way (protective rule/*Schutznorm*).
(2) *Relevant breach* of this (superior) EU law by a legislative or administrative measure by an EU institution or body. Whether a breach is relevant to trigger liability depends on the extent of discretion the institution or body enjoyed when taking the decision. A wide margin of discretion requires a sufficiently serious or manifest breach (gross maladministration); in cases of restricted or no discretion, plain breach of the law (unlawfulness) will suffice. In recent case law, a third category emerged: situations without discretion but with high factual and legal complexity. Here, some sort of institutional fault may be required to trigger liability.
(3) Damage or injury sustained by the private party.
(4) Causal link between the damage/injury and the relevant breach of the protective rule.

II. Member States' Liability

326. In cases of liability of Member States, attention has to be paid to the complex interface between EU law (ground of liability) and national remedies (enforcement of liability). The liability for breach of EU law follows two main paths:

(1) Vertical direct effect cases

These cases cover primarily unduly levied duties or discrimination committed by Member States authorities. Starting with the *Brasserie du pêcheur* judgment, from the mid-1990s onwards the EGC and ECJ have consistently applied the same principles as in cases of breach of EU law by Union institutions. The liability is, however, not restricted to public bodies. Every emanation of the 'State', public or private, can meet the condition of vertical direct effect.

(2) *Francovich* Doctrine

The scope of application of this type of Member States' liability is much closer. It is restricted to an infringement of the obligation to transpose directives in due time and in appropriate form into national law. The last three conditions of Union liability apply in principle. Incidences of non-transposing a directive in the prescribed time period are clear-cut cases of breach of EU law. If the directive confers in a clear and unconditional way a right to private parties, the plain infringement of the Member States' obligation under Article 288(3) will lead to liability. A sufficiently serious breach is required in cases of timely but incorrect transposition of a directive.

327. However, this system of non-contractual liability of Member States for damage caused by breach of EU law does not apply in '*purely internal situations*'. This has recently been confirmed in the lengthy and extensive Belgian case complex of *Ullens de Schoten*.[708] Purely internal situations concern cases which are confined in all respects within a single Member State and where any link between the circumstances of the dispute at issue and EU law (especially the four economic freedoms) is missing. Those damages actions are inadmissible before EU courts. Details of this concept may nevertheless be lacking in definite clarity.

III. Private Parties' Liability

328. The liability of private parties for breach of EU law was for a long time a privilege of the national law of the Member States. The prominent field of application was EU competition law. By the turn of century, with the *Courage Ltd* and *Manfredi* judgments, the judicial realignment of liability law for breach of EU law reached the world of private parties' litigation. In analogy to EU public liability, four conditions must be met for a damages action against a private party to be founded:

(a) Horizontal direct effect: that is, the provision of EU law must intend the protection of a conferred right or defined legal interest of a private party, and other private parties must be under an obligation not to infringe it. Here, the single market's fundamental freedoms may collide with fundamental constitutional rights. Additionally, breach of EU law may suffice to legitimate a competitor's action for damages.
(b) Relevant breach of the provision of EU law. The conditions of relevant breach in these cases can only be defined in a context-specific way.
(c) Damage/Injury.
(d) Causation.

§2. Vicarious Liability of the Union

329. Somewhat neglected by courts and scholars and misallocated in the breach-of-law division of the Union's non-contractual responsibility, vicarious liability struggles to be recognized as an independent and separate field of the EU liability law under Article 340(2). It requires regular torts of the public servants and EU

708. Case C-268/15, *F. Ullens de Schoten v. Etat belge* EU:C:2016:874, paras 50–60 and case law cited.

bodies 'in the performance of their official duties' and remains in so far more closely under the umbrella of common principles of the law of delict/torts of the Member States.

§3. Commentary

330. The *full effectiveness of EU law*, the promotion of which was the paramount target of the EU judicature and which was used as a justificatory formula in nearly every judgment in the early case law when developing the law of non-contractual liability for breach of EU law, has rarely had an equivalent in the practical outcomes of the procedures before the Luxembourg courts. One scholar spoke aptly of 'triumphs for the law and hollow victories for the aggrieved private parties'.[709] The overwhelming majority of actions for damages against legislative acts have been unsuccessful.[710] The cases decided since the 1990s seem to evince a more liberal attitude towards establishing liability. But to achieve this result, it often needed two separate procedures. First, the Court would decide only on the ground of liability and leave it to the litigants to arrange on the amount of damages in out-of-court settlements. If this failed, the party had to return to the Court again. Suing in Luxembourg was, and still is, a time and money consuming endeavour.[711] Another reason for settling cases out of court emerges when Member States are the defendants. It is the intricate problem of transposing the principles of EU breach-of-law liability into the legal systems of the Member States with their fault grounded liability.

331. One main reason for these disastrous statistics is the extreme uncertainty of the EU law of breach-of-law liability. The outcome of the procedure depends nearly exclusively on highly indeterminate legal categories: protective rule, emanation of 'State', wide discretion, high complexity, 'sufficiently serious breach', to name just the most important ones. Often the preliminary rulings of the ECJ remain opaque and ambiguous, forcing the parties before national courts into out-of-court settlements. In addition, the standard of proof in proceedings before the European courts is supposedly very high. And another aspect should not be completely forgotten. In these cases in tort, it is EU courts ruling on EU institutions and on spending EU money.[712] The neutrality of courts, present in ordinary civil litigation, might here (sometimes) be missing.

---

709. W. van Gerven, *Bridging the Unbridgeable* (1996) 45 ICLQ 507.
710. A study, published in 1998, stated that only in one of twenty-five cases in Luxembourg could the damaged party finally recover. Compare H. Rasmussen, *European Court of Justice* 192 (Copenhagen 1998): analysing ECJ cases until 1990. On the final outcome of Member States' liability cases in England and Germany, compare T. Lock, *Is Private Enforcement of EU Law through State Liability a Myth?* (2012) 49 CML Rev 1675.
711. The same holds true for suing before Member States' courts for breach of EU law. Compare the drastic example of Case C-445/06, *Danske Slagterier* (fn 337).
712. On Member States' institutions and Member States' money respectively.

Be that as it may, for a private party to bring an action for damages in Luxembourg remains a risky, unpredictable undertaking.[713] The old saying, 'on the high seas and before judges we are alone in God's hand', was never more true than in cases before the European courts.

713. I finish this section with a lengthy quotation of van Dam's telling summary of EU tort law in C. van Dam, *European Tort Law* 50 (2d ed., OUP 2013):

> 'The most fundamental issue is that loud barking of the principle of liability rarely leads to bite. In practice, the claimant has many hurdles to overcome in order to succeed in a claim for breach of EU law and it is, therefore, not surprising that most runners never reach the finish line. Although they are not necessarily representative, it is remarkable that in many of the above-mentioned cases in which the principle of liability for breach of EU law was established or elaborated, the claimant achieved renown but lost the case. It is one thing to have a principle of liability to ensure the application and effectiveness of EU law but it is quite another to see what it achieves in practice. *In fact, the case law of the ECJ itself calls into question the effectiveness of the rules of liability for breach of EU law.*' (Emphasis added.)

Table 3 Breach of EU Law Liability

Breach of EU Law Liability

by Member States	by EU Institutions	by Private Parties
(I) protective rule vertical direct effect *van Gend en Loos*	Art. 340(2) TFEU protective rule *Relevant Breach*	protective rule horizontal direct effect *Defrenne II/Angonese*
(II) absence of horizontal direct effect of directives *Francovich* liability	legislative acts *Schöppenstedt* *HNL* administrative acts	competition law *Courage/Manfredi*
(III) State protective duty *Schmidberger*	*Margin of discretion test* *Bergaderm* (1) No-fault/plain breach (2) serious/manifest breach	Implied Rights of Action *Muñoz*
(IV) State courts of last instance *Köbler*	(3) *High complexity test* institutional fault?	conflict of fundamental freedoms & fund. rights *Viking/Laval*
(V) Vicarious liability?		

– relevant breach *Brasserie* *Hedley Lomas* *Bergaderm*		– relevant breach ? context specificity !
Procedural autonomy of Member States	– damage – causation	Procedural autonomy of Member States

Part VI. Special Cases of Responsibility of the European Union

332. This Part deals with two fields of responsibility of the Union *without breach of EU law* by its institutions and *without torts* by public servants and bodies.

Chapter 1. Compensation for Damage by Lawful Acts

§1. History

333. In 1996, *H.J. Bronkhorst* stated that the issue of the Union's responsibility for adverse consequences of lawful acts by EU institutions is 'at an embryonic stage',[714] and this in nearly every respect. Some Member States' laws recognize an obligation of the State to compensate severe losses of private parties caused by official acts which do not fulfil the precondition of breach-of-law (wrongful act of the State) or of a tort by a public servant or body. The rationale for this approach is the *principle of equality of public burdens*. The principle of equal treatment includes the obligation for the public authorities not to hold a limited number of private parties financially responsible for adverse consequences of acts taken in the public interest. This principle is infringed if, on behalf of the general public, by lawful official acts a private party had to sustain a *special sacrifice* of assets.[715] In German law, the concept of *Aufopferung* was already incorporated in the Prussian Code (General Land Law) of 1794.[716] The so-called *Aufopferungshaftung* is considerably older than the fault grounded governmental liability from the end of the nineteenth century but restricted to fair compensation of personal injuries. In French law, this concept was based on the principle of '*rupture de l'égalité devant les charges publiques*' resulting in a '*préjudice spécial et grave à un petit nombre de personnes*', a principle which supposedly is traceable to Article 13 of the *Déclaration des droits des hommes et citoyens* of 1789.[717]

334. It is considered a command of distributive justice that the private party is not left alone with this hardship but that it is passed on to the general public. Being an independent and autonomous variant of the public law system of remedies for compensation, it should not be brought into relationship with categories of liability

---

714. H.J. Bronkhorst, *The Valid Legislative Act as a Cause of Liability of the Communities*, in *The Action for Damages* 153 (Heukels & McDonnell eds, KLI 1997).
715. Recognized already in an old Dutch case of 1611, cited by Bronkhorst, l.c., pp. 153, at 155.
716. Prussian Law Gazette 1794; Introduction to the Act, §74,: 'Individual rights and privileges of the residents of a State shall be inferior to the rights and obligations serving the promotion of the common good, if a real collision occurs between them.' §75: 'The State shall compensate the person who was forced to sacrifice his concrete rights and privileges for the public interest.' – The theory of *Sonderopfer* referred to in the various Opinions of Advocates General is misleading. The determination of a loss as *Sonderopfer* served to justify compensation in cases of *unlawful acts* (sic!) of the State. Cf. N. Luhmann, *Öffentlich-rechtliche Entschädigung rechtspolitisch betrachtet,* 48 et seq. (Berlin, Duncker & Humblot 1965).
717. For cases where the action for compensation was based on the French concept of 'égalité devant les charges publiques' and the German theory of 'Sonderopfer' (fn. 16), compare Joined Cases 9 and 11/71, *Compagnie d'Approvisionnement et Grands Moulins de Paris v. Commission* [1972] ECR 391 and Case 59/83, *SA Biovilac NV v. EEC* [1984] ECR 4057 (plus AG Slynn, Opinion [1984] ECR 4091).

and with Article 340(2) TFEU. In *Brasserie*, the Court has meticulously (but incorrectly)[718] stated that the principle of non-contractual liability is 'simply an expression of the general principle familiar to the legal systems of the Member States that an *unlawful act or omission* gives rise to an obligation to make good the damage caused'.[719] This principle, 'inherent in the system of the Treaty' (sic!), however, does not cover responsibility for *lawful* acts or omissions. The term no-fault liability or strict liability is misleading. The issue here it is not about liability and damages, but about 'fair compensation'.[720] Thus, being not a regular 'breach of EU law' case scenario and hence not grounding in Article 340(2), it is at least treated by the Courts as a 'new plea in law' which cannot be introduced in that course of proceedings.[721]

335. In 1984, the Committee of Ministers of the Council of Europe adopted a 'Recommendation Relating to Public Liability.'[722] Principle II(1) of the Recommendation reads:

> 1. Even if the conditions [of faute de service] are not met, reparation should be ensured if it would be manifestly unjust to allow the injured person alone to bear the damage, having regard to the following circumstances: the act is in the general interest, only one person or a limited number of persons have suffered the damage and the act was exceptional or the damage was an exceptional result of the act.

Due to the complexity of the subject, the International Law Commission, however, decided in 1997 to refrain from formulating general principles of compensation for damage caused by public lawful acts (International liability for injurious consequences arising out of acts not prohibited by International Law). Instead, it shifted to the narrower focus of 'prevention of transboundary damage from hazardous activities' and of 'international liability in case of loss from transboundary harm arising out of hazardous activities'.[723]

336. *Legislative* acts are, as usual, in the limelight of case law and academic discussion. The public law of *expropriation* has here to be taken into consideration. In nearly all Member States, an expropriation of private property by legislative acts is

---

718. *See supra* text (para. 229).
719. Joined Cases C-46 and 48/93, *Brasserie du pêcheur and Factortame III* [1996] ECR I-1131, para. 29.
720. A similar term, 'appropriate compensation', has been introduced by AG Lenz, Opinion, in Joined 'Christmas butter' Cases 279–280/84 and 285–286/84, *W. Rau Lebensmittelwerke v. Commission* [1986] ECR 1085, para. 188.
721. Article 42(2) Rules of Procedure of the Court of Justice; Case C-104/97 P, *Atlanta AG and Others v. European Community* [1999] ECR I-6983, para. 27.
722. Council of Europe, Recommendation No. R (84) 15 (Strasbourg 1985). For a Member State's legislative initiative *see* the Dutch draft bill 'Codification of State Liability in Respect of Lawful Activities and Unlawful Decisions by Public Authorities', Documents of the Second Chamber of Parliament (2010–2011) 32 621.
723. Yearbook of the International Law Commission 1997, vol. II, part 2, paras 162–168 (UN ed., New York/Geneva 2000).

only lawful if compensation is provided for in the same act.[724] A famous non-European example is the 'Taking Clause' of the US Constitution: 'nor shall private property be taken for public use without just compensation',[725] which was the primary historical exception to sovereign immunity in US law. Measures of public taking which are in substance equivalent to expropriation are 'special sacrifices'. They require compensation equivalent to the reparation granted in cases of regular expropriation. This issue has been discussed by the AG *Roemer* and *Reischl* in the wheat mill cases of the 1960s. Both ultimately denied an action for damages in cases of purely illegal measures 'without grave culpability'.[726]

337. The crucial problem in these cases is less the assessment of an 'actual and certain damage', but more so the intricate adducing of evidence that the applicant has made any particular and/or disproportionate sacrifice in comparison with the other parties affected by the measure in question. *Inter alia*, in the *Bosphorus* case the ECJ stated correctly that even fundamental rights do not constitute absolute prerogatives, so that their exercise may be subject to restrictions justified by objectives of general interest.[727] Any measure imposing sanctions has, by definition, consequences which affect the right to property and the freedom to pursue a trade or business, thereby causing harm to persons who are in no way responsible for the situation which led to the adoption of the sanctions. Therefore, at the end the courts always have to answer the question whether the public measure at the root of the alleged damage is justified by some fundamental general interest.[728] One helpful step could be to show that one private party alone or only a small group was affected by the measure, so that their position was clearly distinguishable from the generality of comparable persons or businesses in a like position.

338. The legitimacy of claims to fair compensation for lawful acts under EU law had already, more cursorily, been considered by the ECJ in the 1970s and 1980s.[729]

---

724. Compare, e.g., Art. 14(3) German Constitution (Grundgesetz): 'The compensation has to be assessed weighing *justly* the interests of the public and of the private parties concerned.' (Emphasis added).
725. Amendment V. to the Constitution of the United States of America (last sentence).
726. In modern terminology: breach of law without 'sufficient seriousness'. Compare AG Roemer, Opinion, Joined Cases 63–69/72, *Werhahn Hansamühle and Others v. Council* [1973] ECR 1255, at 1273 et seq.; AG Reischl, Opinion, Joined Cases 56–60/74, *Kampffmeyer and Others v. Council and Commission (Kampffmeyer KG* [1976] ECR 748, at 765.
727. Case C-84/95, *Bosphorus Hava Yollari Turtim ve Ticaret AS v. Minister for Transport, Energy and Communication and others, Ireland (Bosphorus*) [1996] ECR I-3953: Irish impoundment of a Yugoslavian airplane operated by a Turkish airline. *Bosphorus'* application against the legality of the impoundment to the ECtHR in Strasbourg remained without success: ECtHR, 30 Jun. 2005, *Bosphorus v. Ireland* 42 EHRR 1.
728. Case C-84/95, *Bosphorus*, para. 26; *see also* Joined Cases 9 and 11/71, *Compagnie d'Approvisonnement et Grands Moulins de Paris v. Commission* (*Grands Moulins*) [1972] ECR 391.
729. Joined Cases 9 and 11/71, *Grands Moulins* (fn. 728) paras 45, 46; Case 54/76, *Compagnie industrielle et agricole du comté de Loheac and Others v. Council and Commission* (*Loheac*) [1977] ECR 645, para. 19; Case C 267/82, *Développement and Clemessy v. Commission* [1986] ECR 1907, para. 33; C 59/83, *Biovilac v. EEC* [1984] ECR 4057, para. 28; Case 265/85, *van den Bergh en Jurgens BV and van Dijk Food Products (Lopic) BV v. Commission* [1987] ECR 1155, para. 46.

These claims were from the outset, if at all, introduced as a subsidiary aspect of the damages actions for breach-of-law under Article 340(2). Telling examples of the treatment of responsibility for legislative acts were the so-called *Christmas butter* cases.[730] Around Christmas time, the Commission made available to the public in the EU quantities of butter from intervention stocks at low prices. The producers of vegetable margarine arguably suffered losses. They sued under Article 340(2), contending the illegality of the Commission's regulation which was the legal basis of the Christmas butter campaign.[731] Thus, it does not come as a great surprise that also the potential claims for fair compensation were straightforwardly treated in the liability language of damages actions for breach of law. The Court simply transferred concepts of breach-of-law liability from the disputes about measures which involve choices of economic policies[732] to this field of law. Nevertheless, the wrong course has already been set for the cases to come. These future cases, where liability for lawful actions became a prominent issue were claims of victims of retaliatory measures in political and economic conflicts.

§2. Dorsch Consult

339. Such a case was *Dorsch Consult.*[733] The dispute was about the legality of a legislative measure. The Courts followed the well-trodden path of liability for breach-of-law. *Dorsch* was a German engineering company with long-term contracts in Iraq. It sued the EU for losses arguably resulting from the Union's trade embargo on Iraq,[734] following the invasion of Kuwait in 1990. Iraq refused to pay debts arising out of earlier contracts on engineering consultancies. *Dorsch* alleged that this refusal was part of retaliatory measures and had its origin in the embargo. According to *Dorsch*, 'liability' of the EU arose by virtue of the principle of its responsibility for lawful acts, in that it (the *Dorsch* company) had suffered an impairment of its property rights equivalent to expropriation, or, alternatively, by virtue of the principle of the Union's liability for unlawful acts, inasmuch as the EU legislator failed to provide for compensation in respect of possible and foreseeable damages.

340. The EGC implicitly considered Article 340(2) TFEU legal ground for compensation. It did not find the embargo an unlawful act. Therefore, it addressed the subject of 'liability' for lawful legislative measures and formulated some general

730. Joined Cases 279, 280, 285 and 286/84, *Rau v. Commission* [1987] ECR 1069; Case 27/85, *Vandemoortele v. Commission* [1987] ECR 1129; Case 265/85, *van den Bergh en Jurgens v. Commission* [1987] ECR 1155. *See also* AG Lenz, Opinion, *Rau v. Commission* [1986] ECR 1084, paras 188, 189: 'sacrifice which threatened their very existence'.
731. Implementing Council Regulation (EEC) 2956/84, OJ 1984 L 279/4.
732. *See* supra text (paras 103 and 104).
733. Case C-237/98 P, *Dorsch Consult Ingenieurgesellschaft mbH (Dorsch) v. Council and Commission* [2000] ECR I-4549.
734. Council Regulation (EEC) 2340/90 preventing trade by the Community as regards Iraq and Kuwait, OJ 1990 L 213/1, amended by OJ 1990 L 216/28.

rules,[735] which on appeal were without reservation approved by the ECJ. The Court restated the current state of the law as follows:

> '(t)hat it is settled law that if the Union is to incur non-contractual liability as a result of a lawful or unlawful act, it is necessary in any event to prove that the alleged damage is real and that a causal link exists between the act and the alleged damage.'[736] … (t)he Union cannot incur non-contractual liability in respect of a 'lawful' act, as in the present case, unless three conditions, namely the reality of the damage allegedly suffered, the causal link between it and the act on the part of the EU institutions, and the unusual and special nature of that damage, are all fulfilled.[737]

341. The Court's decision in *Dorsch* was purely practical. It does not contribute substantially to the law of EU responsibility for lawful acts. Like the EGC, the ECJ denied the existence of 'actual and certain damage'. Nothing further needed to be said then about what constitutes an *unusual and special damage* or what characterizes a special sacrifice. Does it suffice that the damage goes beyond the normal risks inherent in the activity in the economic sector concerned, or must the very existence of the applicant party be threatened by the Union's act? Additionally, the Court did not have the opportunity to deliberate about the identical or non-identical grounds of responsibility in cases of lawful and unlawful measures of the EU institutions.

§3. FIAMM

342. This opportunity came up in 2008, when the collateral damages of the so-called *banana war* between the EU and the US were brought before the European courts. In 1993, the EU adopted a system that allowed African, Caribbean, and Pacific countries (ACP States) to export a certain amount of bananas to the EU without paying customs duty. Bananas from Latin America did not have access to the duty-free tariff rate quota. This provoked complaints by several WTO members, including the USA, where producers of South American bananas were located. The dispute came before the World Trade Organization (WTO). Its Dispute Settlement Body (DSB) found the EU regulations governing the import of bananas to be incompatible with the WTO rules. It authorized the US to levy a customs duty on imports from the EU as a sanction against its banana import regime. Due to these US measures, European exporters, whose products were affected by the increased US customs duty from 1999 to 2001, suffered losses for which they sought compensation from the Union.

---

735. Case T-184/95, *Dorsch Consult* [1998] ECR II-667, para. 59.

736. Case C-237/98 P, *Dorsch*, para. 17.

737. Paragraph 19. For follow-up decisions compare, *inter alia*, T-196/99, *Area Cova v. Council and Commission* [2001] ECR II-3597 and T-195/00, *Travelex Global and Financial Services Ltd v. Commission* [2003] ECR II-1681.

343. The EGC held that the WTO agreements could not be qualified as rules inferring rights to residents of the EU. Breach of them by Council regulations did not give rise to non-contractual liability of the Union under Article 340(2) TFEU. It then considered compensation for lawful legislation and stated that, as a general principle of EU law, the Union can incur 'liability' even in the absence of unlawful actions by its institutions, if the conditions indicated in the *Dorsch* judgment are met. The EGC, however, refused to acknowledge that the damage suffered by the applicant was unusual since it did not exceed the limits of the economic risks inherent in their export operations.[738]

344. On appeal, AG *Maduro* dissented. He undertook a grand attempt to deliver a justification of what he called the 'principle of no-fault liability' of the Union. Even though only a few Member States recognize such a principle, the decisive question is whether such a solution would best meet the specific needs of the legal system of the EU. The establishment of a principle of no-fault Union liability could take its inspiration from the notion of the equality of citizens in bearing public burdens on which French administrative law has based liability for legislation.[739] Turning to the core element of the conditions specific to the regime of no-fault liability, *unusual and special damage*, he stated:

> Damage must be classified as unusual when it appears to be such by reason both of the conditions in which it occurs and its intrinsic characteristics. Unusual use is, first of all, damage that exceeds the limits of the economic risks inherent in operating in the sector concerned, in other words, damage stemming from the materialisation of a risk that the victim could not reasonably have foreseen, against which he could not protect himself. But that is not sufficient. It must also be serious. Otherwise the burden cannot be regarded as unusual, and the damage would not verge on expropriation that cannot be left uncompensated in view of protection that must be given to property. That does not mean that the damage must be equivalent to total or definitive loss of ownership, but it must nevertheless entail sufficiently serious harm to the attributes of the right to property.[740]

345. The ECJ, however, straightforwardly and unequivocally disagreed. It ruled: When the EGC affirmed the existence of a regime providing for non-contractual liability of the Union on account of the lawful pursuit of its activities falling within the legislative sphere, it erred in law. The Court of Justice repeated the well-known formula that the non-contractual liability of the Union under Article 340(2) depends on the satisfaction of a number of cumulative conditions. It went on to hold:

---

738. Case T-69/00, *Fabbrica Italiana Accumulatori Motocarri Montecchio SpA (FIAMM) and Others v. Council and Commission* [2005] ECR II-5393; Case T-135/01, *G. Fedon & Figli SpA and Others v. Council and Commission* [2005] ECR II-29. *See also* Case T-83/00, *Beamglow v. European Parliament, Council and Commission* [2005] ECR II-5459; Case T-151/00, *Laboratoire du Bain v. Council and Commission* [2005] ECR II-23.

739. Joined Cases C-120/06 P and 121/06 P, *FIAMM and Fedon v. Council and Commission* [2008] ECR I-6513, paras 54–62.

740. Paragraph 76. A definition of the notion of 'special damage' was delivered in para. 77.

> Finally, it is clear that, while comparative examination of the Member States' legal systems enabled the Court to make the finding ... concerning convergence of those legal systems in the establishment of a principle of liability in the case of unlawful action or unlawful omission of the authority, including of a legislative nature, that is in no way the position as regards the possible existence of a principle of liability in the case of a lawful act or omission of the public authorities, in particular where it is of a legislative nature.[741]

346. Nevertheless, the Court ultimately embraced also the positions of its honourable AG, from *Roemer* and *Lenz* to *Slynn* and *Maduro*, and granted one proviso:

> With regard, ... , to the right to property and the freedom to pursue a trade or profession, the Court has long recognised that they are general principles of Union law, while pointing out, however, that they do not constitute absolute prerogatives, but must be viewed in relation to their social function. ...
> It follows that a Union legislative measure whose application leads to restrictions of the right to property and the freedom to pursue a trade or profession that impair the very substance of those rights in a disproportionate and tolerable manner, perhaps precisely because no provision has been made for compensation calculated to avoid or remedy that impairment, could give rise to non-contractual liability on the part of the Union.[742]

But the Court could not find that in the instant case there was an infringement of a right to property. So far, the conditions for compensation have not been found to be satisfied in any case of lawful acts.

§4. Post-FIAMM

347. As the law stands after *FIAMM*, it is supposedly settled law that a right to fair compensation of losses caused by lawful acts, especially of a legislative nature, of Union institutions does not exist under EU law. An exception has been made with *FIAMM* for measures which are expropriation in substance. But even in such a case, the Court might prefer to address the issue in terms of violation of the right to property rather than the theory of special sacrifice.

The ECJ did not take up the substantive arguments brought forward by AG *Maduro*. Deprived of their wrong connotations (no-fault liability), they presented the genuine rationale of this concept of fair compensation: equality and distributive justice. This indicates, too, that the legal ground for it is not Article 340(2) TFEU, rather it is an independent and autonomous remedy entailed in the legal system of the Union, not necessarily in those of the majority of the Member States. On this

741. Joined Cases C-120 and 121/06 P, *FIAMM and Fedon* [2008] ECR I-6513, para. 175.
742. *FIAMM*, paras 183, 184. *See also* A. Thies, *The Impact of General Principles of EC Law on Its Liability Regime Towards Retaliation Victims after FIAMM* (2009) 34 EL Rev 889.

basis the dispute on the pros and cons of compensation for lawful official acts will surely continue.[743]

348. In 1996 *H.J. Bronkhorst* said, the EU law of compensation of losses by lawful acts 'is still at an embryonic stage'. It still is, even twenty years later. For the birth of a new legal principle, the European courts have been in labour for a long time. Fortunately, they have obstetricians – the AG.

743. *See*, *inter alia*, Case T-196/99, *Aera Cova and Others v. Council and Commission* [2001] ECR II-3597; Case T-83/00, *Beamglow v. European Parliament, Council and Commission* [2005] ECR II-5459.

Chapter 2. Liability of the EU as Public Principal of the Civil Service

§1. General Rules

349. According to Article 270 TFEU, the European courts have jurisdiction in any dispute between the Union and its officials and employees within the limits and under the conditions laid down in the Staff Regulations or the conditions of employment. Under Articles 90, 91 of the Staff Regulations, such disputes include those between an official or servant and the institution in charge as appointing authority concerning compensation for damage arising out of the relationship of employment between the public servant concerned and the respective Union institution. These damages actions lie outside the field of application of Articles 268, 340(2) TFEU.[744] Temporarily, from its establishment in 2005 until its abolishment in 2016, the ECST[745] had the exclusive jurisdiction to hear and determine at first instance disputes between the EU and its servants pursuant to Article 270 TFEU. These disputes represent some 120 cases a year for approximately 35,000 members of the staff of the Union's institutions. This includes the disputes between all bodies or agencies and their staff.[746]

350. Due to the special character of the public servant-principal-relationship, damages actions of the servant are only admissible if the concrete measure of the institution arguably causing the damage is target of an annulment or an equivalent procedure. Within three months after having filed a complaint against the allegedly wrongful measure, the servant has to bring before the court an action concerning the measure adversely affecting him and with respect to the financial consequences which might have arisen.

351. Written EU law does not define the principles which apply to the liability of the institutions vis-à-vis EU officials. The principles which the ECJ has laid down in civil service law as ground of liability comprise three factors: *faute de service*/maladministration, damage, and a causal link between the two factors.[747]

The core elements comprise the closeness of the employer-employee-like relationship and the requirement of *faute de service*. The latter has its roots in French administrative law and means an administrative failure, an act or omission that constitutes maladministration. One may additionally have recourse to a general duty to

744. Case 9/75, *Meyer-Burckhardt v. Commission* [1975] ECR 1171. *See also* Case 48/76, *Reinarz v. Commission* [1977] ECR 291, para. 10; Case 317/85, *Pomar v. Commission* [1987] ECR 2467, para. 7; Case 401/85, *Schina v. Commission* [1987] ECR 3911.
745. Council Decision 2004/752/EC, Euratom establishing the European Union Civil Service Tribunal, OJ 2004 L 333/7, abolished by Regulation (EU, Euratom) 2016/1192, OJ 2016 L 200/137.
746. Inasmuch as jurisdiction is conferred by primary EU law or statutes to the European Courts.
747. Joined cases 19–20/69, 25/69 and 30/69, *Richez-Parise v. Commission* [1970] ECR 325; Case 11/86, *Delauche v. Commission* [1987] ECR 5345, para. 30.

have regard to the interests of the employee (*Fürsorgepflicht*)[748] of the EU institution as appointing authority (principal) towards its staff. Administrative failure or breach of duty of care constitutes wrongfulness in the sense of common law or objective negligence in the sense of civil law. In this context, a reference to the notion of 'sound administration' as comparative normative standard makes sense.[749] An additional condition of unlawfulness[750] is not required and should be completely avoided in this framework of civil service liability. That is the basic difference to the breach-of-law liability under Article 340(2) TFEU.

§2. PROTECTED INTERESTS

352. Most of the claims for financial compensation by officials are related to regular matters of civil service, i.e., pay, career progress, recruitment, disciplinary measures, etc. These disputes are of no interest for the analysis undertaken here. But there are also tort-like claims. These refer to health injuries[751] or infringement of personality rights and lead to compensation claims inasmuch as these harms are not covered by the EU insurance of officials. The 'Rules on the Insurance'[752] grant protection against the risk of accident at work and occupational disease. A lump sum is paid to cover the financial consequences of the accident or disease.

353. Therefore, actions for compensation of non-pecuniary loss are primarily concerned. In this field of law, the courts consistently take psychological and non-physical consequences into account.

In the case of *Berti,* compensation was sought for a scar which remained as a permanent disfigurement in the face of a child of a public servant after the injuries were healed.[753] The defendant Commission had to pay BEF 60,000.

354. In the *Leussink* case, the subject matter was loss of amenities or enjoyment of life.[754] Mr *Leussink*, an EU official, was involved in a road accident while travelling on mission in a car belonging to the EU and driven by an EU servant. The applicant was seriously hurt. As a consequence, he suffered from a number of

---

748. Compare Case 125/80, *Arning v. Commission* [1981] ECR 2539; Case 11/86, *Delauche v. Commission* [1987] ECR 5345, paras 25 et seq.
749. Insofar (though in a non-staff case) the Court correctly stated: 'The duty of care is inherent in the principle of sound administration.' Case C-47/07 P, *Masdar (UK) Ltd v. Commission* [2008] ECR I-9761, para. 92.
750. Compare the three-tiered concept of delict, stemming primarily from the Germanic civil laws. Cf. H. Koziol, *Basic Questions of Tort Law from a Germanic Perspective* Ch. 6, 171: elements of liability (Vienna, Sramek 2012); as critique *see* Brüggemeier, *Modernising Civil Liability Law* 50 et seq.; Brüggemeier, *Haftungsrecht*, 20–42.
751. *See, inter alia*, Case 152/77, *Miss B. v. Commission* [1979] ECR 2819; Case 131/81, *Berti v. Commission* [1985] ECR 645; Joined Cases 136 and 169/83, *Leussink and Brummelhuis v. Commission* [1986] ECR 2801.
752. Compare Art. 73 Staff Regulations, and the Rules on the Insurance of Officials of the EC, OJ 2005 L 8/1.
753. Case 131/81, *Berti v. Commission* .
754. Joined Cases 136 and 169/83, *Leussink and Brummelhuis v. Commission* [1986] ECR 2801. *See* already *supra* text (fn 182).

lasting sequelae, and he could never return to service. The financial consequences were borne by his official's insurance. He sued the Commission/Union for compensation of his non-pecuniary damage. In his private life, his relations with his wife, children and friends had been irreversibly disrupted. He could no longer enjoy the pleasures of everyday life. The Court ruled on a basis of presumed negligence of the Commission[755] and awarded BEF 3 million as non-pecuniary damages.

In *Leussink*, his wife and children also sought to recover for their own mental distress they experienced due to the extremely serious injuries of husband and father respectively. Though there could be no doubt about the reality and causation of these effects, the Court considered them to be too remote. 'This is borne out by the fact that the legal systems of the Member States make no provision for compensating such effects.'[756]

355. An interesting incident of injury to health came up in the *Nijmann* case.[757] Mr *Nijmann*, an EU official at the Ispra centre in Italy, had regularly for more than ten years during the course of his employment undergone the annual 'medical check-up'.[758] With a new medical officer in service, the existence of a pulmonary emphysema in an advanced stage of development had been diagnosed. Mr *Nijmann* alleged that this could have been noticed earlier and with this information he could have taken appropriate measures in due time to prevent this development. He sued the Commission for damages. The Court determined service-related fault by the EU medical service and went on to state correctly that the plaintiff suffered damage in the form of an aggravation of his illness. This objective (not curable) deterioration of his health condition should be compensated by an award of non-pecuniary damages.[759] Nevertheless, the court missed the point. The aggravation of his illness was not the consequence of a medical treatment. It was an iatrogenic process. In other words: The medical service did not cause the aggravation. Mr *Nijmann* was, by the fault of the medical service, deprived of a chance to combat this development of the illness in an earlier stage of evolution. Correctly seen, the *Nijmann* case is a case of *loss of a chance.*[760]

356. The European courts also grant non-pecuniary damages in cases of defamation or improper critique, though sometimes only by a symbolic compensation.[761] In the *Caronna* case,[762] the French satiric weekly '*Le Canard Enchainé*' published an article denouncing the behind-the-scenes lobbying of the construction industry in Brussels. Mr *Caronna* was named as a 'friend in the right place' of this lobby brotherhood within the Commission and was accused of blatant favouritism

755. The accident occurred because the tread came away from one tyre. The expert report gave as possible reasons for it: poor maintenance or inadequate inspection of the official cars.
756. Paragraph 22.
757. Case T-36/89, *Nijmann v. Commission* [1991] ECR II-699.
758. Provided for in Art. 59(4) of the Staff Regulations.
759. The court stated also contributory (comparative) negligence (50%) on the part of Mr *Nijmann* and awarded finally BEF 50,000.
760. On the treatment of loss of a chance cases by the European courts *see supra* text.
761. *See*, e.g., Case 343/87, *A. Culin v. Commission* [1990] ECR I-240.
762. Case T-59/92, *R. Caronna v. Commission* [1999] ECR II-1129.

in the performance of his duties. He sued the Commission for non-pecuniary damages because the Community breached its duty to have regard for the welfare of its servants by failure to take any action in time to vindicate his honour publicly, which had been called into question by that press article. The EGC held up his claim and determined a service-related fault by the Commission. It evaluated the damage *ex aequo et bono* and awarded a compensation of BEF 50,000.[763]

357. In a number of staff cases, the courts granted compensation for non-material impairments without a bodily injury, such as, e.g., 'shock', 'disturbance' and 'uneasiness' caused by the prospect of an unlawful dismissal,[764] or 'state of uncertainty' regarding the state of health[765] or the professional future,[766] arising from the inaction or another form of maladministration of an EU institution. In this context also belong cases of damages actions brought by EU officials against the European Anti-Fraud Office (OLAF). OLAF, established in 1999,[767] is responsible, *inter alia*, for carrying out internal administrative investigations intended to investigate serious facts linked to the performance of professional activities which may constitute a breach of obligations by bodies, agencies and officials of the Union.[768]

358. These latter cases underscore once more the qualitative and structural difference to general tort law. The focus here is not on direct bodily injury and consequential non-material impairments. At the fore is the special principal-official relationship that delivers the ground for compensation. It suffices that a *faute de service* – a breach of the 'duty to have regard to the legitimate interests of the officials/ employees' – occurred to lead to the compensation of purely mental or psychological consequences.

763. Case T-59/92, *R. Caronna v. Commission* [1999] ECR II-1129.
764. Compare as early cases: Joined Cases 7/56 and 3–7/57, *D. Algera and Others v. Common Assembly of the ECSC* [1957–58] ECR 39, at 66/67, and Case 110/63, *A. Willame v. Commission of the EAEC* [1965] ECR 649, at 667.
765. Joined Cases 10 and 47/72, *di Pillo v. Commission* [1973] ECR 763; Case 75/77, *Mollet v. Commission* [1978] ECR 897.
766. Case T-63/89, *Latham v. Commission* [1991] ECR II-19; Case T-68/91, *G. Barbi v. Commission* [1992] ECR II-2128.
767. Commission Decision 1999/352/EC, ECSC, Euratom of 28.4.1999, OJ 1999 L 136/20.
768. *See*, *inter alia*, Case T-309/03, *M. Camós Grau v. Commission* [2006] ECR II-1173; Case T-48/05, *Y. Franchet and D. Byk v. Commission* [2008] ECR II-1585.

Table 4 Non-contractual Responsibility of the European Union (II)

Non-contractual Responsibility of the European Union (II)

Responsibility for Lawful Acts	Article 340(2) TFEU	Staff Cases
'*égalité devant les charges publiques*'/'*Aufopferung*'	I Vicarious Liability for torts	principal-official-relationship *faute de service*
'fair compensation' no damages/ no strict liability	II Breach of Law by EU institutions	special remedies compensation of non-material impairments:
Dorsch Consult *FIAMM*	– protective rule – relevant breach – damage – causation	– shock – disturbance – state of uncertainty

Book II. Civil Non-contractual Liability

Chapter 1. Introduction

359. Beyond the liability systems for public torts and breach of EU law featured in Book I, there is no comparable regime of *civil* non-contractual liability established by secondary EU law. The EU legislator has harmonized only a few peripheral sectors of private liability law through directives or regulations, and many initiatives failed politically. The eminent exception is still the product liability directive which was passed in 1985 after more than ten years of controversial deliberations. It will be considered below in greater detail. The ambitious project of EU environmental liability which began with promising drafts of directives in the late 1980s finally ended up with a non-liability directive in 2004. Various fields of technical risks – railways, steamships, automobiles, airplanes, nuclear power plants – are covered by international conventions, ratified by most EU Member States and incorporated into their national law. Only one of these conventions has been adopted by an EU regulation in 1997: the Warsaw/Montreal Convention on international air carriage.[769]

Increasingly, another economic sector has come to the fore: information technology and free flow of personal data within the EEA. In 1995, the EU passed a data protection directive. Currently, it is in the process of being superseded by a General Data Protection Regulation. This field of law will be taken up in the last section.

769. *See also* the stock-taking of approximation of tort law within the EU by C. von Bar, *The Common European Law of Torts* vol. I, 375–418 (OUP 1998).

Part VII. Liability for Defectiveness

360. Some national laws, e.g., the Brazilian, Finnish, Russian and Spanish Consumer Protection Acts, take an embracing regulatory approach to both defective *products* and defective *services*. Whether this is a reasonable legal project does not need to be answered here. The European Commission intended to pursue a similar path. It first presented a directive on product liability, and shortly after passing the directive, the Commission began to work on a directive on liability for supplied services, which closely followed the model of liability for defective products. The defective service liability directive did not succeed. A first proposal was presented in 1990 but was repealed in 1994, and no new initiatives have been undertaken so far. Therefore, this part features primarily EU product liability and sketches only briefly the subject of service liability.

Chapter 1. Product Liability

§1. History

361. Relief for injuries caused by defective products became a serious problem in most developed industrial countries in the second half of the last century – from the US to Japan and Western Europe. Re-established large-scale production in these countries after the Second World War swamped the markets with products. The law available to determine the enterprises' responsibility in case of injuries was without exception the traditional fault-based law of delict or torts, i.e., *producers' liability* for negligence (*Produzentenhaftung*).[770] But negligence on the side of the enterprises when organizing complex industrial production processes was difficult to prove by the remotely injured parties, even after the courts went over to shifting the burden of proof for due care to the defendant manufacturer.[771]

362. A decisive change of the legal situation occurred when in the US the Supreme Court of California in its landmark judgment *Greenman v. Yuba Power Products* in 1963[772] decided that injuries caused by defective products were no longer governed by the tort of negligence, but by a new no-fault regime of non-contractual liability – strict products liability in tort. This new type of strict products liability started its triumphant progress through the jurisdictions of the US, when *W. Prosser*, then the reporter for the American Law Institute's (ALI's) new Restatement of Torts, adopted the concept and incorporated it into the Restatement (Second) of Law: Torts in 1965 as §402A.[773] This special liability of *sellers*[774] of products combined the remedies and directness of tort actions with the strictness of contractual warranty claims.

363. In the Europe of the 1960s, the reform of products liability law in the Member States of the (then) European Economic Community also became a matter of rising concern.[775] The EEC Commission started working on a directive on products liability in 1968, under the impression of the *Thalidomide* disaster in the UK and

---

770. *See* for the US: *MacPherson v. Buick Motor Co*, 217 NY 382, 111 NE 1050 (1916); for Germany: RG, 25 Feb. 1915, RGZ 87, 1; for UK: *Donoghue v. Stevenson* [1932] AC 562 (HL).
771. *See* for the US: *Escola v. Coco Cola Bottling Co. of Fresno*, 24 Cal 2d 453, 150 P 2d 436 (1944); for Germany, BGH, 26 Nov. 1968, BGHZ 51, 91 (fowl pest). As comparative accounts *see, inter alia, The Development of Product Liability. Comparative Studies in the Development of the Law of Torts* (S. Whittaker ed., CUP 2010); M. Tulibacka, *Product Liability Law in Transition. A Central European Perspective, Markets and the Law* (Ashgate 2009); *Product Liability in Comparative Perspective* (D. Fairgrieve ed., CUP 2005).
772. 59 Cal 2d 57, 377 P 2d 897 (1963).
773. ALI (ed), *Restatement (Second) of Law: Torts,* vol. II (ALI Publ. 1965). On the development of this field of US law *see Restatement (Third) of Law: Products Liability* (ALI Publ. 1998); D. Owen, *Products Liability* (2d ed., Thomson/West 2008).
774. That is every member in the distribution chain from the manufacturer of product components to the last retailer.
775. Reform of products liability was, e.g., a prominent subject of the 47th German Lawyers Convention (Deutscher Juristentag) 1968.

the *Contergan* catastrophe in West Germany.[776] The work, interrupted at the beginning of the 1970s during the preparation of the first enlargement wave (Denmark, Ireland and UK), took a long time coming. In 1976, the first proposal of a directive was presented by the Commission.[777] It took another nine years until the Council of Ministers finally reached a unanimous vote[778] and adopted *Directive 85/374/EEC* in 1985.[779] The Member States were obliged to implement the directive within a three-year time period until mid-1988. One of the first countries to transpose the directive into its domestic law was the UK;[780] the last among the 'founding EEC Member States' to implement was France in 1998.[781]

364. In the meantime, the Directive has been incorporated into the private law of twenty-eight EU Member States. Many countries in Central and Eastern Europe implemented the Directive already prior to their accession to the EU, e.g., Croatia in 2005. So did the three EFTA-States of Norway, Iceland and Liechtenstein, forming together with the EU the EEA.[782] Even Switzerland, a former EFTA country but not a member of the EEA, has adopted the product liability directive.[783] Many countries outside the EU followed this model.[784]

365. The Directive was based on ex-Article 100 TEEC (Article 115 TFEU): achievement of the common market. Its purposes are entailed in its first recital: to assure undistorted competition between producers, to facilitate the free movement of goods and, predominantly, to promote an equal level of consumer protection across the Member States.

Since 1995, the European Commission has published four reports on the application of the Directive.[785] In its first report of 1995, the Commission stated no appreciable effect on product liability insurance and on the level of industrial

776. In the US, the drug was to be marketed under the brand name 'Kevadon', but finally did not get the approval by the Federal Food and Drug Administration (FDA). – In Germany, the Contergan catastrophe led to compensation provided through state-funds and to the incorporation of a strict product liability regime into the Act on Pharmaceuticals (1976/1978).
777. OJ 1976 C 241/9. – In 1977, the Council of Europe passed a 'Convention on [Strict] Products Liability in regard to Personal Injury and Death' (Strasbourg Convention) which, however, never entered into force.
778. This was due to the historical coincidence of a personal change in the post of the federal minister for economic affairs in West Germany, a country which blocked the directive from the beginning. A former member of the European Parliament, Mr M. Bangemann, became the new minister (1984–1988). European minded and new in office, he did not hesitate to give his consent on behalf of West Germany. From 1989–1999, Mr Bangemann was EU Commissioner.
779. Directive 85/374/EEC on the approximation of the laws, regulations and administrative provisions of the Member States concerning liability for defective products, OJ 1985 L 210/29 (as amended).
780. Part I, Consumer Protection Act 1987.
781. Act of 19 May 1998 (Loi 98-389), incorporating the provisions of the Directive into the French civil code (Arts 1386-1 to 1386-18 C. civ.).
782. Compare *supra* text and fn 21.
783. Produktehaftpflichtgesetz 1993.
784. On the supposed attraction of the Directive to third countries *see* M. Reimann, *Product Liability in a Global Context: The Hollow Victory of the European Model*, 11 ERPL 128 (2003).
785. COM(1995) 617 final (13 Dec. 1995); COM(2000) 893 final (31 Jan. 2001); COM(2006) 496 final (14 Sep. 2006); COM(2011) 547 final (8 Sep. 2011).

research and development. It also noted that fewer than ten cases using the special EU product liability rules were reported from all (then) eleven Member States which had implemented the Directive. At least the latter changed in the meantime. In its fourth report of 2011, the Commission communicated that the number of liability claims and out-of-court settlements on the basis of the Directive had increased. But solid empirical data are not available. As in the reports before, the Commission did not find any reason to propose a thorough amendment of the Directive.[786] The 5th report on the application of the Directive, covering the period 2011–2015, was due by 2017, but has not yet been published (as of November 2017).

§2. Liability under Directive 85/374/EEC

366. Directive 85/374/EEC is said to have introduced a no-fault regime of civil liability for damage caused by defective products. Still today, the nature of this EU product liability is controversial. It is not strict liability in the sense of the German *Gefährdungshaftung*, which provides for civil liability regardless of any defectiveness, especially in cases of materialization of technical risks.[787] The very term 'strict liability' is itself far from being unambiguous. In English common law, 'strict liability' is an indeterminate category. It is used as an umbrella term to lump together anything from near-absolute liability to little more than a reversed burden of proof in negligence cases.[788]

367. Finally, every qualification depends on the understanding of the notion of defect: whether the Directive has introduced a uniform category of objective product defect that is free from any negligence elements, or whether there exists a distinction between manufacturing defects (flaws) and design (and instruction) defects, with the latter arguably containing elements of 'corrective conduct', i.e., negligence. The former understanding is the predominant European approach;[789] the latter is correlated to the German and US American point of view. This issue will be discussed in greater detail *infra* the text under the heading of 'product defects'. With this proviso having been made, EU product liability is qualified in this monograph as *quasi-strict liability*, that is, as a hybrid between negligence liability and no-fault liability or *Gefährdungshaftung*.

---

786. In its Green Paper on Liability for Defective Products, COM(1999) 396 final, the Commission examined whether a revision of the Directive is justified on more than ten points, *inter alia*, extending the coverage to non-material damage and damage to goods put to professional use.

787. Compare, *inter alia*, J. Esser, *Grundlagen und Entwicklung der Gefährdungshaftung* (C.H. Beck 1941); Brüggemeier, *Risks and Strict Liability* (2013) 21 ERPL 923; H. Koziol, P. Apathy & B.A. Koch, *Gefährdungs-, Produkt- und Eingriffshaftung. Österreichisches Haftpflichtrecht*, vol. III (Sramek 2014).

788. Compare, *inter alia*, *Winfield & Jolowicz on Tort* paras 1–38 (18th ed., Sweet & Mawwell 2010). For a European (and beyond) stock-taking of strict liability compare *Unification of Tort Law: Strict Liability* (B.A. Koch & H. Koziol eds, KLI 2002).

789. Compare, *inter alia*, H.C. Taschner, *Produkthaftung* 28 (C.H. Beck 1986).

I. Maximum Harmonization and Article 13 of the Directive

368. Originally, it was disputed whether the liability regime of the Directive introduced a minimum harmonization or maximum harmonization. The former would mean that it provided only a common basis of product liability across all Member States while not precluding Member States from retaining or adopting stricter protective measures.[790] With three judgments, handed down on 24 April 2002, the Court left no doubt that the Directive introduced a regime of *maximum harmonization.*[791] According to this concept, the Member States are bound to the protective scope determined by the Directive. Any departure from its rules is excluded, except where it is expressly provided for by the Directive. (These optional extensions concerned three aspects: development risk defence, caps on liability in serial personal injury cases, and liability for primary agricultural products.[792]) This clarification by the judgment was of no real surprise. More interesting was the Court's reasoning to the scope of Article 13, that is, which domestic law of the Member States remains unaffected by the Directive. Article 13 provides three categories: (i) general contract law, (ii) general law of non-contractual fault liability, i.e., law of delict and torts, and (iii) 'special liability systems' existing at the moment when this Directive was notified. Only the latter category was a subject of dispute.

369. One of the three cases, the case of Ms *Sánchez,* dealt with the Spanish Act on Protection of Consumers and Users of 1984 providing in Spain for a system of strict liability which enables consumers and users to obtain compensation for damage by the use of a defective thing, product or service. Following accession to the EC in 1986, Spain implemented the Directive 85/374/EEC. A provision in the transposing Act explicitly clarified that the Spanish consumer protection law of 1984 shall not apply to civil liability for damage caused by defective products mentioned in Article 2 of the Directive. Ms *Sánchez* received a blood transfusion in a medical establishment belonging to the defendant company. In the course of that transfusion, she allegedly became infected with Hepatitis C. The blood used for the transfusion had been treated by a transfusion centre. Ms *Sánchez* sued the defendant for damages. Though arguably within the scope of both laws, she sought compensation under the Spanish consumer protection law, which was more favourable to the victim of damage. The Spanish court, referring for a preliminary ruling, wanted to know from the ECJ whether the exclusion of the provisions on strict liability in the consumer protection law of 1984 through the Spanish transposing Act was compatible with EU law, here with Article 13 of the Directive.

370. In 1985, two 'special regimes' of non-contractual no-fault liability for defective products could be found in Western Europe: the German liability law for

790. In this regard reference had been made to Art. 169(4) TFEU (ex-Art. 100 TEEC).
791. Case C-183/00, *M.V.G. Sánchez v. Medicina Asturiana SA* [2002] ECR I-3901; *see also* already Taschner, *Produkthaftung* 2 (1986).
792. Compare Arts 15(1)(a) + (b) and 16(1). The last point has been repealed in 1999. *See infra* text and fn 827.

pharmaceuticals, introduced in 1976 after the Thalidomide/*Contergan* catastrophe of the 1960s, and the Spanish consumer protection law, introduced after the cooking oil scandal of 1981. When Directive 85/374/EEC was notified, only one special regime existed *within* the then European Economic Community: the German liability for pharmaceuticals which was even stricter than the law of the Directive, in so far as development risks were included. This exception has been expressly recognized by the 13th recital of the Directive.[793] However, Article 13 focuses unambiguously on the existence of special liability systems before July 1985. Spain joined the EU in 1986; its consumer protection law dates from 1984. Whether these circumstances suffice to make a substantial difference is more than questionable.

Therefore, the Court additionally referred to the regulation of specific sectors of production, like pharmaceuticals (or cooking oil). It concluded:

> [a] system of producer liability founded on the same basis as that put in place by the Directive and not limited to a given sector of production does not come within any of the [special] systems of liability referred to in Article 13 of the Directive. That provision cannot therefore be relied on in such a case in order to justify the maintenance in force of national provisions affording greater protection than those of the Directive.[794]

Thus, 'special liability schemes' are ruled to be limited to a given sector of production.

371. In *Commission v. France,*[795] the French implementing law was found in contradiction to the Directive when it allowed recovery for the first EUR 500 of property damage;[796] and for making distributors liable on the same basis as producers. This restrictive line has been endorsed afterwards in the case of *Skov Æg* where the Danish legislator extended the catalogue of the parties to sue to any last seller of a product and made distributors jointly liable with producers.[797] Sellers' liability for defective products is admissible outside EU product liability law – under the general laws not excluded by Article 13 – only if it is either contractual liability or (fault-based) non-contractual liability. An EC initiative to introduce into the Directive the possibility for Member States to extend product liability to distributors remained unsuccessful.[798]

793. The question of whether Germany, *after* the notification of the Directive, is still entitled to autonomously regulate its liability law of pharmaceuticals, has been answered by the ECJ in the affirmative. *See* case C-310/13, *Novo Nordisk Pharma GmbH v. S.* EU:C:2014:2385.

794. Case C-183/00, *Sánchez*, para. 33 (emphasis added).

795. Case C-52/00, *Commission v. France* [2002] ECR I-3827. As a sequel compare Case C-177/04, *Commission v. France* [2006] ECR I-2461.

796. On this, *see also* the third judgment of 24 Apr. 2002, Case C-154/00, *Commission v. Greece* [2002] I-3879.

797. Case C-402/03, *Skov Æg v. Bilka Lavprisvarehus A/S and Others* [2006] ECR I-199.

798. Council decision of 19 Dec. 2002, OJ 2002 C 26/2.

II. Conditions of Liability

372. The basic conditions of EU product liability can be found in Article 1 of the Directive. Article 1 reads: '*The producer shall be liable for damage caused by a defect in his product.*' Therefore, EU product liability is conditional on the proof of: (1) damage, (2) a product, (3) a defect, and (4) causation (Article 4).[799] Differently to the American law, the EU product liability is restricted to producers. This category of producer (5) needs some clarification. Additionally, the rules on exclusionary grounds (6) are of relevance, for which the defendant producer bears the burden of proof.

A. Damage

373. 'Damage is the centrepiece of all delict law'.[800] At first regard, the Directive seems to follow the famous French regulatory model. Article 1 focuses on a broad and undifferentiated category of damage à la ex-Article 1382 C.civ.[801] This impression is, however, misleading. Article 9 limits the compensable damage to cases of infringements of a few legally protected interests, thus letting the German regulatory approach of §823(1) *BGB* back in through the backdoor. Only damage resulting from personal injury and from impairment or destruction of property is recoverable. Against this background, three basics need to be recalled from the outset:

(i) Assessing damage under the law of the Directive is a two-step operation: first, determining *injury* to person or property; second, assessing *material damage* resulting therefrom. Non-material damage (especially pain and suffering) is beyond the scope of EU product liability law (Article 9 subparagraph 2).
(ii) EU law does not provide for an elaborated law of torts. Therefore, beyond the specific legal definitions given by the Directive and without further judicative authority by the case law of the European courts, reference has to be made to the general principles common to the tort law of the Member States. This methodological approach is well known from Article 340(2) TFEU.
(iii) Application of national rules shall not impair the effectiveness of the Directive, and the national court has to interpret its implemented domestic law in the light of the wording and the purposes of the Directive.

1. Death and Personal Injury

374. The first instance covered is 'damage caused by death or personal injury' (Article 9(a)). In other words, the bodily integrity of a person must be injured.

799. Evidently, it is an editorial mistake that the drafters did not list the term 'product' as a subject of proof in Art. 4 of the Directive.
800. C. von Bar, *The Common European Law of Torts* 6, vol. 2 (OUP 2000).
801. After the reform of the French contract law in 2016, the French law of delict comprises Arts 1240–1245 C.civ.

375. According to common understanding, human life begins with birth and ends with death. From a liability law perspective, this conventional view needs further clarification, particularly in respect of the beginning of life. Biologically, human life begins with the fertilization of the female egg by the male sperm. Internationally, the question as to when human life *legally* begins is controversial. The ECtHR in 2004 abstained from an answer to this question due to the heterogeneity of the laws of the Signatory States of the Council of Europe.[802] EU law, too, does not contain any detailed information from when 'life before birth' can be considered a legally protected interest. The ECJ has not yet had a possibility to touch this question with a preliminary ruling for the law of EU product liability. National courts shall have to refer to their respective domestic rules of law, if there are any.[803] Anyway, an embryo or foetus should be entitled to damages for bodily or health injuries to her or him in the womb of the pregnant woman caused by intoxicated food or prenatal medical maltreatment with defective drugs, which she or he can claim in her or his own name after birth.

376. Human life terminates upon death. Death was traditionally characterized by respiratory failure, cessation of heartbeat and circulatory arrest. In Western States predominantly – in Europe and North America – the concept of brain death has overtaken. In practice, the difference between these two modes of determining the time of death is only relevant in exceptional cases. This does not need to be deepened here. Special problems arise with regard to the legal consequences in cases of fatal injuries, as the injured person is deceased and cannot bring any claim for compensation. The questions as to which third persons can pursue which claims, and of whether claims of the deceased are subrogated to third persons are not touched by the Directive and are left to the discretion of Member States' law.[804]

377. Personal injuries comprise injuries to the human body and to human health. *Injury to body* is any injury to the bodily integrity of a human being, typically brought about by external forces. *Injury to health* concerns the inner influence of an activated disturbance to a person's bodily state. An injury to health does not require the person to be in a healthy condition and it may also exist if the possible improvement of an illness is not undertaken or is made impossible.

378. The latter variant was brought before the Court in the Danish case of *Veedfald*.[805] The plaintiff was due to undergo a kidney transplant surgery at a district hospital. The kidney, donated by his brother, was prepared for transplantation through flushing with a perfusion fluid manufactured in cooperation with another district hospital. A defect of the fluid made the kidney unusable for transplantation. Mr

---

802. ECtHR, 8 Jul. 2004, *Vo v. France* 40 EHRR 259.
803. For a comparative account, *see* E. Özsunay, *Rights of Embryo and Foetus in Private Law,* in *International Academy of Comparative Law, Convergence of Legal Systems in the 21st Century. General Reports at the XVIth International Congress of Comparative Law* 1275 (Bruylant 2006).
804. On bereavement damages, *see* supra text (para. 301).
805. ECJ, Case C-203/99, *Veedfald v. Århus Amtskommune* [2001] ECR I-3569. *Veedfald* was the first substantive product liability case before the ECJ, fifteen years after the notification of the Directive.

Veedfald sued the Regional Authority (*Amtskommune*) as owner and operator of the hospitals for damages. Next to the question of whether the fluid, manufactured exclusively for internal medical use by the district hospitals, was a 'product' in the sense of Article 2 of the Directive,[806] the additional problem was: which head of material damage was concerned? Did it result from a personal injury (body or health) or from an impairment of property? Directly impaired through the defective fluid was an item of property, the kidney, which was made unusable for transplant. But who was the owner of the donated kidney in the hands of the hospital medical staff prior to transplantation – property of the donor, possession of the hospital, expectant right of the intended recipient? Indirectly injured was the health of the intended recipient Mr *Veedfald*, whose real chance of improvement of his malaise was destroyed.

379. The AG pleaded for a personal injury, though neither specifying whether to the body or health, nor indicating which person is injured when an explanted organ is impaired or destroyed: the donor of the organ[807] or the intended recipient?[808] Both the AG and the Court avoided unambiguous answers to these questions and finally left it to the Danish court to determine the respective head of damage (and the person concerned).

380. In the two cases of *Boston Scientific Medizintechnik GmbH*, the German Federal Court of Justice wanted to know from the ECJ whether the costs for replacement of an implanted potentially defective pacemaker and defibrillator could be regarded as recoverable damage resulting from injury to body or health (Article 9(1)(a) of the Directive).[809] The supposedly defective medical product, however, did not cause a concrete injury to the bodily integrity or health of the plaintiffs suffering from heart disease. Maybe its potential defectiveness led to emotional distress of the patients, but pain and suffering are not recoverable under the law of the Directive. Basically, it is a contractual warranty case when the replacement of a purchased defective medical product is pursued. The replacement of implanted defective devices implies necessarily a violation of the bodily integrity by surgical operation as does any regular implantation of medical products.[810] But the authorized surgery

806. Compare *infra* text.

807. This has been found in a German case of sperm destruction. Before undergoing a surgery, a man deposited his frozen sperm in a sperm bank where it was destroyed through negligence of the bank's staff. The Federal Court of Justice found an injury to the body of the sperm donor. In both cases, *Veedfald* and the sperm case, determining a personal injury was the condition to claim compensation for pain and suffering under national law. Compare BGH, 9 Nov. 1993, BGHZ 124, 52 (in English available: www.iuscomp.org/gla/judgments/bgh/BGH.htm).

808. AG Colomer, Opinion, Case C-203/99, *Veedfald* [2000] ECR I-3572, paras 31 et seq.

809. BGH, 30 Jul. 2013, VersR 2013, 1450/1451. Compare Joined Cases C-503/13, *Boston Scientific Medizintechnik GmbH v. AOK Sachsen-Anhalt*, and C-504/13, *Boston Scientific Medizintechnik GmbH v. Betriebskrankenkasse RWE*, EU:C:2015:148.

810. Compare Brüggemeier, *Schadensersatz für implantierte fehlerhafte Medizinprodukte*, MedR 2014, 537 (*id.*, *Risarcimento del danno da prodotto impiantato diffetoso*, Rivista di diritto civile 2014, 1056); F. Werro and A. Tolou, *Le défaut potentiel et les mesures préventives dans la responsabilité du fait des produits défectueux*, in *Die Schweiz und die europäische Integration/La Suisse et l'intégration européenne* 261(A. Epiney & S. Affolter eds, Zurich 2015).

here serves to *prevent* (future) personal injuries through the defective product. It does not itself constitute an injurious act in the sense of liability law.

381. The AG and the Court argued that (potentially) defective[811] active implants such as pacemakers and defibrillators constitute an 'abnormal potential for damage', so that the necessary costs of preventing this risk for patients' life to materialize should be treated *like* a personal injury damage.[812] The Court, in its brief but ambiguous ruling, held:

> damage caused by a surgical operation for the replacement of a defective product, ..., constitutes 'damage caused by death or personal injuries' for which the producer is liable, if such an operation is necessary to overcome the defect in the product in question.[813]

Taking these general terms literally, this would mean that the Court herewith introduces a third category of damage, i.e., an unwritten lit. c of Article 9(1): in addition to damage through injury to person and property, the *costs of necessary measures to prevent personal injury and injury to property* are now recognized as product damage. In any case, at least as far as defective (active) implantable medical devices (pacemakers, defibrillators etc.) are concerned, where patients are in a particularly vulnerable situation, costs of recommended prophylactic measures are from now on compensable *as* personal injury damage under EU product liability law.

382. There is no further specification of the extent of compensable damages resulting from personal injury given by the Directive. Therefore, the general rules and principles regarding such damages under non-contractual liability in the national laws of the Member States apply. In Germany, the *Produkthaftungsgesetz* includes specific provisions requiring that compensation be paid for: (i) the cost of medical treatment, pecuniary loss incurred during illness, funeral expenses, (ii) loss of financial support suffered by a third party dependent on the deceased, and (iii) future loss of earnings or future needs or support of a third party.[814]

383. EU product liability law relates only to 'material' damage. Remedies for *non-pecuniary loss*, especially compensation of pain and suffering, are left outside the scope of the Directive (Article 9(2)). In this regard, the EU legislator referred the victims of personal injury to the domestic law of the Member States. The Directive contains no optional departure from this exclusion.[815] Member States' law also determines the definition of non-material damage. The respective amounts awarded

811. On the category of 'potential defect', *see infra* text.
812. AG Bot, Opinion, Joined Cases C-503 and 504/13, EU:C:2014:2306.
813. Joined Cases C-503/13, *Boston Scientific Medizintechnik GmbH v. AOK Sachsen-Anhalt*, and C-504/13, *Boston Scientific Medizintechnik GmbH v. Betriebskrankenkasse RWE*, EU:C:2015:148, para. 55. Compare also the final judgment of the Bundesgerichtshof, 9.6.2015, NJW 2015, 3096.
814. §§7–9 Produkthaftungsgesetz (as amended), transferring the respective rules of the BGB law of delict (§§842–845) into the Produkthaftungsgesetz.
815. Compare Art. 15 with its optional departures from the rules of the Directive.

under national law in the Member States for similar incidents still vary considerably.[816]

384. On the other side, it is incompatible with the maximal harmonization approach when Member States subsequently extend the scope of application of their transposing law to this explicitly excluded issue. In 2002, when the ECJ handed down its three judgments on maximum harmonization,[817] the German legislator amended the domestic law of damages. *Inter alia*, it introduced for the first time in the German legal history a recovery of pain and suffering into the various heads of *Gefährdungshaftung* for technical risks. It used this opportunity also to amend the *Produkthaftungsgesetz* with its supposedly strict liability and, contrary to Article 9(2), extended compensation in personal injury cases to pain and suffering.[818] To achieve this result, it needs an amendment of the Directive 85/374 by the EU legislator, which expressly provides for compensation of pain and suffering in personal injury cases or at least makes such an extension optional. Therefore this German amendment of the *Produkthaftungsgesetz* contradicts EU law and is inapplicable.

2. Property

385. Property in a thing is the classical 'absolute' subjective right. It enshrines the competence to dispose of the thing, e.g., to sell, to possess and use it at will, as long as the rights of others or legal prohibitions do not stand in the way of that use (Article 544 C. civ., §903 *BGB*). This 'absolute' property right is *not* the target of the Directive. The scope of protection is restricted to impairments of the physical integrity of movable and immovable things, i.e., *damage*, including spoiling, and *destruction* (Article 9(1)(b)). Compensation covers the costs of repair of the damaged thing and the current market price of the destroyed thing or the costs of new acquisition respectively. For the same reason, loss of use as consequential damage is not recoverable.

Pure economic losses are per se excluded.

386. The impairment must affect *something other* than the defective product itself. If one defective part affects other defect-free components of an integrated complex industrial product (*Weiterfresserschäden*), this does not constitute damage to property under the Directive.[819]

387. The Directive contains additional qualifications of damage to property.

One major purpose of the Directive was the *protection of consumers*. That is the reason why Article 9(1)(b) finally wants to restrict the scope of compensation of

816. Compare Munich Re-insurance Co., *Compensation for Pain and Suffering. Actual Trends in Europe and USA* (MunichRe 2012); S.D. Sugarman, *Tort Damages for Non-Economic Losses: Personal Injury* 323 in *Comparative Tort Law* (M. Bussani & A.J. Sebok eds, Cheltenham Elgar 2015).
817. *See* fns 781 et seq.
818. §9(ii) Produkthaftungsgesetz (as amended).
819. Differently, e.g., the German general law of delict (§823(1) BGB) with its contested doctrine of 'Weiterfresserschäden'. Compare BGH, 24 Nov. 1976, BGHZ 67, 359; BGH, 18 Jan. 1983, BGHZ 86, 256; BGH, 12 Feb. 1992, BGHZ 117, 183.

property damage to consumer interests. But instead, to focus straightforwardly on defective consumer goods which lead to personal injury or causes property damage,[820] liability has been made conditional on whether the *damaged item of property*, movable or immovable, was a consumer good. This definition of a consumer interest in EU product liability law is twofold:

(i) the damaged thing must be 'ordinarily intended for private use or consumption' (consumer good); and
(ii) must in fact be 'used by the injured person mainly for his own private use or consumption'.[821]

The first element – nature of consumer good – focuses on the objective purpose of the damaged item of property; the second element on the concrete, individual-subjective aspect of the use. In cases of dual-use things, e.g., hire cars operated for private and professional use, the second element is at the fore. The nature of the concrete use at the moment of the injury is decisive.

388. Finally, Article 9(1)(b) provides for a particularity, uncommon to the liability law of the Member States. Property damage is only recoverable with a threshold of EUR 500. The intention was to abolish litigation on minor damage, but to keep property damages in the scope of protection. Liability insurers lamented the disproportionately high administrative costs of these damages.[822]

Commercial property, that is, professionally used goods and materials, remains outside the scope of the Directive. These damages are only recoverable under the national law of delict/torts.[823]

B. *Product*

389. Damage must be caused 'by a product'. Although consumer protection is a main objective of Directive 85/374/EEC, its application is not limited to consumer goods. That is basically an ill-fitting approach.[824] Instead, the term 'product' is borrowed from general products liability in tort. Article 2 defines 'product' as any movable or good 'even if incorporated into another movable or into an immovable' (or implanted into the human body). This definition as such is insufficient. It needs concretization and specification by other provisions of the Directive. These specifications are given by Article 7(c), where they appear in the context of exclusionary grounds. To be a product, the movable thing or good must: (i) be *manufactured*, (ii)

820. This is the politically correct approach, *inter alia*, of the Brazilian, Finnish, Russian and Spanish consumer protection law.
821. Article 9(1)(b)(i)(ii) Directive.
822. Compare Taschner, *Produkthaftung*, 136 (1986).
823. Compare Case C-285/08, *Société Moteurs Leroy Somer v. Société Dalcia France and Société Ace France* [2009] ECR I-4733.
824. *See* already *supra* text.

this process must be done 'for sale or any form of distribution for *economic purposes'*, and finally (iii) the good must in fact be manufactured and distributed '*in the course of business'*.

390. With these specifications, '*product*' in the sense of EU product liability law can be defined as follows: *any movable thing manufactured professionally and for economic purposes* (Article 2 in conjunction with Article 7(c)), regardless of the different attribution of the burden of proof for these conditions.

1. Manufactured: Not Manufactured

391. 'Manufactured' means produced by industrial processes, craftsmanship or artists' work, notwithstanding that industrially produced goods are clearly at the fore.[825] Therefore, goods not produced by men but *by nature*, i.e., primary agricultural products and game, were originally excluded.[826] Such agricultural products comprised products of the soil, of stock-farming and of fisheries. Only after they had undergone initial (industrial) processing, they would then come into the reach of the Directive. This law was amended in 1999 after the 'mad cow disease' or BSE disaster in the UK.[827] Since then, primary agricultural products have been treated like manufactured goods.

392. Emphatically not manufactured are *parts of the human body*: organs such as heart, kidney and liver, used for transplantation; blood, used for transfusion; sperm, used for (heterologous) in-vitro-fertilization. Explanted from the human body, these organs are movable things, capable of property, but they are not products in the sense of EU product liability law. However, beyond doubt seems to be that after processing and storage in organ-, blood- or sperm-'banks', these former parts of the human body are considered products. Therefore, in the various cases of infection with Hepatitis C or HIV after blood transfusion, the blood has been treated without exception as a product.[828]

393. *Industrial waste* is not manufactured in the strict sense of the term. Waste is a production residue, that is to say, an object not sought as such. The first waste framework directive of 1975 defined waste as 'any substance or object which the holder intends to discard or is required to discard'.[829] Economically, it is more reasonable to avoid the 'production' of waste. Damage through (toxic) waste appears

825. Compare recital no. 3 of the Directive. The wording of Art. 2 does not to contain any restrictions to industrial production.
826. However, the Member States were allowed to extend the coverage of EU product liability law to these products in their national law (ex-Art. 15(1)(a)).
827. Directive 1999/34/EC, OJ 1999 L 141/20. For a discussion on further revisions of the Directive compare Green Paper on Liability for Defective Products, COM(1999) 396 final.
828. Compare Case C-183/00, *Sánchez* (fn.) and the English Hepatitis case complex *A and Others v. National Blood Authority and Others* [2001] 3 All ER 289 with manifold references.
829. Article 1 of the Directive 75/442/EEC on waste, OJ 1975 L 194/23; codified in 2006 and revised in 2008: Directive 2008/98/EC on waste, OJ 2008 L 312/3.

to be primarily a problem of environmental liability, that is, of liability regardless of defectiveness.[830] Industrial waste may be dangerous, but this quality does not turn it into a defective product.

However, goods, materials or raw materials resulting from a manufacturing or extraction process which is not primarily intended to produce that item may constitute not a residue but a by-product which the enterprise does not wish to discard. If instead it intends to exploit or market the materials on economically advantageous terms in a subsequent process without prior processing, the product liability directive may be applicable to these goods.[831]

394. Often discussed is the product nature of computer software. Here, the frontiers between product and service liability get blurred. The conventional answer is that, as long as the software is stored on a tangible medium (DVD, Flash-drive), it is treated as a product.[832]

2. Economic Purpose

395. The good must be manufactured for sale or 'any form of distribution for economic purpose' (Article 7(c)). This question was raised in the above-mentioned case of *Veedfald*.[833] The hospitals produced the (defective) perfusion fluid for internal medical use by the district hospitals only. Regardless of whether the hospitals were private enterprises or publicly funded establishments, the fluid was not an object intended for sale on the market, but for exclusive application in medical services through the district hospitals, here for kidney transplantation. It is the medical service that is paid for by the patient or his health insurer, and there is no purchase of the fluid by the patient or anybody else. That is the difference to contracts on implantation of medicinal products. In the latter cases, the patient pays twice: for medical service (implantation) and for acquisition of property (medical product). Therefore in *Veedfald*, the perfusion fluid was not a product (Article 2) and no product liability should ensue. *Veedfald* was basically a case of liability for (defective) medical services.[834]

3. Professionalism

396. The good must be manufactured 'on the job' by work of an employee in the scope of his or her employment or by paid work of a self-employed person. Any hobby activity is outside the reach of EU product liability. A telling example is the food made by 'housewives or househusbands' at home for the purpose of a street or

830. Compare *infra* text (Part VIII, Ch 1).
831. On the classification of materials as waste compare ECJ, Case C-188/07, *Commune de Mesquer v. Total France and Total International Ltd*, EU:C:2008:359 with reference to other case law.
832. Compare the answer of the EU Commission to a parliamentary question, OJ 1989 C 114/42.
833. Compare fn 805.
834. Stated correctly by AG Colomer. Compare Case C-203/99, Opinion, *Veedfald* [2000] ECR I-3572, paras 17–20.

neighbourhood party and sold at a price roughly covering the costs of manufacturing. If a customer suffers health problems after consumption of a piece of intoxicated food, the way to EU product liability is barred because no product is present. Damages can only be claimed under the provisions of general law of delict/torts.

4. Additional Characteristics

397. A manufactured movable remains a product even after it has been incorporated as a component into another small or large product (ship or airplane), or after having been built into an immovable. Examples for the latter are elevators, escalators or heating and ventilator systems installed in buildings. The same holds true for blood after transfusion and medical devices after implantation into the human body.

A final clarification has been made by Article 2 of the Directive: *Electricity* is legally treated like a product.[835] The same is supposed to hold true for gas. The Spanish legislator explicitly included gas when transposing the Directive.

C. Defect

398. It is not the causation of damage through a product that triggers liability. The product must be *defective*. Therefore, the term defect became the central category of EU product liability, constituting as well its ambiguous character as quasi-strict liability. Being the core element, it is at the same time the most controversial topic in the debates on EU product liability and on 'strict' products liability in general.

Internationally, three categories of 'product defect' are recognized in the law of product liability in tort: *manufacturing defects* (flaws), *design/construction defects* and *instruction/warning defects*.[836] An additional fourth category is the producer's failure of post-marketing control.[837] The first three are covered by the Directive; the fourth variant of defect as a fault category is not. The drafters of the Directive started with the regulation of manufacturing and construction defects. Their understanding was that these two defects are thoroughly objective and therefore one uniform no-fault approach would be appropriate. Instruction defects were included rather late in the legislative process. This section will discuss whether and how these two elements, different categories of product defect and a uniform definition and treatment of defect, fit together.

399. Article 6(1) gives the definition of a product defect. It reads: 'A product is defective when it does not provide the safety which a person is entitled to expect,

---

835. Compare as an example BGH, 25 Feb. 2014, BGHZ 200, 242.

836. Compare W. van Gerven et al., *Common Law of Europe Casebooks: Tort Law* 674–683 (Hart 2000); ALI (ed.) *Restatement (Third) of the Law of Torts: Products Liability* (1998), §2(a)(b)(c).

837. Compare *Restatement: Products Liability*, §10 (post-sale failure to warn); W. van Gerven et al., *supra* fn 836.

taking all circumstances into account.' Additionally three examples for circumstances, which may determine the safety expectation, are given (Article 6(a)(b)(c)):

- the presentation of the product;
- the use to which it could reasonably be expected that the product would be put; and
- the time when the product was put into circulation.

400. Defectiveness is a normative attribute of the product. It shall be 'reasonably safe'. Thus, defect is lack of reasonable safety. To determine this normative standard, the Directive refers the courts to the safety expectations of the general public. This approach originates from the consumer expectation standard, adopted from the US American law. Being not exclusively consumer protection law, however, the Directive has generalized this approach. These expectations of the public are defined *culturally* and *regionally*, that is, they may be different, e.g., in northern and southern parts of Europe; *objectively*, i.e., not from the individual perspective of an injured person; and *contextually*, depending on the concrete circumstances of the case. To the extent that consumer goods are concerned, the safety expectation of an average consumer of the product in question is decisive. Alternatively, neither the public nor the average consumer may have any actual safety expectations, e.g., in relation to newly developed products. Finally, it is anyway the courts which function as impartial and objective instances to articulate reasonable expectations of product safety.

401. Against this background, the three exemplary circumstances can be understood as follows:

> *The* presentation *takes into account the way the product has been marketed by the producer. This covers description, labelling, package instructions and operation manuals, warning of misuse. It may also cover information provided by advertising campaigns. The modes of product presentation determine the assessment of instruction defects.*

402. The *reasonably expected use* is a complex category. The product must be usable this way without endangering the personal integrity or property of the user. The category of reasonably expected use relates to three variants of product use:

- *Specified normal use* is the most restricted category of product use. It means the possible use as it is defined by the producer itself. Statutory regulations of product safety in EU law and national law often apply this narrow term.
- *Foreseeable use* or reasonably foreseeable misuse. This is the core reach of reasonably expected use in tort law; it dominates also the scope of application under EU product liability law. The product must be safe under these conditions of possible use.

- *Gross misuse* is a way of handling the product which is contrary to any reasonable expectation. Gross misuse is imputable self-damaging, which does not trigger liability. An example is the famous (often cited, though imaginary) case of the cat put into the microwave for drying.

403. The *time of marketing* is relevant in various respects. First, decisive is the time when the *concretely* damaging product has been put in circulation. For assessing its defect, one has to focus on the safety expectations at this point of time, which implies a relativity of safety expectations. Second, Article 6(2) makes clear that (improved) products, marketed afterwards, do not turn the former products per se into defective goods. Third, the time of the marketing of the product is relevant for the determination of the *development risk*. According to the definition provided by Article 7(e), a development risk is present when the risk in question could not be discovered given the 'state of scientific and technical knowledge' at the time the producer put the product in circulation. The development risk defence, which is only optional for the Member States to exclude, and the 'state of the art defence' will be discussed below in the text.

404. Some legal systems refer additionally to *risk-utility tests* to determine a product defect, especially in design cases.[838] These tests are used to establish proper product safety standards by balancing costs and benefits of a product. The drafters of the Directive rejected these tests.[839]

1. 'Product Defects': Uniformity or Diversity?

405. It is a widely held view among EU lawyers that the Directive has introduced a uniform category of product defect and does not differentiate between different notions of defect, and that this liability regime is 'strict', that is, it is free from elements of fault and unlawfulness.[840] However, this is but half of the truth.

a. Design and Instruction Defects

406. EU product liability is neither absolute liability, i.e., liability for causation,[841] nor *Gefährdungshaftung*.[842] It is liability for defectiveness, for lack of required safety. Safety of products is a normative category, to be determined by reasonable safety expectations of the public. It is not the supposed objectivity of the product defect that makes the difference to negligence liability. It is the other way

838. For US law compare *Restatement of the Law (Third): Torts*, p. 40 (1998).
839. *See* Taschner, *Produkthaftung*, 82 (1986).
840. Compare from Taschner, *Produkthaftung*, 27 et seq. (1986), to D. Wuyts, *The Product Liability Directive – More than Two Decades of Defective Products in Europe*, 5 JETL 1 (2014) with further references.
841. One of the rare cases of absolute liability is provided for damage caused by space objects on the surface of the earth. Compare UN Convention on International Liability for Damage Caused by Space Objects of 1972.
842. I deliberately avoid the diffuse term of 'strict liability'. Compare *supra* text and fn. 788.

around. The *normativity* of the defect and safety category constitutes the structural analogy to negligence liability. The courts proceed in the same way as they do in cases of negligence. To assess a product defect, they have to determine a normative alternative standard of safety, taking all the relevant circumstances of the case into account. As a first step, they have to assess the correct level of precaution required for the product in question. Then they have to compare the characteristics of the concrete product which caused the injury with the determined normative safety standard. Does the product comply with the safety standard or not? If it complies, a defect is missing; if it does not comply, a defect is present. Then the producer just did not invest enough in safety.

Negligence has been aptly defined as 'absence of due care according to the circumstances'.[843] A product defect can be defined as 'absence of due safety according to the circumstances'. As the standard of due care in the 'negligence lottery',[844] in product liability the alternative safety standard too is characterized by endemic instability.[845]

407. This is at least true for design or construction defects. The same principles apply for self-evident reasons to *instruction defects*. Hence, there are good reasons to qualify the liability for these defects as negligence, grounded on objective (enterprise) organizational fault.[846] That is how they are predominantly treated in the American jurisdictions under the US 'strict' products liability law.[847]

408. Private liability law is but one mechanism to promote the production and sale of safe products. Another is the administrative safety regulation by public law. For this purpose, in addition to the product liability directive, the EEC in 1992 passed a general product safety directive (GPSD),[848] amended in 2001.[849] The objective of the GPSD is to ensure a high level of product safety throughout the single market of the EEA. This concerns consumer products that are not covered by specific legislation, such as pharmaceuticals, medical devices and food. The GPSD confers market monitoring and surveillance obligations to the national enforcement authorities.[850] A new product safety regulation comprising all consumer products is in preparation.[851]

843. Compare *Palsgraf v. Long Island R. Co.*, 248 N.Y. 339, 162 N.E. 99 (N.Y. 1928), by B. Cardozo. *See also* ALI (ed.), *Restatement of the Law (Third): Torts: Liability for Physical and Emotional Harm* (2010), §3: Negligence, p. 29.
844. Compare M.A. Franklin, *Replacing the Negligence Lottery* (1967) 53 Va. L. Rev. 774; P.S. Atiyah, *The Damages Lottery* (Hart 1997).
845. Compare, *inter alia*, J. Stapelton, *Product Liability* 233: 'defect' requirement (Butterworths 1994).
846. On enterprise liability and negligence, *see* already *supra* text and fn 308.
847. Compare *Restatement (Third) of Torts: Products Liability*, §2.
848. Directive 92/59/EEC on general product safety, OJ 1992 L 228/24.
849. Directive 2001/95/EC on general product safety, OJ 2002 L 11/4.
850. Compare in greater detail C. Hodges, *European Regulation of Consumer Product Safety* (OUP 2005).
851. Compare COM (2013) 78, Proposal for a Regulation on consumer product safety and repealing Council Directive 87/337/EEC and Directive 2001/95/EC.

409. Specific product safety legislation under the umbrella of the GPSD, e.g., directives on toys, chemicals, cosmetics, machinery, and separate legislation e.g., on medical devices contain in their anneces essential safety requirements. Products designed in compliance with these safety requirements are prima facie regarded as defect-free. To facilitate this conformity proof, technical standards harmonized at EU level are drawn up by private law bodies (CEN, Cenelec etc.) which retain their non-binding status.[852] The conformity with safety requirements can be documented by a *CE marking*. A CE marking is a manufacturer's declaration that the product at issue complies with the essential safety requirements of the relevant EU product safety legislation. The conformity declaration is issued by a so-called notified body (certification body notified to the EU). These bodies must have successfully undergone an accreditation procedure for verification of their competence.[853] Products bearing the CE marking can unimpededly be marketed throughout the EEA. The presumption of conformity with the safety requirements can be refuted in two ways: by proof of product defect in a concrete liability trial, and on the regulatory level by a special 'safeguard procedure' between Member States and Commission.[854]

b. Manufacturing Defects

410. But there are still the manufacturing defects, the so-called flaws. Unlike the approach of uniformity supposes, the legal perspective is different here. The normativity of an alternative safety standard is missing. A flaw is a single product that individually departs from a product series that is free from defects. The defectiveness does not result from not meeting the requirements of a normative alternative standard, determined by the courts, but by a factual deviation from other items of the same series of production. Here, the design is the safety standard. If the deviation is of relevance for the safety of persons and property,[855] then this individual product is defective. The deviation constitutes the product defect, regardless whether this deviation was avoidable or discoverable by final inspections. In other words: liability for flaws under the Directive is a veritable no-fault liability. This mixed character of negligence, as far as design (and instruction) defects are concerned, and of no-fault with respect to flaws is the reason why it seems to be justified to qualify EU product liability as quasi-strict liability.

c. The 'One-Offs' (*Ausreißer*) Defence

411. A further particularity of product liability for flaws has been tellingly demonstrated in a judgment of the German Federal Court of Justice of 1995.[856] The

852. *See* on this in greater detail the website 'New Approach Standardization in the Internal Market.'
853. On the monitoring duties of these notified bodies and their liability in fault under national tort law, *see* Case C-219/15, *E. Schmitt v. TÜV Rheinland* EU:C:2017:128.
854. On the withdrawal of a CE marking under the Directive 98/37/EC on machinery, OJ 1998 L 207/1 (amended 2006), compare Case C-470/03, *A.G.M.-COS.MET* [2007] ECR I-2798.
855. A deviation in colour or taste may constitute a defect in sales law, but is irrelevant from a product liability point of view.
856. BGH, 9 May 1995, BGHZ 129, 353 (sparkling water bottle; available in English: www.iuscomp.org/gla/judgments/tgcm/z950509.htm). *See also* W. van Gerven et al., *Tort Law*, 655

defendant company bottled and distributed carbonated mineral water in returnable glass bottles. The plaintiff, a then 9-year-old girl, was fetching two bottles from the cellar of her parents' house. She had placed them on the floor outside the cellar in order to close the door and was about to pick them up when one of the bottles exploded. Splinters of glass entered her left eye and caused serious injuries. She sued the bottling company for compensation of material damage and for recovery of pain and suffering.

412. The expert report noted two possible causes for the explosion: a chip about 4 mm broad off the surface of the bottle, or a very fine hairline crack. It remained uncertain whether one of these causes was already present when the bottle was delivered or whether they came into existence after the delivery of the bottle. Under EU product liability law the producer can escape liability if it can adduce evidence that the defect in question did not exist at the time when the product was delivered or that the defect arose afterwards (Article 7(b)). This evidence had not been shown. The defendant bottling company contended additionally that the defects could not have been detected notwithstanding what was found to be a technical supervisory procedure in accordance with the very latest state of technology. In other words, the defendant brought forward the development risk defence (Article 7(e)). The Federal Court held on this central point as follows:

> The potential danger of returnable glass bottles filled with carbonated liquids has long been recognised and has indeed frequently engaged the courts. … (t)he danger of such glass bottles lies in the fact that even a tiny hairline crack which spreads can cause it to explode. Such a defect may arise at the stage of filling or pre-exist unnoticed, but in neither case is it a development risk resulting from construction. Liability in respect of it cannot be excluded under Article 7(e) of the Product Liability Directive. In such cases of so-called one-offs ('Ausreißer') the producer can only avoid liability if evidence can be adduced that the hairline crack was not in the bottle when it had been refilled and put into circulation.[857]

413. This judgment provides aptly for another significant difference between manufacturing defects and design defects. 'One-offs' are rare manufacturing specimens being different from the other products of the same series. They are by definition undetectable and unavoidable. Even with a quality control of high technical level, a given number of products may leave the assembly line in a defective condition and cause injury. Therefore, under regular producer liability for fault in the general law of delict or torts, this would not lead to liability (so-called one-offs defence). But this is different from the EU product liability regime, which insofar indeed has the character of a clear-cut strict liability.

---

et seq. (Hart 2000). It has been discussed in the English Hepatitis C case complex: *A and Others v. National Blood Authority and Others* [2001] 3 All ER 289, paras 44 and 53.

857. BGHZ 129, 353, at 360 (The translation in the German Law Archive (fn 856) is incorrect.). On the necessity of a request for a preliminary ruling to the ECJ, compare W. van Gerven et al., *Tort Law* 659 (Hart 2000).

414. One-offs fall within the reach of EU product liability law because they are defective products but do not constitute development risks. *Development risks are product defects resulting from design and construction of new products*[858] containing detrimental side effects, which were unknown and could not have been detected and avoided when applying the current state of scientific and technical knowledge. This concept is not transposable to flaws such as 'one-offs'. They are *singular defective specimens* in an otherwise non-defective product series.[859] There is knowledge about their existence, but technical impossibility to detect them in particular products. It is only in respect of unknown development construction defects that producers can exclude responsibility under EU product liability law.

415. Another clarification has to be made in this context. Pre-manufacturing risks such as contamination of blood products[860] raise similar questions. The risk that donated blood can be infected by Hepatitis C or HIV is well known. The fact that such infected blood products are defective is beyond question. Hence, the task for the processors of donated blood is to establish high-quality control techniques which serve to identify and exclude infected blood. By no means does infection result from the industrial processing of the donated blood. The situation of blood banks and of other processors of blood is comparable to manufacturers who must be aware that a given number of products leave in a defective condition in spite of high tech control mechanisms. Similarly, it cannot be excluded that in rare cases specimens of infected blood enter the further stages of processing. From that, it is clear that contaminated blood products cannot be considered development risks. Therefore, they are outside the reach of the development risk defence of Article 7(e). Like one-offs (*Ausreißer*), they are covered by 'strict' EU product liability law. To do away with this result in EU product liability law, it would need an amendment of the Directive by the EU legislator introducing a specific blood shield provision.[861]

858. In this respect correctly, compare Taschner, *Produkthaftung*, 114 (1986).

859. On the question of whether a bunch of one-offs may constitute a presumption of defectiveness of the whole product series, compare ECJ, Joined Cases C-503 and 504/13, *Boston Medizintechnik* EU:C:2015:148, and *see infra* text: potential product defect.

860. *See* especially the judgment of the High Court (M. Burton J) in the English Hepatitis C case complex (with 112 plaintiffs): *A and Others v. National Blood Authority and Others* [2001] 3 All ER 289 with a remarkable comparative stock-taking. From the author's point of view, the judgment is misled in so far as it operates with the comprehensive category of a 'non-standard product'. Thus it ignores both, that there is not one uniform alternative standard rendering a product defective, but a *factual* one (flaws) and a *normative* one (design defects), and that the difference between manufacturing and design defects is central for the correct understanding of the development risk defence. Finally, however, the High Court followed the tracks of the Bundesgerichtshof, that is, not allowing the development risk defence in cases of known but undiscoverable defects. *See*, *inter alia*, G. Howells & M. Mildred, *Infected Blood: Defect and Discoverability – A First Exposition of the EC Product Liability Directive* (2002) 65 MLR 9 ; M. Brooke & I. Forrester, *The Use of Comparative Law in A & Others v. National Blood Authority*, in *Product Liability in Comparative Perspective* 13 (D. Fairgrieve ed., CUP 2005).

861. In so far it does nothing other than restate the current state of the law when France and Spain exclude blood products from the development risk defence in their transposition of the Directive.

d. Potential Product Defect

416. Recently the Court had to decide on product defectiveness in two cases of implanted medical devices (pacemakers and cardioverter defibrillators (ICDs)).[862] The manufacturer informed the physicians about a higher risk of malfunctioning of its products in certain production series. In relation to the pacemakers, the risk of failure was between 0.3% and 0.9%. With regard to the ICDs, in four cases out of 46,000 the devices were found defective (!). Patients decided to get their implants replaced. Their health insurers sued the producer for reimbursement of the costs of replacing the devices.[863] In both cases, the affected devices were destroyed after removal, so that the plaintiffs could not adduce evidence of a product defect. Does the mere suspicion of a defect constitute a product defect? AG *Bot* and ECJ acknowledged an 'abnormal potential for damage' (death or cardiac failure) in the cases of implants of the production batch in question. Therefore, the Court held:

> Accordingly, where it is found that such products belonging to the same group or forming part of the same production series have a potential defect, it is possible to classify as defective all the products *[!]* in that group or series, without there being any need to show that the product in question is defective.[864]

417. This implies an extraordinary broadening of the concept of product defect and it raises more questions than it answers. It remains unclear how to qualify products that create an 'abnormal potential of damage' and products that have a lower or normal risk profile. No specification is given how many specimens of a production series must be defective to constitute such a potential of damage and to trigger product batch liability (zero defect consumer expectation?). Any form of risk-utility analysis, is it dispensible in these cases? Must there be a recommendation of preventive action by experts? This extension of the concept of defect also undermines the apportionment of the burden of proof as provided for under Article 4.

2. Diversity of Defects and Quasi-Strict Liability

418. To put the record straight: EU product liability is a hybrid. It is 'strict' (no-fault) with respect to manufacturing defects. It is also strict to the extent that Member States do not adopt the 'development risk defence'.[865] It is objective fault liability of enterprises with regard to regular construction and instruction defects (but without the element of a duty of care).

862. Joined Cases C-503/13 and 504/13, *Boston Scientific Medizintechnik GmbH v. AOK Sachsen-Anhalt*, and *Boston Scientific Medizintechnik GmbH v. Betriebskrankenkasse RWE* EU:C:2015:148.
863. Compare *supra* text (paras 380 and 381).
864. *Boston Scientific Medizintechnik*, para. 41.
865. Only Finland and Luxembourg seem to have excluded the 'development risk defence'.

D. Causation and Proof

1. General Rules

419. Article 4 provides that the injured person has to prove the defect, the damage, and the causal relationship between defect and injury/damage. Additionally the existence of a product has to be established. This is exceptionally an explicit regulation of the distribution of the burden of proof in a European Directive. Procedural rules are widely regarded as a matter of the laws of the Member States ('procedural autonomy'). Standard of proof and what evidence is sufficient to meet that standard are not harmonized by the Directive. Additionally, a shift of the burden of proof to the producer can be found in Article 7(b), dedicated to one specific defence of the producer.[866] Unlike the terms of product, defect and producer, the notion of causation is not defined in the Directive. The concept of causation is assumed by the drafters as well known and as more or less common to the laws of delict/torts of the Member States.[867] In view of the authority of national law for procedural matters, the question may be raised whether given facilitations of evidence in the law of a Member State, such as *res ipsa loquitur* or presumptions of facts, comply with Article 4 of the Directive.

2. Presumption of Causation and Defect

420. This topic came before the Court with the French case of *Sanofi Pasteur.*[868] It concerns an action for damages brought by a patient and his family, based on ex-Article 1386-1 *Code civil.* The plaintiff was vaccinated against Hepatitis B through injections of a vaccine produced by *Sanofi.* Shortly afterwards, the plaintiff began to suffer from various troubles which led to a diagnosis of multiple sclerosis. Under the French law of delict a causal relationship may be presumed where a disease manifests itself shortly after administration of an allegedly defective vaccine in circumstances where there are no personal or family antecedents related to the disease (*'présomptions graves, précises et concordants'*).[869] The Court of First Instance upheld the action. Two courts of appeal dismissed the action. The *Cour d'appel de Paris* held that the short period between the injection of the vaccine and the appearance of the first symptoms of multiple sclerosis, in conjunction with lack of any personal or family antecedents of that disease, could not give rise to 'serious, specific and consistent presumptions' of a causal link between the vaccine and the plaintiff's illness. The court noted that there was no scientific consensus to support such a causal relationship and that the cause of multiple sclerosis was unknown.

866. *See infra* text.
867. On causation and proof in EU public liability law, *see supra* text.
868. Case C-621/15, *N.W. and Others v. Sanofi Pasteur MSD SNC and Others* EU:C:2017:484. Compare also C-310/13, *Novo Nordisk Pharma* EU:C:2014:2385.
869. Cour de cassation Civ. 1re, 22.5.2008, Bull. Civ I, Nos 147, 148 and 149; RTD civ 2008, 492 with comments P. Jourdain. Compare G. Viney, *La responsabilité des fabricants de médicaments et de vaccins, les affres de la preuve*, D. 2010, 391.

Finally, it referred to epidemiological studies showing that 92% to 95% of persons with multiple sclerosis had no antecedent in their family.[870] The *Cour de cassation*, in its request for preliminary ruling, wanted to know whether this presumption of causation (and defect), as permitted under French law, is consistent with Article 4 of the Directive, notwithstanding the finding that medical scientific evidence was missing.[871]

421. The ECJ made another attempt at Solomonic judgments.[872] It held on the one hand that national evidentiary rules that exclude any recourse to circumstantial methods and require instead proof based on medical research of the existence of a causal link between the allegedly defective vaccine and the appearance of the disease disregard the requirements of Article 4. On the other hand, the application of these evidentiary rules should undermine neither the apportionment of the burden of proof provided for under Article 4 nor the effectiveness of the system of EU product liability. Whether the circumstances of the case in question constitute 'serious, specific and consistent evidence' has to be assessed by the national court's ruling on the merits of the action. – Thereupon, the *Cour de cassation* finally dismissed the appeal and upheld the judgment of the *Cour d'appel de Paris*.[873]

422. Partisans of patients' rights may welcome the ECJ's judgment. From the point of view of legal doctrine, it is another step towards loss of clarity of EU product liability law. Article 4 requires that the plaintiff first has to prove the defect of the product when it was put into circulation. Then, next to damage, she has to prove the causal relationship between defect and injury/damage. In this judgment the Court tolerates the French approach of presuming a causal relationship. This presumption of causation then leads to a presumption of defectiveness of the vaccine. Whether this inverse double presumption of central conditions of liability is compatible with the unambiguous content of Article 4 is more than questionable. – The second effect is the loss of harmonization. The Directive intends to establish an equal regime of liability of manufacturers and of protection of consumers throughout the twenty-eight Member States and to completely harmonize the matters regulated by it. By tolerating within the scope of EU product liability law a broad variety of national evidentiary rules (for proof of defect and causation), the Court produced the opposite effect on this harmonized law.

423. Final remark: With or without 'circumstantial evidence', the liability of a manufacturer who develops and markets a vaccine, where medical research neither establishes nor rules out the existence of a causal link between the vaccine and the disease in question, is *de lege lata* not feasible under EU product liability law! When the manufacturer *Sanofi Pasteur* put the vaccine in circulation, given this state of medical research, the presumed defect could not be discovered. If one

870. Cour d'appel de Paris, 7.3.2014.
871. Cour de cassation Civ 1re, D. 2015, 2602 with note Borghetti.
872. Case C-621/15, *Sanofi Pasteur* EU:C:2017:484, paras 18–43.
873. Cour de cassation Civ.1re, 18.10.2017, No. 14-18118.

vindicates, for whatever legitimate reasons, another result, one has to call upon the EU legislator to repeal the 'development risk defence' of Article 7 lit. e of the Directive.[874]

E. Producer

424. Liability for defective products under the Directive is liability of producers, not of sellers.[875] Article 3 presents three categories of 'producer': the manufacturer of the finished product, the quasi-producer and the EEA importer. Product liability is clear-cut enterprise liability. Neither executives nor employees are addressees of liability.

425. The model producer is the manufacturer of the finished product. This will also include assemblers. Equally treated are the producers of raw material and the manufacturers of component parts. If the defect originates from the used raw material, it is conceivable that all three categories of producers are jointly and severally liable for defectiveness.

Article 3(1) also mentions the so-called *quasi-producer*. A quasi-producer is factually a non-producer who pretends to be a producer. That occurs by putting one's name, trademark or other distinguishing feature on the product, manufactured somewhere and by somebody else. Endemic examples of quasi-producers are the big European trade firms who outsource production to Asia and market the products under their brand name in the EEA.

By way of exception non-producers (third-country importers and distribution companies) under certain conditions have also been qualified as producer. This importer must be a commercial trader. Import for private use is irrelevant, as is the inner-Union trans-border movement of goods. Only the importer of third-country products *into the EEA* is treated like a producer. It is the party in the distribution chain who imported the risk into the EEA and can be made responsible under European law.

426. Finally, Article 3(3) provides for a chance of last resort for the injured EU citizen to claim compensation for damage caused by a defective product – *the distributor*. The distributor will mostly be a retailer, wholesaler or internet trader. But also, restaurants can be qualified as sellers of food and beverages. However, only if no producer, no quasi-producer and no EEA importer can be identified, any distributor of the product can be sued for damages. The trader can avoid this liability if it can name the party who supplied him with the defective product.

427. If the plaintiff makes an error as to the identity of the producer, it is for the national procedural law to determine the legal consequences. However, substitution

874. *See infra* text.
875. Some national laws, however, put also distributors under the umbrella of 'strict' products liability, e.g., China and the US. For Chinese law compare Brüggemeier, *Modernising Civil Liability Law*, p. 188; for US law compare *Restatement (Third): Products Liability*, §2.

of the wrong defendant by the right producer is only admissible within the ten-year cut-off period of Article 11.[876]

F. Exclusionary Grounds

428. Article 7 lists six grounds that may exclude the liability of the producer. They are exhaustive, but of different nature. Some mean nothing else than shifting the burden of proof; others are genuine defences which must be brought forward by the defendant producer.

429. A shift of the burden of proof concerns the characteristics of the product.[877] As already discussed *supra*, Article 7 makes clear that the presence of a product in the sense of Article 2 requires manufacturing for *economic purpose* and manufacturing *in the course of business*. According to the Directive, these characteristics of the product are presumed with the onus of proving the absence of these two characteristics falling on the supposed producer.

The other grounds are genuine defences, that is, they contain new facts contended by the defendant producer which would exclude liability. The burden to show the evidence is here, too, on the producer.

430. The first exclusionary ground concerns the fact that the damaging product has not been brought *into circulation* by the producer. 'Brought into circulation' means that the process of manufacturing including final testing and inspections must be completed. That is, the product, be it raw material, component part or finished good, left the factory and entered into distribution. The term 'putting into circulation' has to be interpreted uniformly throughout the Directive.[878] In the English case of *O'Byrne I*, the ECJ had the opportunity to clarify the meaning of this term in the context of the ten-year cut-off period (Article 11).[879] In *O'Byrne I*, two questions were raised: (i) when has a product been put into circulation; and (ii) under which conditions is a substitution of a wrong defendant admissible? The latter issue will be treated shortly *infra* the text.

431. In 1992 the plaintiff, then a 1-year-old child, suffered serious injury from a defective vaccine administered to him in a hospital. The producer of the vaccine was a French company. It sent the unit with the defective vaccine to its distribution company in the UK, wholly owned by the French producer. The English subsidiary sold the vaccine to the UK Department of Health, which delivered it to the hospital where it had been administered to the plaintiff. In 2001, the plaintiff brought an action for damages against the English sales company under EU product liability

876. Compare Case C-127/04, *O'Byrne I* [2006] ECR I-1313 (sales company sued instead of producer). *See* in greater detail *infra* text.
877. *See supra* text.
878. It is used in Arts 6(1)(c), 6(2), 7(a)(b)(e), 11 and 17 of the Directive.
879. Case C-127/04, *O'Byrne v. Sanofi Pasteur MSD Ltd and Sanofi SA (O'Byrne I)* [2006] ECR I-1313.

law. Informed about the true producer, in 2002 he sued the French company, a claim which was time-barred by a margin of one month (Article 11). Therefore, the plaintiff applied for the English subsidiary to be substituted by the French producer in the first, non-time-barred action. To assess the expiry of the cut-off period in this case, the question had to be answered: When has the defective vaccine been 'put into circulation'? In France, when it was given for dispatch to England, or in the UK, when it was delivered by the English subsidiary to the Health Department?

432. The Court ruled that the examination of a close relationship between companies in this context must not be influenced by the question whether or not distinct legal persons are involved. Instead, it needs to be determined whether the subsidiary in question is exclusively part of the distribution chain or whether it is in reality involved in the manufacturing process. According to the Court, a product has been put into circulation when it left the manufacturing process for distribution in the form in which it is finally offered to the public.[880]

433. The second exclusionary ground exempts the manufacturer from liability if it can prove that it is more probable than not that the defect which caused the damage did not exist at the time the product was put into circulation or that it originated afterwards. That is, preponderance of evidence suffices. It is the only time in the Directive that implicitly a standard of proof has been addressed. This does not mean that this standard of proof applies thoroughly in EU product liability law. On the contrary, the fact that the standard of preponderance of evidence has been expressly and exclusively used in this subparagraph indicates that it is not generally applicable in EU product liability law. With respect to the general standard of proof applied under the Directive, any information is missing.[881]

434. Third, producers' liability does not exist if the defect is due to compliance of the product with mandatory regulations issued by public authorities. This is an obvious consequence. Compliance with law cannot lead to liability. This is then a case of governmental liability of the public authorities who passed faulty regulations. However, the exclusionary ground of Article 7(d) is restricted to *mandatory* regulations and technical standards. Hence, it does *not* concern the technical standards of private standardization bodies like AFNOR, BSI, DIN, CEN or ISO.

435. The 'New Approach to Technical Harmonization', launched by the EU institutions in the mid-1980s, is also *not* covered by this provision.[882] It is still in the discretion of the producer how to develop and design its products that they comply with the fundamental EU safety requirements. The CE conformity marking, awarded by notified certification bodies, implies only a presumption of the compliance with safety requirements. The plaintiff can adduce double evidence: (i) The

880. Case 127/04, *O'Byrne I*, paras 29–32. But *see also* the dissenting Opinion of AG Geehoed, *O'Byrne I* [2005] ECR I-1325, paras 43 et seq.
881. Compare also *supra* text on the liability under primary EU law.
882. Correctly stated by Taschner, *Produkthaftung*, 111 (1986). Compare Council Resolution of 7 May 1985 on a New Approach to Technical Harmonization and Standards, OJ 1985 C 136/1.

concrete product in question does not comply with fundamental safety requirements, turning it defective. (ii) In spite of compliance with the safety requirements, the product in question is defective in the sense of Article 6 of the Directive. Having shown this evidence, the national public authorities are obliged under EU product safety law to take the appropriate market surveillance measures like the safeguard procedure to abolish the presumption of safety compliance.[883]

In this respect, it can be stated that a 'regulatory compliance defence' does not exist in EU product liability law.

436. The fourth one is the most important exclusionary ground – the development risk.[884] Research and development of new products shall be fostered in the EU to promote economic growth and technical progress, but societies have to pay for this path to growth and progress with contingent risks of newly developed products. To whom should these risks be attributed: to the producer or the victims concerned? Article 7(e) gives the answer: The manufacturer can exclude liability if it adduces the evidence that the product defect was undetectable when the product was put into circulation, given the current '*state of scientific and technical knowledge*'. This answer was a political compromise. Without this exclusionary exit for the industry, the Member States would not have unanimously passed the Directive. As a quid pro quo, the Directive grants individual Member States the opportunity to autonomously extend the producers' liability to these contingent product risks (Article 15(1)(b)). Only Finland and Luxemburg completely removed this exclusionary rule. Spain made an exception for high-risk products like drugs, foodstuffs and food products intended for human consumption. France did it for body parts and products derived from body parts.[885]

437. Article 7(e) provides for the so-called *development risk defence*. Development risks are restricted to design or construction defects. It is a whole newly developed product series that is affected. Therefore, flaws, especially so-called one-offs, being only individual deviants from an otherwise faultless product series, are not covered.[886] Decisive point of time for the determination of the current state of knowledge is the first time when a product of the defective new product series has been put into circulation.

Finally, it is the state of scientific and technical knowledge *anywhere and of anyone* in the world that matters, provided it is reasonably accessible. Under the Directive, the producer cannot avoid liability by showing that it complied with the acknowledged state of scientific and technical knowledge. That is the commonly labelled *state of the art defence*. In EU product liability law the state of knowledge is not the technical benchmark for producer conduct but the focus for scientific discoverability of design defects.[887]

883. Compare Regulation (EC) No. 765/2008 setting out the requirements for accreditation and market surveillance relating to the marketing of products, OJ 2008 L 218/30.
884. From an English point of view compare M. Mildred, *The Development Risks Defence*, in *Product Liability in Comparative Perspective* 167 (D. Fairgrieve ed., CUP 2005).
885. As far as blood products are concerned, compare *supra* text.
886. *See supra* text and fns 412–414.
887. Correctly stated by Taschner, *Produkthaftung* 116 (1986).

438. The state of knowledge and its accessibility were addressed by the ECJ in 1997.[888] The UK transposed the formula of the 'state of scientific and technical knowledge' into its Act on Consumer Protection as follows:

> that the state of scientific and technical knowledge at the relevant time was not such that a producer … might be expected to have discovered the defect if it had existed in his products while they were under his control.[889]

The Commission took the view that inasmuch as section 4(1)(e) of the Act refers to what may be expected of a producer, its wording conflicts with Article 7(e) in that it permits account to be taken of the subjective knowledge of producers taking reasonable care, having regard to the standard precautions taken in the industrial sector in question.

439. The Court made clear that Article 7(e) is not directed at the practices and standards *in use* in the industrial sector in question (state of the art) but, unreservedly, at the state of scientific and technical knowledge, including the most advanced level, at the time of marketing the product. The focus is not on what the concrete producer actually or subjectively was or could have been aware of, but on the objective and most advanced state of scientific and technical knowledge worldwide.

But this knowledge must have been accessible to the producer at the time when the defective product was put into circulation. This question of accessibility and its conditions, however, were not developed further by the Court. It was left to the national courts to resolve it.

440. Lastly, Article 7(f) deals with a special problem of liability of producers of components (and raw materials). Covered are two cases: (i) A delivered component part without defect becomes defective due to inappropriate further processing or installation, or (ii) the defect results from the design of the final product or from instructions given by its manufacturer. If the producer of component parts can prove these facts, it is exempted from liability. The same holds true for producers of raw materials though they are not expressly mentioned in Article 7(f).

G. Additional Provisions

441. If the conditions featured above are met, the producers' duty to compensate the damage caused by their products under EU product liability law is in principle founded. The Directive provides for some additional rules.

442. Article 16 authorizes the Member States to introduce caps for damages in cases of serial losses, that is, damages resulting from a death or personal injury and caused by identical products with the same defect. Three categories have to be distinguished: regular individual damage by one product; multiple damages caused by

888. Case C-300/95, *Commission v. United Kingdom* [1997] ECR I-2649.
889. Section 4(1)(e) of the Consumer Protection Act of 1987, Part I.

one product, e.g., a defective bus or airplane; and *serial losses*. With respect to the latter, Member States can provide for a ceiling of at least EUR 70 million. Germany, Portugal and Spain have exercised this option. In contradiction to the Directive, the German *Produkthaftungsgesetz* also extended its ceiling of EUR 85 million to multiple damages caused by *one* defective product.[890]

443. Article 10 provides a rule on prescription. A limitation period of *three years* shall apply to actions for damages under the Directive. The limitation period begins to run when the plaintiff becomes aware or should reasonably have become aware of: (i) the damage, (ii) the defect, and (iii) the identity of the producer. Unavoidable error on the producer and suing the wrong one leaves the period of limitation towards the 'right' producer unaffected.

444. Whereas the start of the limitation period is conditional on a subjective factor, the *extinction of rights* within the cut-off period according to Article 11 seems to be exclusively conditional on an objective factor: The right to bring an action for damages under the Directive shall be extinguished *ten years* after the producer has put the defective product into circulation. In the case of *O'Byrne I*, the ECJ also had to decide, next to the question when a product had been put into circulation,[891] the issue of whether the substitution of a wrong defendant mistakenly sued is admissible after the expiry of the ten-year cut-off period.[892] In *O'Byrne I,* the plaintiff commenced an action against the English sales company within the cut-off period. Informed about his error, he sued the French producer, a claim which in the meantime was time-barred (Article 11). Therefore, he applied for a substitution by the French producer in the original procedure. As the Directive says nothing to this issue, the Court held that it is a matter for national procedural law to regulate the circumstances in which substitution of parties would be permitted.[893] In England, this topic was governed by section 35 of the Limitation Act. In accordance with section 35(6), substitution is admissible if either there is a relevant mistake as to name, or if an existing claim against the original party could not be maintained without the joinder or substitution for the new party. In *O'Byrne I*, substitution was admitted by the High Court.[894]

445. The defendant French producer appealed twice. The (then) House of Lords, notwithstanding their Lordships' preparedness to dismiss the appeal, was, however, not unanimous as to the meaning of the ECJ's ruling. Thus, the House of Lords brought the same issue a second time before the ECJ. This time more straightforwardly, the Court held that, in principle, Article 11 excludes any damages action being brought against a producer after the expiry of the ten-year cut-off period.

890. §10(1) Produkthaftungsgesetz.
891. *See supra* text and fn 879.
892. Case C-127/04, *O'Byrne I* [2006] ECR I-1313.
893. Case C-127/04, para. 39.
894. *O'Byrne v. Aventis Pasteur MSD Ltd* [2006] EWHC 2562 (QBD), [2007] 1 WLR 757. *See also* beforehand *Horne-Roberts v. SmithKline Beecham plc* [2001] EWCA Civ 2006, [2002] 1 WLR 1662.

However, given two conditions, the national courts are not precluded from admitting substitution in accordance with their national procedural law:[895]

(1) The putting into circulation of the product in question by the subsidiary was, in fact, determined by the parent producer company.
(2) The factual producer was not reasonably identifiable and the mistakenly sued company did not inform the plaintiff, promptly and on its own initiative, of the identity of the producer.[896]

In any case, the UK Supreme Court found that the French producer did not determine the delivery of the vaccine by its English subsidiary. Already in its first *O'Byrne* ruling, the ECJ had stated that the French company had put the vaccine into circulation. Therefore, the UKSC now allowed the producer's appeal, and *O'Byrne* could not substitute the English subsidiary by the French producer.[897]

446. Nearly twenty years after suffering serious brain damage through a vaccine and after eight years of proceedings, *O'Byrne* lost the case, seemingly due to a time-bar of a margin of one month. At second glance, *O'Byrne* is an extremely sad story of a victim of a defective product, who got lost in the brave new world of EU product liability law with its malfunctioning of the inter-judicial cooperation between ECJ and national courts.

447. EU product liability cannot be excluded or limited (Article 12). This rule is primarily of declaratory effect because in most cases of product liability, unlike in cases of service liability, regularly there is no privity of contract between producer and injured person.

§3. Conclusion

448. The piecemeal approach of harmonizing civil liability law has its unavoidable deficits. It is limited to the narrow sector regulated by the directive and to the few legal categories (such as product, defect, producer) autonomously interpreted by the ECJ. The harmonization project, however, remains embedded in the heterogeneous structure of the domestic liability law of the Member States, as concerns the categories and extents of damages, e.g., in cases of fatal injuries; apportionment of damages among jointly and severally liable producers; or procedural rules like presumption of facts, standard of proof, substitution of parties, etc.

449. Thirty years after its entry into force, the Directive still does not cover two core areas: commercial property and non-material damage. Both issues have been on the agenda of possible subjects for revision in the Commission's Green Paper of

895. Case C-358/08, *Aventis Pasteur SA v. O'Byrne* (*O'Byrne II*) [2009] ECR I-11305.
896. This proviso seems to refer to the alternative liability of distributors according to Art. 3(3).
897. *OB v. Aventis Pasteur SA* [2010] UKSC 23.

1999.[898] The latter is an indispensable issue for a legal regime that focuses primarily on the protection of bodily integrity. Time is ripe for the EU legislator, through an amendment of the Directive, to introduce compensation for pain and suffering for personal injury victims. Initiatives of individual Member States to extend, contrary to Article 9(2) of the Directive, the coverage of EU product liability law to non-material damage are barred by the maximum harmonization doctrine. Therefore, in *any* case of personal injury and property damage, to get full compensation,[899] the victims of defective products in the EEA have no alternative other than to sue under the pre-harmonized national law of delict or torts. (For cross-border litigation within the EU, the jurisdiction is determined by the Brussels Ia Regulation of 2012[900] and the applicable national law by the Rome II Regulation of 2007.[901] Rome II contains special rules for product liability (Article 5)).

450. As a matter of fact, development risks for design defects are excluded in EU product liability law, notwithstanding the optional faculty for the Member States to do away with the development risk defence (Article 15(1)(b)). Seemingly, only two Member States exercised this option. A Directive regulating product liability in the meanwhile thirty-one countries of the EEA should address this relevant situation of lacking liability. By a supplementary provision therefore, the Directive should require that the law of the Member States shall provide a remedy in cases of producers' failure to monitor the products they put into circulation and to react in an appropriate manner if defects occur after marketing, e.g., by post-sale warning or products recall.[902]

It has been criticized as less convincing to distinguish between liability for undiscoverable manufacturing defects and pre-manufacturing risks on the one side and non-liability for unavoidable design defects due to the development risk defence on the other side.[903] Be that as it may, the Directive 85/374/EEC was not the result of rational academic lawmaking, but the imperfect political compromise through an EU legislator who wanted to promote the accomplishment of the common market, growth of the economies and a little bit of common consumer protection.

451. As the Directive had not been subject to any evaluation, the Commission decided in 2016 to carry out a fully fledged assessment of the performance of the Directive, which will be supported by an external study. The evaluation was foreseen for the end of 2017. As part of the evaluation, the Commission has launched

898. Green Paper on Liability for Defective Products, COM(1999) 396 final.

899. For example, to do away with the threshold of EUR 500 and to get compensation of loss of use in cases of damage to private property.

900. Regulation (EU) No. 1215/2012; compare *supra* text, paras 32–35.

901. Regulation (EC) No. 864/2007 on the law applicable to non-contractual obligations (Rome II), OJ 2007 L 199/40 (not applicable in Denmark). *See Rome II Regulation* (P. Huber ed., Sellier 2011).

902. In *Commission v. France* (fn. 795), the ECJ held that the French attempt to make the development risk defence conditional on an established system of post-sale monitoring by the producer is incompatible with the law of the Directive.

903. Compare J. Stapelton, *Product Liability* (Butterworths 1994); J. Stapelton, *Bugs in Anglo-American Products Liability*, in *Product Liability in Comparative Perspective*, 295, at 330 et seq. (D. Fairgrieve ed., CUP 2005).

a public consultation. The aim of the consultation is to collect stakeholders' feedback on the application and performance of the Directive. A special focus is on the challenges raised by new technological developments, e.g., the so-called internet of things (IoT).[904] However, as of November 2017, no results of these initiatives were available.[905]

904. The IoT is a network of digital products, communicating and interacting with the environment and other devices.
905. *See* http://ec.europa.eu/growth/single-market/goods/free-movement-sectors/liability-defective-products.

Chapter 2. Liability of Service Suppliers

§1. Draft Service Liability Directive

452. On 9 November 1990, the Commission presented a proposal for a directive on the liability of suppliers of services.[906] The proposal closely followed the model of the product liability directive. It sought to harmonize the rules on non-contractual liability for services in the law of the Member States. The Commission simultaneously announced to present supplementary proposals concerning the construction sector and the health sector.[907]

The basic content of the proposal was as follows: Suppliers of services should be liable for damage resulting from injury to persons and to the physical integrity of movable or immovable property. Unlike in the product liability law, the damage must be caused by fault committed in the performance of the service. The burden of proving the absence of fault was on the service supplier. The injured person had to adduce evidence for his or her injury/damage and causation by the service supplied.

453. Service in the sense of the proposal meant any transaction carried out on a commercial basis or by way of public service and in an independent manner. The transaction should not have as its direct and exclusive object the manufacture of movable goods or the transfer of rights in rem or intellectual property rights. Addressee of liability was the service enterprise or the service supplying public body, not executives organizing or employees providing the service. Most of the supplementary provisions were borrowed from the product liability directive.

454. The reception of the proposal was restrained, its discussion within the parliamentary institutions controversial. In 1993, the Commission was asked to present an amended proposal. Instead, for various reasons, the proposal was withdrawn in 1994.[908] The field of respective services was too heterogeneous. A workable concept of 'defective service' as different from fault was not at hand. The fact that, unlike in product liability, the supply of services is closely interwoven with contractual relationships made an exclusively non-contractual approach less convincing.

The issue was supposedly taken up again by the consumer policy action plan for 1999–2001, which announced 'new initiatives' concerning liability for damage caused by the provision of services. No further concrete steps have, however, been

906. COM(90) 482 final – SYN 308; OJ 1991 C 12/8. Compare, *inter alia*,, *Entwurf einer Richtlinie über die Haftung bei Dienstleistungen/The Draft Directive on the Liability of Suppliers of Services/ Project de directive sur la responsabilité en matière de prestations de services* (S. Littbarski ed., Bundesanzeiger 1982). – For a comparative account of service liability in six European countries (plus the EU and US), *see Liability for the Safety of Services* (U. Magnus & H.W. Micklitz eds, Nomos 2006).

907. For a comparative account of liability in the health sector compare *Medical Liability in Europe* (B.A. Koch ed., de Gruyter 2011); *The Development of Medical Liability* (E. Hondius ed., CUP 2010).

908. COM(94) 260 final: Communication from Commission on new directions on the liability of suppliers of services.

undertaken. The Directive on Services of 2006[909] did not address the liability aspect any further.

455. Outside the EU, the Council of Europe had taken up a narrow field of service liability with its 'Convention on the Liability of Hotel-Keepers Concerning the Property of their Guests' of 1962.[910] Contracting parties were European countries inside and outside the EU.

§2. Case Law of the ECJ

456. The jurisdiction of the ECJ occasionally tried to subsume service liability under product liability. *Veedfald,* though undoubtedly a case of a defective medical service, was brought by the ECJ, then still inexperienced in products liability, under the product liability directive, notwithstanding that the perfusion fluid in question was not a 'product' in the sense of Article 2 of the Directive.[911] The Court has recently corrected this approach. In the case of *Dutrueux*, a patient sustained damage resulting from the failure of a defective heated mattress used in the course of a medical treatment.[912] What was a matter of course is from now on also recognized by EU secondary law: A hospital is not liable under EU product liability law for defective equipment applied in the performance of medical services if this item has been produced by a third party. Suppliers of services are not producers of goods in the sense of Article 3 of the Directive. In *Dutrueux*, too, the Court noted that any *national* regime of no-fault liability on the part of service providers, additional to product liability, can contribute to enhancing consumer protection.[913]

457. In *Schmitt v. TÜV Rheinland,*[914] the Court also addressed service providers' liability, though somewhat indirectly. The case concerned liability of certification bodies ('notified bodies') within the framework of the EU product safety regulation.[915] The products here were breast implants covered by the Directive on medical devices.[916] The 'notified bodies' state with their conformity declaration that the products at issue comply with the safety and health requirements of the

909. Directive 2006/123/EC on Services in the Internal Market, OJ 2006 L 376/36.
910. Entered into force in 1979. For a text compare http://conventions.coe.int/Treaty/en/Treaties/Html/041.htm.
911. Compare *supra* text (para. 378).
912. Case C-495/10, *Centre hospitalier universitaire de Besancon v. T. Dutrueux and Caisse primaire d'assurance maladie du Jura* [2011] ECR I-14155.
913. C-495/10, *Dutrueux* [2011] ECR I-14155, para. 35.
914. Case C-219/15, *F. Schmitt v. TÜV Rheinland* EU:C:2017:128.
915. New approach to technical harmonization and standards, OJ 1985 C 136/1, and Global approach to conformity assessment, OJ 1990 C 10/1.
916. Directive 93/42/EEC concerning medical devices, OJ 1993 L 169/1; amended by Directive 2001/104/EC, OJ 2002 L 6/50; in the meantime replaced by Regulation (EU) 2017/745 on medical devices of 5.4.2017, OJ 2017 L 117/1.

Directive.[917] *TÜV Rheinland* was the accredited and notified body in charge of the safety declaration for the breast implants in question, produced in France. The breast implants contained defective silicone. Many recipients of the defective implants got their devices replaced. They brought actions for damages. Since the French manufacturer had fallen into insolvency, Mrs *Schmitt* sued the 'notified body' for insufficient control of the manufacturing process before German courts. German law of delict applied.

458. On request through the German Federal Court of Justice, the ECJ had to clarify the scope of the auditing and monitoring obligations of 'notified bodies' under the EU product safety law for medical devices. The Court held that the 'notified bodies' are in principle not obliged to carry out unannounced inspections to examine the manufacturer's business. Only in face of evidence indicating that a medical device may not comply with the safety requirements, the notified body must take all steps necessary to ensure that it fulfils its obligations under the Directive.[918] Therefore, the Federal Court finally denied fault of the 'notified body' TÜV Rheinland and dismissed the action.[919]

917. On the applicability of the Directive on Services (OJ 2006 L 376/36) on 'certification bodies' compare ECJ, Case C-593/13, *Presidenza del Consiglio dei Ministri and Others v. Rina Services SpA and Others* EU:C:2015: 399.

918. C-219/15, *F. Schmitt*, paras 40 and 48.

919. Bundesgerichtshof, 22 Jun. 2017, VII ZR 36/14, NJW 2017, 2617. – In France, on 20 Jan. 2017, the Court of First Instance in Toulon ruled that TÜV Rheinland and its French subsidiary have to pay EUR 60 million compensation to 20,000 plaintiffs. The final amount of damages remained to be assessed. An appeal is pending before the superior court in Aix on Provence.

Part VIII. Additional Civil Liability Regimes

Chapter 1. Environmental Liability

459. The concept of environmental liability comprises two dimensions: (i) relief for individual damage caused by environmental pollution, and (ii) compensation of impairments of the natural environment (ecological/environmental damage). The first dimension belongs to classic civil liability in tort; the second tends to be under a private-public or purely public law regime of compensation and restoration remedies. Both dimensions were covered by an advanced piece of legislation: the Council of Europe's 'Convention on Civil Liability for Damage resulting from Activities Dangerous to the Environment' of 21 June 1993.[920] This so-called Lugano Convention, however, never entered into force. Up to now, it has been ratified by just one country – Portugal.

460. Next to the national law of the Member States, such as the German *Umwelthaftungsgesetz* of 1990,[921] some ratified international conventions are of relevance in this field of law, to mention but two:

- The International Convention on Civil Liability for Oil Pollution Damage of 1969, as amended in 1992 (Liability Convention).[922] It governs the liability of ship owners for damage caused by the spillage of persistent oil from oil tankers. It introduced strict (no-fault) liability on the part of owners and charterers, limited to an amount calculated by reference to the tonnage of the ship, and established a system of compulsory liability insurance.
- The International Convention on the Establishment of an International Fund for Compensation for Oil Pollution Damage of 1971, as amended in 1992 (Fund Convention).[923] It complements the Liability Convention by establishing a system for compensating victims which is financed by contributions from the oil industry.

920. For a text cf. http://conventions.coe.int.
921. Act on Environmental Liability of 10 Dec. 1990, Federal OJ 1990 I, p. 2634.
922. Compare OJ 2004 L 78/32.
923. Compare OJ 2004 L 78/40; by Protocol of 2003 supplemented by an additional compensation fund (OJ 2004 L 78/24).

Most of the Member States are parties to these Conventions. However, the EU has not acceded to these international conventions and therefore, they are not EU law.[924] The same holds true, *inter alia*, for the nuclear liability conventions.[925]

§1. History

461. Originally, the EU Commission was focused on a civil environmental liability directive, grounded on the polluter-pays principle and relying on the deterrent effect of liability law.[926] It should cover individual cases of personal injury and property damage caused mostly by industrial sources of emission. Pure economic loss was also concerned: for example, hotels without customers in the vicinity of beaches contaminated by oil; bathing facilities downstream of polluted rivers. Questions of remoteness and imputability assumed increased importance. Sector-specific attempts had been undertaken in the 1990s: On the basis of the waste framework directive of 1975, a remarkable proposal of a 'directive on civil liability for damage caused by waste' was presented in 1989 and amended in 1991.[927] According to its Article 3, every industrial 'producer' of waste should be strictly liable for injuries to private parties (personal injury and damage to property) caused by its waste. Certain quasi-producers were put in the same category, e.g., importers of waste, site operators. Liability would not only arise for individual damage, but also for impairment of the natural environment (ecological damage). This initiative had been complemented in 1993 by a proposal of a 'directive on the landfill of waste', providing for a no-fault liability of operators of waste disposal sites.[928]

However, these proposals remained in the stage of drafts and never entered into force. One possible explanation of this failure was the uncertainty of whether insurance coverage would be afforded by the European liability insurers. Today, these drafts count as missed chances for a European environmental liability law.

§2. 'Non-Liability' Directive 2004/35/EC

462. Instead, the Commission was oriented towards a more comprehensive approach. The dimensions of the conceived new EU liability regime were then laid down in the *White Paper on environmental liability* of 2000.[929] This White Paper

924. On the litigation following the oil spillage caused by the sinking of the oil tanker 'Erica' *see* ECJ, Case C-188/07, *Commune de Mesquer* [2008] ECR I-4501.
925. Convention on Third Party Liability in the Field of Nuclear Energy of 1960 (Paris Convention) and supplementary conventions.
926. Compare L. Krämer, *The Single European Act and Environmental Protection* (1987) 24 CML Rev. 659.
927. COM(89) 282 final; [1989] OJ C 251/3; amended in 1991: COM(91) 219 final – Syn 217; OJ 1991 C 192/6.
928. COM(93) 275 final – Syn 335; OJ 1993 C 212/33. *See also* the Green Paper on remedying environmental damage of 1993: COM(93) 47 final.
929. COM(2000) 66 final; *see also Umwelthaftung in der EU/Environmental Liability in the EU* (J. Hamer ed., Bundesanzeiger 2002).

proposed a framework directive imposing no-fault liability for damage by EU regulated dangerous activities. It should still cover both losses of private parties and ecological damage. Fault liability should be introduced for damage to biodiversity caused by non-dangerous activities.

463. Intensive and controversial disputes among institutions, experts and stakeholders, following the publication of the White Paper, led finally to a disappointing decision of the Commission: The civil liability aspect was completely deleted and the content of the intended directive was restricted to restoration of environmental damages by public authorities. A first proposal for what was still called an environmental liability directive was published in 2002.[930] Two years later the Directive 2004/35/CE on Environmental Liability with Regard to the Prevention and Remedying of Environmental Damage was passed.[931] It focuses primarily on the prevention of ecological damage. Embodying concepts similar to the natural resource damage regime under US law, it makes Member States' authorities responsible for ensuring that 'damage to water, land and biodiversity is either prevented, by taking appropriate measures in cases of imminent threats, or effectively remedied, by restoring the previous condition if the damage has already been done'. Industrial undertakings, including transporters or disposers of waste, whose operations have resulted in the discharge of dangerous substances resulting in potential environmental damage to land, water and protected habitats and species may be subject to liability under the Directive. Here, 'liability' means that public authorities are entitled to reimbursement of the costs spent for damage prevention or restoration from the commercial undertakings responsible for the ecological damage.

464. The question of whether an infringement of the EIA Directive 85/337/EEC[932] designed to prevent environmental harm by carrying out environmental impact assessments and to inform the public thereon can also result in compensation for economic loss has been treated in the case of *Leth v. Austria.*[933]

930. COM(2002) 17 final.

931. OJ 2004 L 143/56. Compare, *inter alia*, L. Krämer, *Directive 2004/35/EC on Environmental Liability* (2004) 3 ELM 5; M. Hinteregger, *Environmental Liability*, in *Tort Law of the European Community*, 108 (Koziol & Schulze eds, Springer 2008); *Environmental Liability and Ecological Damage in European Law* (M. Hinteregger ed., CUP 2008): comparative stock-taking.

932. Directive 85/337/EEC on the assessment of the effects of certain public and private projects on the environment, OJ 1985 L 175/40, as amended.

933. ECJ, Case C-420/11, *J. Leth v. Austria and Land Niederösterreich*, compare *supra* text and fns 344 and 481.

Chapter 2. Liability for Automobile Traffic, Air Carriage and Nuclear Energy

§1. Automobile Traffic

465. The invention of railways, steamships, automobiles and airplanes caused many European countries to introduce new regimes of no-fault liability (*Gefährdungshaftung*).[934] Today, most of the continental civil law systems acknowledge this type of liability, whereas in the common law countries negligence liability is still at the fore. Within the EU, no steps towards harmonization of the respective liability law have been undertaken.

466. With regard to automobile keepers' liability for road traffic accidents,[935] only the compulsory liability insurance schemes have been harmonized across the Member States. The five directives, passed from 1972 onwards,[936] were codified in 2009.[937] They require that Member States ensure that civil liability for road traffic accidents in their countries is covered by insurance, and they specify, *inter alia*, the types of damage to be covered by motor vehicle insurance. These directives influence the substantive law, if at all, only indirectly.

467. *Jurisdiction* and *applicable law* in cross-border road traffic accidents in the EEA are governed by two Regulations: the Brussels I Regulation (recast 2012,[938] and the Lugano Convention) and the Rome II Regulation of 2007.[939] With regard to the applicable national tort law in road traffic accidents, Article 4(1) of the Rome II Regulation provides for a general rule: The applicable law shall be the law of the country in which the *direct or primary injury/damage* occurred, 'irrespective of the country in which the event giving rise to the damage occurred and irrespective of the country in which the indirect consequences of that event occur'. The respective national law determines the basis and extent of liability, including the parties liable and the persons entitled to compensation (Article 15 Rome II Regulation).

468. 'Indirect consequences' of a car accident (Article 4(1) Rome II Regulation) are not restricted to consequential damages. They cover in principle also 'secondary

934. Compare Brüggemeier, *Risks and Strict Liability* (2013) 21 ERPL 923.
935. In that respect compare the report for the EU Commission: Compensation of victims of cross-border road traffic accidents, 2009.
936. Starting with Directive 72/166/EEC on the approximation of the laws of Member States relating to insurance against civil liability in respect of the use of motor vehicles, and to the enforcement of the obligation to insure against such liability, OJ 1972 L 103/1.
937. Directive 2009/103/EC relating to insurance against civil liability in respect of the use of motor vehicles, and the enforcement of the obligation to insure against such liability, OJ 2009 L 263/11.
938. Regulation (EU) 1215/2012 on jurisdiction and the recognition and enforcement of judgments in civil and commercial matters, OJ 2012 L 351/1. In an important judgment, the ECJ established that the injured victim of a car accident can bring an action directly against the liability insurer of the party who caused the accident at the courts for the place where the plaintiff victim is domiciled. Case C-463/06, *FBTO Schadeverzekeringen NV v. J. Odenbreit* [2007] ECR I-11321.
939. Regulation (EC) No. 864/2007 on the law applicable to non-contractual obligations, OJ 2007 L 199/40.

injuries' or *dommages par ricochet*. This has been stated by the Court for *bereavement damages* of close relatives of a deceased accident victim who resided in another EU Member State.[940] Their damages claims are determined by the law of the Member State where the primary injury/damage occurred.

469. In *Haasová* the Court addressed the problem of whether automobile liability insurers are obliged to compensate non-material damage sustained by close relatives resulting from the death of a road traffic accident victim. It held that personal injury damages under EU law comprise both, material and non-material damages. In principle, also third parties such as relatives of a deceased person are entitled to compensation. Compulsory liability insurers, however, are obliged to pay only where the applicable national tort law provides for such compensation.[941]

470. In a whole lot of cases the Court affirmed limitations of liability contained in substantive national laws, e.g., due to contributory fault of the plaintiff, as far as the coverage of insurers is concerned.[942] In contrast, a complete exclusion of claims against the insurer, be it by contract or statute, is regularly regarded as incompatible with the motor vehicle insurance directives.[943] In line with its settled case law in these matters is the Court's judgment in the *Petillo* case.[944] Here the Italian Private Insurance Code established a specific compensation scheme for inferior non-material damage caused by road traffic accidents. These damages were less favourable to victims than those provided for under the ordinary rules of civil liability. The Court stressed once more the freedom of the Member States to determine the rules of civil liability applicable to road accidents, but seems to be willing to retain a certain control of the disproportionateness of limitations of road traffic victims' rights to compensation. Finally, it upheld the Italian legal provisions.

§2. International Conventions

471. International conventions tried to fill this gap of lacking harmonization of liability law, however, with little success.[945]

The Convention on Civil Liability for Damage Caused during Carriage of Dangerous Goods by Road, Rail and Inland Navigation Vessel of 1989 has never been ratified.[946] It would have introduced no-fault liability of the respective carrier for

---

940. Compare ECJ, Case C-350/14, *Florian Lazar v. Allianz SpA* EU:C:2015:802, paras 25–30: claim of a Romanian father whose daughter was killed in a road traffic accident in Italy.

941. Case C-22/12, *K. Haasová v. Rastivlav Petrik and Other* EU:C:2013:692, with reference to EFTA Court Case E-8/07, *Celina Nguyen v. the Norwegian State*, EFTA Court Rep. [2008] 224.

942. *See, inter alia*, Case C-484/09, *Marques Almeida v. Companhia de Seguros Fidelidade-Mundial SA and Other* EU:C:2012:656.

943. *See* Case C-537/03, *Candolin and Others v. Vahinkovakuutusosakeyhtio Pohjola and Other* [2005] ECR I-5745 (refusal or limitation of payment by insurer in cases of getting into the car of a drunk-driver).

944. Case C-371/12, *E. and C. Petillo v. Unipol Assicurazioni SpA* EU:C:2014:26 with further references.

945. *See also* C. von Bar, *The Common European Law of Torts* 390 (vol. I, OUP 1998).

946. Text at www.unece.org/trans/danger/publi/crtd/doc/crtd_e.doc.

damage by any dangerous goods during their carriage, be it national or international. Liability was subject to the standard defences and to monetary limitations, coupled with compulsory liability insurance.

The Convention Concerning International Carriage by Rail of 1980 established a uniform system for the international carriage of passengers and goods by rail.[947] It has been ratified by most EU Member States and incorporated into their national law.

The same holds true for the various conventions on maritime transport.[948] Not being EU law, these conventions will not be regarded in further detail in this monograph.

§3. Air Carriage

472. The only exception to the rule that international liability conventions were not incorporated into EU law is the case of the conventions on air carriage. The *Warsaw Convention* was transposed into EU law by Regulation (EC) No. 2027/97, the *Montreal Convention* by Regulation (EC) No. 889/2002. The EU legislation on air passengers' rights, such as the Regulation No. 261/2004,[949] can be neglected in this tort monograph. The Regulation No. 261/2004 grants air passengers rights to assistance and financial relief against air carriers in cases of serious delay or cancellation of flights.

I. Air Carriage Conventions

473. Concerning the *international* carriage of passengers and cargo by air, national law had been replaced early by international conventions. Already in 1929, the *Warsaw Convention* (WC) was passed.[950] It originally provided for a non-contractual regime of quasi-strict liability of air carriers (i.e., presumption of fault).[951] This was a compromise between the strict liability of French contract law (*obligation de résultat)* and the no-fault liability of other continental European countries like Germany (*Gefährdungshaftung*) on the one side, and the respect for the supposed needs of the developing juvenile aviation industry on the other side.

---

947. Text at www.unece.org/trade/cotif/cotif02.htm.

948. Compare B.A. Koch, *Other Strict Liabilities*, in *Tort Law of the European Community* 135, at 150 et seq. (Koziol & Schulze eds, 2008) with further references.

949. Regulation (EC) No. 261/2004 establishing common rules on compensation and assistence to passengers in the event of denied boarding and of cancellation or long delay of flights, OJ 2004 L 46/1.

950. [Warsaw] Convention for the Unification of Certain Rules Relating to International Carriage by Air of 12 Oct. 1929 (amended at The Hague on 28 Sep. 1955 and by Protocol No. 4 of Montreal 1975).

951. Article 17. The air carrier could rebut the presumption by showing that it has taken 'all necessary measures' to avoid the damage (Art. 20). This liability regime of Arts 17 and 20 WC comes close to the strict liability under §7(1)(2) of the German Act on Liability of Keepers of Automobiles (1909).

Liability was limited by fixed amounts for death or personal injury of the passengers.[952] Although Article 17 WC focused on an 'accident', its interpretation has been stretched by courts from the materialization of technical risks to man-made incidents (including terrorist acts or sexual assaults by co-passengers).[953]

474. The WC was succeeded by the *Montreal Convention* of 1999 (MC).[954] It was less a newly conceived legal document than a consolidation of the WC and its amendments hitherto into a single treaty. The MC established a two-tiered system of responsibility of air carriers (Articles 17 and 21):

(1) Strict liability up to an amount of SDR 113,100[955] for each killed or injured passenger. Force majeure and acts of god are not recognized as exclusionary grounds.
(2) Unlimited quasi-strict liability for exceeding amounts of damages. The carrier can exonerate itself from this liability by showing evidence that: (i) the damage was not due to its fault, or that (ii) it was solely caused by the fault of a third party.

475. The principles of contributory negligence apply in both cases (Article 20). Any damages claim of a passenger falling in the ambit of this Convention is bound to its rules and limits. (The crew members are under their respective national social insurance or workers' compensation schemes.)

Claims have to be filed within two years starting from the date of effective or planned arrival of the plane at the destination, or from the date on which the carriage stopped (Article 35).

476. Steps have been undertaken to work out an international convention on air carriers' liability for *damage to third parties on the ground* (Rome Convention). A first convention was passed in 1952 but was ratified only by a few countries. During the work on the MC, there was consent to undertake a redrafting of the Rome Convention. These redrafting works have not yet come to a final result. So far, this scenario remains under the respective national law.

---

952. Article 22. Liability was unlimited if the passenger (or his/her relative) could prove that the accident was caused by intentional or reckless behaviour of the carrier's personnel (Art. 25).
953. As landmark case compare *Air France v. Saks*, 470 U.S. 392 (1985); on this in general (albeit exclusively from an Anglo-American law perspective) *see* G. Leloudas, *Risk and Liability in Air Law* (Informa Law 2009).
954. [Montreal] Convention for the Unification of Certain Rules Relating to International Carriage by Air of 28 May 1999.
955. Special Drawing Rights of the International Monetary Fund (= USD 175,800, as of December 2011).

II. Regulation (EC) No. 889/2002

477. This non-contractual liability regime of the Montreal Convention has been incorporated into EU law by Regulation (EC) No. 8892002.[956] It extended the liability rules of the MC to all air carriages effectuated by EU or EEA air carriers, regardless of whether they are domestic flights within one single Member State or intra-union or international flights. The Regulation stipulates that air carriers furnish advance payments to victims 'as may be required to meet immediate economic needs on a basis proportional to the hardship suffered' (Article 5 Regulation 889/2002).

Unlike under WC and Regulation 2027/97, compensation is now extended from damage resulting from personal injury of passengers to cases of passenger delay[957] and destruction and loss of baggage. The category of damage in international convention law and under the EU Regulation comprises, in principle, material and non-material damage.[958]

478. This EU liability regime is bolstered by minimum insurance requirements governed by Regulation (EC) No. 785/2004.[959]

§4. Nuclear Energy

479. After the Second World War, the fast-spreading civil use of nuclear energy brought an unprecedented new technical risk into existence and raised new legal problems, too. The devastating cross-boundary consequences of a nuclear incident required an international nuclear liability regime. Already in the early 1960s, two international conventions were passed which addressed this liability problem:

- *Paris Convention* of 1960,[960] comprising sixteen Western European States (incl. Turkey). The Convention entered into force in 1968 and was amended by protocols in 1964, 1982 and 2004 (not yet in force).
- *Vienna Convention* on Civil Liability for Nuclear Damage of 1963,[961] comprising Non-Western European States.

---

956. Regulation (EC) No. 889/2002 on air carrier liability in the event of accidents, OJ 2002 L 140/2, amending the Council Regulation (EC) No. 2027/97 (OJ 1997 L 285/1) which beforehand had transposed the Warsaw Convention into EU law.
957. On passengers' delay compare also Regulation (EC) No. 261/2004. *See* Joined Cases C-402 and 432/07, *C. Sturgeon and Others v. Condor Flugdienst GmbH* and S. *Böck and Other v. Air France SA* [2009] ECR I-10923; Case-257/14, *C. van der Lans v. Koninklijke Luchtvaart Maatschappij NV* EU:C:2015:618 (also on the exclusionary ground of 'extraordinary circumstances').
958. Compare Case C-63/09, *A. Walz v. Clickair SA* [2010] ECR I-4239.
959. Regulation (EC) No. 785/2004 on insurance requirements for air carriers and aircraft operators, OJ 2004 L 138/1.
960. OECD Convention on Third Party Liability in the Field of Nuclear Energy of 1960 (Paris Convention). For the full text *see* the website of the International Atomic Energy Agency (IAEA): https://www.iaea.org.
961. IAEA Convention on Civil Liability for Nuclear Damage of 1963 (Vienna Convention),which entered into force in 1977.

Both Conventions were aligned by the *Joint Protocol Relating to the Application of the Vienna Convention and the Paris Convention* of 1988.

480. The Conventions' nuclear liability regime provides for the liability of operators of nuclear installations for damage resulting from incidents at their sites or during transport of nuclear substances to and from the site. Liability is strict, i.e., regardless of fault. Material and non-material damage is compensated in cases of death and personal injury. Damage to property is covered, pure economic loss, however, excluded. Liability of the operator is limited in amount; under the Paris Convention originally to SDR 15 million. Under the Vienna Convention the defences of contributory negligence are acknowledged. No liability exists in cases of nuclear incidents caused by armed conflicts, hostilities, civil war and grave natural disasters. Operators must take out third party liability insurance or provide for equivalent financial security. Liability expires within ten years of the nuclear incident. Still, there is no binding EU or EAEC law establishing liability and insurance of operators of nuclear power plants. It is up to the individual Member State's law to determine this liability and its limits, upholding the principles of the Conventions' law.

481. Especially with regard to the crucial point of amounts of liability, the Member States' laws vary extremely. The estimated potential damage of a nuclear incident amounts to hundreds of Bill. Euro. Most Member States liability of operators, however, is limited to hundreds of Mill. Euro. For example in Germany, operators' liability is in principle unlimited; but the mandatory coverage comes only to EUR 2.5 billion and is funded by the community of all operators of nuclear power plants in Germany (so-called Atom Fund).[962] Exceeding damage has to be compensated by the State. In cases of grave natural catastrophes, such as *Fukushima*, the liability is limited to EUR 2.5 billion. Special restrictive rules apply in cases of property damage.[963] Cross-boundary damages are only compensable to an extent that corresponds to the amount of operators' liability granted by the respective Member State law.[964] – In Belgium and the Netherlands the liability is restricted to EUR 1.2 billion, in Sweden and Poland to EUR 380 million, in the UK and Poland to less than EUR 200 million.

482. With a growing number of outdated nuclear power plants, susceptible to breakdowns, in the Member States, the risk of a devastating incident in Europe is rising. It needs both, internationally coordinated nuclear energy politics (EU and beyond) and an effective EU liability and insurance regime for nuclear incidents (such as a European joint atomic fund).

962. *See* §13 Atomgesetz (German Act on Nuclear Energy).
963. *See* §31(3)(i) Atomgesetz.
964. *See* § 31(2) Atomgesetz.

Chapter 3. Protection of Personal Data

483. As EU law currently stands, the right to protection of personal data is established by Article 8 ChFR, Articles 39 TEU and 16 TFEU, and Article 8 ECHR. The right to protection of personal data (privacy) is not an unlimited fundamental right, but must be considered in relation to its function in society and to other potentially affected fundamental rights or freedoms: such as freedom of expression (Article 11 ChFR), freedom to conduct a business (Article 16), protection of intellectual property (Article 17(2)), etc. Article 52(1) ChFR accepts that limitations may be imposed on the exercise, *inter alia*, of the right to data protection, as long as the limitations are provided for by law, respect the essence of these rights, and, subject to the principle of proportionality, are necessary and genuinely met objectives of general interest recognized by the EU or the need to protect the rights or freedoms of others.[965]

§1. Directive 95/46/EC

484. The data protection legislation began in the Member States (West Germany in 1970[966]/Sweden in 1973[967]). In efforts to promote a comprehensive data protection system throughout Europe, in 1980, the Organization for Economic Cooperation and Development (OECD) issued its influential 'Recommendations concerning guidelines governing the protection of privacy and trans-border flows of personal data', which were in 1981 supplemented by the Council of Europe's 'Convention for the protection of individuals with regard to automatic processing of personal data.'

485. Against this backdrop and more than twenty years after the take-off in Germany and Sweden, in 1995, the EU adopted the Directive 95/46/EC which laid the groundwork for personal data protection by EU legislation.[968] Article 1(1) stated its objectives: 'Member States shall protect the fundamental rights and freedoms of natural persons and in particular their right to privacy with respect to the processing of personal data.' The Directive introduced standards for the commercial processing of personal data by private parties, but State bodies were left out. It requires the Member States to provide for efficient legal protection systems.

486. '*Personal data*' is defined as 'any information relating to an identified or identifiable natural person (data subject); an identifiable person is one who can be

965. Compare ECJ, Joined Cases C-92 and 93/09, *Schecke GbR and Eifert v. Land Hessen* [2010] ECR I-11063, paras 65 et seq.
966. In 1970, the Land Hessen passed the world's first data protection act, providing, *inter alia*, for a data protection commissioner. In 1977, a federal act on data protection (Bundesdatenschutzgesetz) was adopted in West Germany, entering into force in 1978 (Federal OJ 1977 I, p. 201).
967. Credit Information Act 1973 and Debt Recovery Act 1974.
968. Directive 95/46/EC on the protection of individuals with regard to the processing of personal data and on the free movement of such data, OJ 1995 L 281/31.

identified, directly or indirectly, in particular by reference to an identification number or to one or more factors specific to his/her physical, psychological, mental, economic or social identity'.[969] Personal data are not restricted to text and figures, but comprise also sound and image data of natural persons. These data remain outside the scope of the Directive if carried out for purposes of public security, defence, national security, etc.[970]

'*Processing*' means 'any operation or set of operations which is performed upon personal data, whether or not by automatic means, such as collecting, recording, storage, … disclosure by transmission, dissemination or otherwise making available', etc.[971] The concept of data processing is extremely broad, extending the scope of application of most laws of the Member States. It expressly covers data processing carried out solely for journalistic purposes or the purpose of artistic or literary expression. Therefore, in these cases Article 9 explicitly provides for derogations from the data protection provisions. Privacy and freedom of expression must be brought to a sort of practical concordance.

487. The processing by a data controller of personal data must comply with five data protection principles.[972] The most important among these is: Processing must be 'fair and lawful', in determining which regard is to be had to the method by which the data are obtained. Article 7 contains criteria defining the legitimacy of data processing. Lawful data processing requires that the data subject has 'unambiguously given his/her consent'.[973] The intricacies of legitimate data processing, detailed in the Directive, cannot be featured further in this monograph.

488. The Directive itself, like other EU legislative measures harmonizing public law areas, does not contain any mandatory *liability rules* in its Articles 22–24. It only stipulates that any individual shall have a judicial remedy in case of breach of rights granted to him or her by national law applicable to the processing in question. Regular sanctions in cases of unlawful processing are rectification, blocking and erasure.[974] The responsibility for compliance rests on the shoulders of the controller.[975]

489. '*Controller*' means a natural or legal person or any other body, which alone or jointly with others determines the purposes and means of the processing of personal data.[976] Article 23(1) stipulates that Member States must make sure that any party who has sustained damage resulting from unlawful processing operations or any act incompatible with the national provisions adopted pursuant to the Directive,

---

969. Article 2(a) Directive 95/46/EC.
970. Directive 95/46/EC, recitals 16 and 17.
971. Article 2(b).
972. Article 6(1).
973. Article 7(a).
974. Article 32(2). Erasure may include the 'right to be forgotten'. Compare Case C-131/12, *Google Spain SL and Google Inc. v. Agencia Española de Protección de Datos (AEPD) and Other* EU:C:2014:317.
975. Article 6(2).
976. Article 2(d).

shall be entitled to claim compensation from the controller. The controller may be exempted from liability, in whole or in part, if he proves that he is not 'responsible for the event giving rise to the damage' (Article 23(2)).

490. Therefore, Member States were obliged to introduce a cause of action for damages either in the form of no-fault liability, or as liability based on fault with a reversal of the burden of proof in their domestic law. No-fault would mean liability for plain illegality, i.e., unlawful processing of personal data. If the national legislator opts for the fault alternative, the controller is released from liability when he adduces evidence that he could not avoid the event leading to damage and the standard of objective negligence is applicable. In the amended German *Bundesdatenschutzgesetz* and in the British Data Protection Act 1998, a quasi-strict enterprise liability has been introduced, that is, negligence liability with a reversal of the burden of proof for fault.[977]

491. The Directive also provided for administrative sanctions and remedies available to supervisory authorities of the Member States.[978] This issue, however, falls outside the strict parameters of civil liability for breach of data protection rights featured in this part of the monograph.

492. Generally, uncertainties about the scope of liability under the Directive persist, thus undermining its harmonizing effects. Telling examples are two famous cases concerning infringement of privacy of celebrities through print media. The German case of *Caroline von Monaco/Hannover* is treated by the German civil courts[979] (and the Federal Constitutional Court[980]) exclusively under general law of delict of the BGB. The courts did not address data protection law at all. In the parallel English case of *Naomi Campell*, both High Court and Court of Appeal applied the transposed British law, the Data Protection Act 1998 (though with contradictory results).[981] The House of Lords, however, ignored the data protection law and decided the case under English common law (breach of confidence).[982] The correct approach across all Member States would be to proceed primarily on the ground of

977. On the concept of quasi-strict enterprise liability *see supra* text.
978. Compare European Union Agency for Fundamental Rights, *Data Protection in the European Union: The Role of National Data Protection Authorities* (Publications Office of the EU, Luxembourg 2010).
979. Bundesgerichtshof, 19 Dec. 1995, BGHZ 131, 332.
980. Bundesverfassungsgericht, 15 Dec. 1999, BVerfGE 101, 361 (constitutional review of the judgment of the BGH). Both judgments have been found in breach of Art. 8(1) ECHR by the ECtHR: 24 Jun. 2004, 40 EHRR 1. To this case complex, *see* Brüggemeier, *Protection of Personality Rights in the Law of Delict/Torts in Europe*, in *Personality Rights in European Tort Law* 34–37 (G. Brüggemeier, A. Colombi Ciacchi & P. O'Callaghan eds, CUP 2010).
981. *Campbell v. Mirror Group Newspapers Ltd* [2002] EWHC 299; [2003] EMLR 2 (CA).
982. *Campbell v. Mirror Group Newspapers Ltd* [2004] UKHL 22; [2004] 2 AC 457; *see also OBG v. Allan* [2008] AC 1.

EU data protection law and only subsidiarily under domestic tort law (privacy, personality rights, breach of confidence, etc.)[983]

493. Criteria are especially missing to determine the *quantum of non-material damage* awards. In this respect, three distinct judicatures are delivering incoherent results: ECtHR, EU courts and Member States' courts. Under the ECHR, parties seeking redress for breach of data protection rights sue for 'just satisfaction' (Article 41). The ECtHR here adopts a rather restrictive approach to award compensation for non-pecuniary damage in Article 8 cases. Where there has been disclosure of information, or a State has failed to put a framework in place to prevent unlawful use or to provide effective judicial remedy, the quantum of financial compensation awarded is usually relatively small.[984] In contrast, the EGC developed in the so-called staff cases a remarkably generous regime of non-material damage compensation.[985] This also covers infringements of personality rights. In the *Franchet and Byk* case, two EU officials contended wrongful disclosure of personal information by the European Anti-Fraud Office (OLAF). They sued the Commission for damage to their reputation. The EGC granted non-material damage awards of EUR 56,000 to each applicant.[986] The transposition of the Directive into national law did not bolster harmonization up either. The German Act, e.g., did not exclude redress of non-material damage explicitly, but only serious violations of privacy/data protection rights were considered compensable.[987] The UK Data Protection Act distinguishes between damage and distress. For recovery of distress, however, the English courts pursue a minimalistic path. A telling case is Halliday, where the judge at first instance awarded only nominal damages of GBP 1 for failure to process financial data correctly. The Court of Appeal held that this did not accord with the case law of the CJEU and reassessed the level of compensation at GBP 750.[988]

494. In 2002, Directive 95/46/EC was supplemented by Directive 2002/58/EC on the protection of privacy in the *electronic communications sector* (so-called e-privacy Directive).[989] The Directive addresses the provider of a publicly available electronic communication service. It must take appropriate technical and organizational measures to safeguard security of its services. The Directive lays down rules

---

983. On the variety of national laws for breach of data protection or privacy rights, *see Tort Law* 141–169 (van Gerven, Lever & Larouche eds, Hart 2000); *Protection of Personality Rights* (G. Brüggemeier, A. Colombi Ciacchi & P. O'Callaghan eds, CUP 2010).

984. ECtHR, *Rotaru v. Romania*, 4.5.2000, Appl. No. 28341/95 (FRF 50,000); *K.U. v. Finland*, 2.12.2008, Appl. No. 2872/02 (EUR 3,000); *Szulc v. Poland*, 13.11.2012, Appl. No. 43932/08 (EUR 5,000).

985. *See supra* text (Part VI, Ch. 2). It needs to be recalled, however, that EU staff cases concern *public* liability, and not wrongful conduct of private parties.

986. Case T-48/05, *Franchet and Byk v. Commission* [2008] ECR II-1585. – *See also* J. Kokott & C. Sobotta, *The Distinction Between Privacy and Data Protection in the Jurisprudence of the CJEU and the ECtHR*, (2013) 3 International Data Privacy Law 222.

987. §7 Bundesdatenschutzgesetz.

988. *Halliday v. Creation Consumer Finance Ltd* [2013] EWCA Civ 333.

989. Directive 2002/58/EC concerning the processing of personal data and the protection of privacy in the electronic communications sector, OJ 2002 L 201/37, as amended by Directive 2009/136/EC, OJ 2009 L 337/11.

to protect the confidentiality of communications. *Inter alia*, listening, tapping, storage or other kinds of interception or surveillance of communications and the related data traffic are prohibited (Article 5).

Articles 6–13 deal with the protection of the right to privacy. Despite detailed provisions, however, the Directive itself again does not provide for a liability system of its own. It refers to the Directive 95/46/EC with its provisions on administrative remedies and civil liability.

495. Both directives were complemented by Framework Decision 2008/977/JHA as a general instrument at EU level for the protection of personal data in the areas of police cooperation and judicial cooperation in criminal matters.[990]

§2. New Approach 2016: General Data Protection Regulation (GDPR)

496. The constitutional acknowledgement of the right to data protection in the Charter and in the Lisbon Treaties on the one hand, and the unprecedented rapidity of the development of information technology on the other led the EU institutions to develop a new legal framework.[991] This framework contains a fragmented approach providing a legislative proposal for private processors and for public authorities:

- a General Data Protection Regulation; and
- a Directive on the protection of individuals with regard to the processing of personal data by competent authorities for the purposes of prevention, investigation, detection or prosecution of criminal offences or the execution of criminal penalties, and the free movement of such data.[992]

497. The centrepiece of the legal framework for the protection of personal data in the EU became the *General Data Protection Regulation*, passed in 2016 and coming into force in May 2018.[993] A Regulation was chosen because its direct applicability reduces legal fragmentation and provides greater legal certainty by introducing a harmonized set of core rules, improving the protection of fundamental rights of individuals and contributing to the functioning of the Internal Market.

990. OJ 2008 L 350/60.

991. COM(2012) 9 final: Safeguarding Privacy in a Connected World – A European Data Protection Framework for the Twenty-First Century.

992. COM(2012) 10 final. This fragmentation of data protection has been criticized by Simitis. Compare S. Simitis, *Der verkürzte Datenschutz* (Nomos 2004).

993. Regulation (EU) 2016/679 on the protection of natural persons with regard to the processing of personal data and the free movement of such data, OJ 2016 L 119/1. For an explanatory memorandum compare COM(2012) 11 final: Proposal for a Regulation on the protection of individuals with regard to the processing of personal data and on the free movement of such data.

498. Chapter VIII deals with remedies, liability and penalties. With regard to civil liability, the Regulation does not offer new elements. It adheres to the formulations of the Directive 95/46/EC. The new head of liability, now directly applicable throughout the twenty-eight Member States, is Article 82(1).[994] It reads:

> Any person who has suffered material or non-material damage as a result of an infringement of this Regulation shall have the right to receive compensation from the controller or the processor for the damage suffered.

Article 82(3) opens again the possibility for controllers and processors to escape liability if they can show that they were not responsible for the event giving rise to the damage (quasi-strict liability). Article 82(4) and (5) provides for joint and several liability of controllers and processors, and for a right of partial reimbursement of the one of the tortfeasors who paid full compensation.

499. Actions for damages against a controller or a processor shall be brought before the courts of the Member State where the controller or processor has an establishment. Alternatively, such proceedings may be brought before the courts of the Member State where the data subject has his or her habitual residence (Articles 79(2) and 82(6)). Subsidiarily, the Brussels Ia Regulation with its extraterritorial effects is applicable.[995]

500. Direct applicability per se is less helpful when the applicable law itself is lacking in content and precision. Article 82(1) makes it at least clear that compensation of non-material damage cannot be made conditional of grave infringements of data protection rights. The discrepancies between the involved jurisdictions with respect to the quanta of non-material damage awards remain. It is up to the European courts – CJEU and ECtHR – to mitigate these discrepancies and to make protection of personal data more effective.

---

994. Compare also Recital 146.
995. Regulation (EU) 1215/2012; compare *supra* text (Introduction, §3, III).

Part IX. Summary and Commentary

501. *Christian von Bar* stated correctly that there is no unified or harmonized law of delict/torts in the EU.[996] Harmonization of civil liability law has been pursued only in peripheral areas, to be more precise – in *one* peripheral area: products liability. In contrast to the evaluation through *H.C. Taschner*,[997] this approach was not a very satisfying one. To obtain full compensation in personal injury and property damage cases, it is still indispensable that the plaintiff brings an action for damages under pre-harmonized national law of delict or torts.[998] The odd problems of forum shopping, etc., that the Directive wanted to do away with, have come up again. In the field of environmental liability, the EU finally abstained from passing a civil liability directive. Harmonization of international traffic and transport is dominated by international conventions, with only one exception: the incorporation of the international air transport conventions into EU law. Thus, civil liability remains the domain of the Member States' domestic law. In the field of data protection legislation, it remains to be seen whether the 2016 Regulation supports an approximation in the field of liability.

502. An example for the heterogeneity of the rare provisions on civil tort liability is compensation for non-material damage. The term itself is left without contours. The product liability directive, though focused on recovery for personal injuries, expressly excludes compensation, e.g., for pain and suffering. It is left to the Member States' law to cover it in their domestic law of torts. In air transport liability law, the ECJ has ruled that the category of 'damage' includes both material and immaterial damage.[999] In the broad field of data protection, it is now free from doubt that material and non-material damage must be compensated, but the quanta of the damages awarded by the jurisdiction of ECtHR, CJEU and Member States' courts vary extremely.

---

996. C. von Bar, *The Common European Law of Torts*, vol I, no. 374 (OUP 1998). Compare also H. Koziol & R. Schulze, *Conclusion*, in *Tort Law of the European Community* 589–610 (Koziol & Schulze eds, Springer 2008).

997. Taschner, *Produkthaftung und Verschuldensfrage*, ZEuP 2012, 560, at p. 567: 'Directive 85/374/EEC has solved the problem of product liability to complete general satisfaction'.

998. *See supra* text.

999. Compare also Case C-168/00, *Leitner v. TUI Deutschland* [2002] ECR I-2631, on compensation of non-material damage in case of non-performance under a (travel) contract.

503. The existing voluminous treatises on 'European Tort Law' do not deal with unified or harmonized European tort law, but contain a comparative stock-taking of the national laws of delict/torts in the EU Member States;[1000] without doubt, comparative work at its best, but by no means with an 'EU tort law' as its subject.

1000. Compare C. von Bar, *The Common European Law of Torts* (2 vols, OUP 1998/2000); W. van Gerven et al., *Common Law of Europe Casebooks: Tort Law* (Hart 2000); C. van Dam, *European Tort Law* (2d ed. OUP 2013). – A rare example of a treatise on genuine EU tort law is W. Wurmnest, *Grundzüge eines europäischen Haftungsrechts* (Mohr Siebeck 2003).

Concluding Remarks

504. Tort law of the European Union is predominantly public liability law. *It is liability for breach of EU law*. What looks at first glance as a concise concept, loses at second regard clear contours. The very core of this breach-of-law liability is the non-contractual liability of the Union and of its institutional organs. It is governed by the second paragraph of Article 340 TFEU. This small paragraph, unchanged in its wording from 1957 onwards, contained two distinct types of liability: vicarious liability of the Union for torts, i.e., traditional wrongful acts, of its public servants, its bodies and institutional organs (the hidden EU tort law), and Union liability for breach of EU law by institutions and bodies of the Union. For the former, reference to (more or less) common principles of the (tort) law of the Member States makes sense. For the latter – breach of EU law – this reference finds no subject. Breach-of-law liability means responsibility for unlawful public acts without fault of EU institutions: legislature, executive, and in principle, judiciary. This category of public liability for unlawfulness, stemming from French administrative law, was unknown to most of the respective Member States' laws. Its principles had to be fleshed out autonomously by the case law of ECJ, fuelled solely by the spirit and purpose of the Treaties. Different conditions were elaborated to trigger liability for legislative (*manifest breach*) and administrative acts (*plain breach*). As far as the consequences of liability are concerned, recourse again was held to common rules of the laws of the Member States.

505. In the meantime, the type of vicarious liability got lost vis-à-vis the emergence and increasing dominance of this new breach of EU law jurisprudence. The *Grifoni* (*I Nos 1 and 2*) case is a telling example for this process of displacement.[1001]

Independent paths within Union liability are the compensation of losses resulting from lawful official acts, and the liability of the Union as principal towards its employees (staff cases). In these staff cases of public liability, the EGC elaborated genuine criteria for compensation of non-material damage.

506. Next to Union liability, the ECJ developed the liability of Member States for breach of EU law; this time without support by any provision of the Treaties. Ground-breaking early judgments served as cornerstones for this judicial architecture: direct effect, supremacy, and protectiveness of EU law. Here again, differentiated approaches were pursued: Liability in vertical direct effect cases and in *Francovich* scenarios builds two main paths of non-contractual Member States' liability for breach of EU law. Responsibility for State courts of last instance and for authorities in breach of State protective duties were special applications.

The case of *A.G.M-COS.MET* raised the intricate problem of whether there exists a vicarious State liability for breach of EU law by State public servants. The Court, however, did not address this issue.

1001. Case 308/87, *Grifoni v. EAEC* [1990] ECR I-1203/[1994] ECR I-341. For the jurisprudence of the EGC *see*, *inter alia*, the staff case T-48/05, *Franchet and Byk v. Commission* [2008] ECR II-1585.

507. Public liability for breach of EU law gained new momentum in the 1990s. From 1989 onwards two courts – ECJ and EGC[1002] – handed down judgments in damages actions. The case law got more differentiated. At the same time the ECJ undertook efforts to consolidate the different strands of public liability. Principles of Union liability and of Member States' liability exercised mutually inspiring influence. This process, from *Brasserie du pêcheur* to *Bergaderm*, led to some oversimplifications. The margin of discretion became the decisive criterion for determining liability of public authorities. The *Brasserie* formula of a 'sufficiently serious breach' developed into an all-embracing mantra for public liability cases, and reading these judgments one is sometimes reminded of a Tibetan prayer wheel.

This monograph tries to re-differentiate the public liability law. The neutral formula of 'relevant breach' was introduced to cover different conditions of liability: plain breach, institutional fault, manifest breach. General conditions of liability were presented under recourse to principles of tort law of the Member States.

508. Unlike in the area of Union liability, *damages actions against Member States* have to be brought before the national courts. The ground of action is provided by EU law and, in principle, ascertainable *via* preliminary ruling by the ECJ; the appropriate remedies, however, have to be supplied by domestic law. Inappropriateness between EU conditions and national consequences of liability can cause considerable problems. The magic formula, invented early to overcome these difficulties, is the requirement to comply with the 'principles of equivalence and efficiency'.

509. A completely independent field of liability law is addressed with the issue of liability of *private parties* for breach of EU law. Core conditions for liability are the protective character and the horizontal direct effect of the infringed provision of EU law. Traditionally recognized cases were violations of competition rules of EU law. Recently, the European courts were kept busy with conflicts of fundamental economic freedoms versus fundamental rights of the European Charter, both claimed by private parties. Efforts to transpose the consolidated principles of public liability to this complex field of law must fail from the outset. Neither does it make sense to apply to private parties principles developed to control acts of the State, nor does the decisive criterion of public liability – margin of discretion – seem to be a workable benchmark to determine liability of individuals and enterprises. Therefore, conditions as well as consequences of liability of private parties for breach of EU law remain ambiguous. Clear contours have yet to be elaborated by the Courts. Until then the national courts will have to muddle through with ad hoc pragmatic outcomes, often resulting in out-of-court settlements. For the time being, this monograph can only present different case scenarios and insist on the context specificity of solutions.

510. In the shadow of this huge but less structured and multi-facetted field of responsibility for breach of EU law, a harmonized *civil liability law* does not exist in the EU. The only peripheral exception is the approximation of products liability.

1002. Former Court of First Instance.

The Directive 85/374/EEC has been critically restated *supra* in the text. The rest are pointillist approaches. Thoroughly inhomogeneous, the conditions of liability remain opaque: fault – no-fault, strict – quasi-strict. The different legislative acts do not provide for a common definition of core categories such as damage,[1003] let alone subcategories like non-material damage.

For the time being, like *Schuman's* vision of a '*Fédération européenne*', the project of an EU civil non-contractual liability law is far from realization.

1003. Even the European Parliament stated that 'European rules governing liability do not yet have a reasonably uniform concept of damage or an idea as regards its definition …,' quoted from COM(2001) 398 final, at 11.

Selected Bibliography

Books

Aalto, P. *Public Liability in EU Law. Brasserie, Bergaderm and Beyond* (Oxford: Hart, 2011).

American Law Institute (ed.). *Restatement (Third) of Law: Torts – Products Liability* (St. Paul, MN: Thomson/West, 1998).

Bar, C. von. *The Common European Law of Torts*. 2 vols (Oxford: OUP, 1998/2000).

Barnard, C. *The Substantive Law of the EU – The Four Freedoms*. 4th ed. (Oxford: OUP, 2013).

Bell, J. & Ibbetson, D. (gen. eds). *The Legal Development: The Case of Tort Law* (Cambridge: CUP, 2012).

Biondi, A. & Farley, M. *The Right to Damages in European Law* (Alphen aan den Rijn: KLI, 2009).

Brüggemeier, G. *Prinzipien des Haftungsrechts* (Baden-Baden: Nomos, 1999) (in English: *Common Principles of Tort Law* (London: BIICL, 2004/2006)).

Brüggemeier, G. *Haftungsrecht. Struktur, Prinzipien, Schutzbereich* (Heidelberg/Berlin: Springer, 2006).

Brüggemeier, G. *Modernising Civil Liability Law in Europe, China, Brazil and Russia* (Cambridge: CUP, 2010).

Court of Justice of the European Union (ed.). *The Court of Justice and the Construction of Europe. Analyses and Perspectives on 60 Years of Case Law* (The Hague: Asser & Springer, 2013).

Craig, P. *EU Administrative Law*. 2nd ed. (Oxford: OUP, 2010).

Craig, P. & de Búrca, G. (eds). *The Evolution of EU Law*. 2nd ed. (Oxford: OUP, 2011).

Craig, P & de Búrca, G. *EU Law. Text, Cases, and Materials*. 5th ed. (Oxford: OUP, 2011).

Dam, C. van. *European Tort Law*. 2nd ed. (Oxford: OUP, 2013).

European Group on Tort Law (ed.). *Principles of European Tort Law* (Vienna: Springer, 2005).

Fairgrieve, D. (ed.). *Product Liability in Comparative Perspective* (Cambridge: CUP, 2005).

Fairgrieve, D., Andenas, M. & Bell, J. (eds). *Tort Liability of Public Authorities in Comparative Perspective* (London: BIICL 2002).

Fenyves, A., Karner, E., Koziol, H. & Steiner, E. (eds). *Tort Law in the Jurisprudence of the European Court of Human Rights* (Berlin: de Gruyter, 2011).

Gerven, W. van, Lever, J. & Larouche, P. *Common Law of Europe Casebooks: Tort Law* (Oxford: Hart, 2000).
Giliker, P. *Vicarious Liability in Tort. A Comparative Perspective* (Cambridge: CUP, 2010).
Hartkamp, A.S., et al. (eds). *The Influence of EU Law on National Private Law* (Deventer: Kluwer, 2014).
Heukels, T. & McDonnell, A. (eds). *The Action for Damages in Community Law* (The Hague: KLI, 1997).
Koziol, H. & Schulze, R. (eds). *Tort Law of the European Community* (Vienna, Springer, 2008).
Laenerts, K., Arts, D. & Maselis, I. *Procedural Law of the European Union*. 2nd ed. (London: Thomson/Sweet & Maxwell, 2006).
Laenerts, K. & van Nuffel, P. *European Union Law* (London: Sweet & Maxwell, 2011).
Magnus, U. (ed.). *Unification of Tort Law: Damages* (The Hague: KLI, 2001).
Micklitz, H.W. & de Witte, B. (eds). T*he European Court of Justice and the Autonomy of Member States* (Cambridge: Intersentia, 2011).
Mosler, H. (ed.). *Haftung des Staates für rechtswidriges Verhalten seiner Organe/ Liability of the State for Illegal Conduct of its Organs/La responsabilité de l'Etat pour le comportement illégal de ses organs* (Cologne: Heymanns, 1967).
Oliphant, K. (ed.). *The Liability of Public Authorities in Comparative Perspective* (Cambridge: Intersentia, 2016).
Spier, J. (ed.). *Unification of Tort Law: Liability for Damage Caused by Others* (The Hague: KLI, 2003).
Steiner, A.Z., *Die außervertragliche Haftung der Europäischen Union nach Art. 340 Abs. 2 AEUV für rechtswidriges Verhalten* (Tübingen: Mohr Siebeck, 2015).
Taschner, H.C. *Produkthaftung* (Munich: C.H. Beck, 1986).
Tridimas, T. *The General Principles of EU Law*. 2nd ed. (Oxford: OUP, 2005).
Viney, G., Jourdain, P. & Carval, S. *Traité de droit civil: Les conditions de la responsabilité*, 4th ed (Paris: L.G.D.J., 2013).
Wakefield, Jill, *Judicial Protection through the Use of Article 288(2)EC* (The Hague: KLI, 2002).
Wurmnest, W. *Grundzüge eines europäischen Haftungsrechts. Eine rechtsvergleichende Untersuchung des Gemeinschaftsrechts* (Tübingen: Mohr-Siebeck, 2003).

ARTICLES

Arnull, A. 'Liability for Legislative Acts under Article 215(2) EC'. In *The Action for Damages in Community Law*, edited by Heukels & McDonnell (The Hague: KLI, 1997), p. 129.
Brüggemeier, G. 'Risks and Strict Liability'. *ERPL* 21 (2013): 923.
Galand-Carval, S. *Comparative Report,* In *Liability for Damage Caused by Others*, edited by J. Spier (The Hague: KLI, 2003).
Gerven, W. van 'Bridging the Unbridgeable: Community and National Tort Laws after Francovich and Brasserie'. *ICLQ* 45 (1996): 507.

Gerven, W. van 'Of Rights, Remedies and Procedures'. *CML Rev* 40 (2000): 501.
Gerven, W. van 'A Common European Law in the Area of Tort Law'. In *Tort Liability of Public Authorities in Comparative Perspective*, edited by Fairgrieve, Andenas & Bell (London: BIICL 2002), p. 125.
Havu, K. 'Horizontal Liability for Damages in EU Law'. *ELJ* 18 (2012): 407.
Lagrange, M. 'Non-Contractual Liability of the Community in the ECSC and in the EEC'. *CML Rev* 3 (1965/1966): 10.
Leczykiewicz, D. 'Horizontal Application of the Charter of Fundamental Rights'. *EL Rev* 38 (2013): 479.
Reich, N. 'The Interrelation Between Rights and Duties in EU Law: Reflections on the State of Liability Law in the Multilevel Governance System of the Union'. *YEL* 29 (2010): 112.
Reich, N. 'Horizontal Liability in EC Law: Hybridization of Remedies for Compensation in Case of Breaches of EC Rights'. *CML Rev* 44 (2007): 705.
Schermers, H.G. & Swaak, C.R.A. 'Official Acts of Community Servants and Art. 215(4) EC'. In *The Action for Damages in Community Law*, edited by Heukels & McDonnell (The Hague: KLI, 1997), p. 167.
Sieburgh, C. 'EU Law and Non-Contractual Liability of the Union, Member States and Individuals'. In *The Influence of EU Law on National Private Law*, edited by A.S. Hartkamp et al. (Deventer: Kluwer 2014), p. 465.
Toth, A.G. 'The Concepts of Damage and Causality as Elements of Non-Contractual Liability'. In *The Action for Damages in Community Law*, edited by Heukels & McDonnell (The Hague: KLI, 1997), p. 179.
Tridimas, T. 'Liability for Breach of Community Law: Growing Up and Mellowing Down'. *CML Rev* 38 (2011): 301.
Woude, M.H. van der 'Liability for Administrative Acts under Article 215(2) EC'. In *The Action for Damages in Community Law*, edited by Heukels & McDonnell (The Hague: KLI, 1997), p. 109.

Table of Cases

The numbers here refer to footnote numbers.

Cases of the ECJ (numerical list)

C-36/02, *Omega Spielhallen- und Automatenaufstellungs-GmbH v. Oberbürgermeisterin von Bonn* [2004] ECR I-9609, 432
C-201/02, *D. Wells v. Sec'y of State for Transport, Local Governments and the Regions* [2004] ECR I-723, 346
C-222/02, *Peter Paul and Others v. Germany* [2004] ECR I-9460, 350
C-234/02 P, *European Ombudsman v. Lamberts* [2004] ECR I-2838, 167, 168
C-281/02, *Andrew Owusu v. N.B. Jackson* [2005] ECR I-1383, 75
C-173/03, *Traghetti del Mediterraneo v. Italy* [2006] ECR I-5177, 442, 445
C-198/03 P, *Commission v. CEVA and Pfizer* [2005] ECR I-6392, 515
C-402/03, *Skov Æg v. Bilka Lavprisvarehus A/S and Others* [2006] ECR I-199, 797
C-470/03, *A.G.M.-COS.MET Srl v. Suomen valtio and T. Lehtinen* [2007] ECR I-2798, 90, 156, 340, 457, 460, 466, 471–473, 854,
C-537/03, *Candolin and Others v. Vahinkovakuutusosakeyhtio Pohjola and Other* [2005] ECR I-5745, 943
C-127/04, *O'Byrne v. Sanofi Pasteur MSD Ltd and Sanofi SA (O'Byrne I)* [2006] ECR I-1313, 876, 879, 880, 892, 893
C-144/04, *W. Mangold v. R. Helm* [2005] ECR I-9981, 614, 615
C-177/04, *Commission v. France* [2006] ECR I-2461, 795
Joined Cases C-295–298/04, *Manfredi and Others v. Lloyd Adriatico Assicurazioni* [2006] ECR I-6618, 544, 665, 667, 668, 680, 701
C-278/05, *Robins and Others v. Secretary of State for Work and Pensions* [2007] ECR I-1054, 503
C-282/05 P, *Holcim (Deutschland) AG v. Commission* [2007] ECR I-2941, 259, 270–272, 491
C-432/05, *Unibet (London) Ltd and Unibet (International) Ltd v. Justitiekanslern* [2006] ECR I-2271, 485
C-341/05, *Laval un Partneri Ltd v. Svenska Byggnadsarbetareförbundet and Others* [2007] ECR I-11767, 583
C-438/05, *International Transport Workers' Federation and Finnish Seamen's Union v. Viking Line ABP and OÜ Viking Line Eesti* [2007] ECR I-10806, 580, 583-586, 589
Joined Cases C-120 and 121/06, *FIAMM and Others v. Council and Commission* [2008] ECR I-6513, 281, 740–744
C-244/06, *Dynamic Medien Vertriebs-GmbH v. Avides Media* [2008] ECR I-505, 432
C-348/06 P, *Commission v. Girardot* [2008] ECR I-833, 676
C-445/06, *Danske Slagterier v. Germany* [2009] ECR I-2119, 337–339, 485
C-463/06, *FBTO Schadeverzekeringen NV v. J. Odenbreit* [2007] ECR I-11321, 938
C-47/07 P, *Masdar (UK) Ltd v. Commission* [2008] ECR I-9761, 63, 64, 749
C-94/07, *A. Racanelli v. Max-Planck-Gesellschaft* [2008] ECR-I 5939, 529
C-188/07, *Commune de Mesquer v. Total France and Total International Ltd* [2008] ECR I-4501, 831, 924
C-385/07 P, *Der Grüne Punkt – Duales System Deutschland v. Commission* [2009] ECR I-6155, 282
Joined Cases C-402 and 432/07, *C. Sturgeon and Others v. Condor Flugdienst GmbH* and *S. Böck and Other v. Air France SA* [2009] ECR I-10923, 927

Cases of the ECJ (Alphabetical List)

Table of Cases

CASES OF THE EGC (FORMER EUROPEAN COURT OF FIRST INSTANCE) (NUMERICAL LIST)

Table of Cases

CASES OF THE EFTA COURT

CASES OF THE EUROPEAN COURT OF HUMAN RIGHTS (CHRONOLOGICAL LIST)

CASES OF COURTS OF SELECTED MEMBER STATES AND THE USA

France (Chronological List)

Germany (Chronological List)

Italy (Chronological List)

United Kingdom (Alphabetical List)

United States (Alphabetical List)

Table of Cases

Table of EU Legislation

The numbers here refer to footnote numbers.

DIRECTIVES

Index

The numbers here refer to paragraph numbers.

Index

www.ingramcontent.com/pod-product-compliance
Ingram Content Group UK Ltd.
Pitfield, Milton Keynes, MK11 3LW, UK
UKHW020136290926
15471UKWH00003B/531

9 789403 500706